W9-CMP-838

CHILDREN'S WAYS WITH SCIENCE AND LITERACY

Science is often a forgotten subject in early elementary grades as various mandates require teachers to focus on teaching young students to achieve mostly reading and mathematical competencies. This book offers specific examples and empirical evidence of how integrated science-literacy curriculum and teaching in urban primary-grade classrooms give students opportunities to learn science and to develop positive images of themselves as scientists.

The Integrated Science-Literacy Enactments (ISLE) approach builds on multi-modal, multidimensional, and dialogically oriented teaching and learning principles. Readers see how, as children engage with texts, material objects, dialogue, ideas, and symbols in their classroom community, they are helped to bridge their own understandings and ways with words and images with those of science. In doing so, they become learners of both science and literacy. The book features both researcher and teacher perspectives. It explores science learning and its intersection with literacy development in schools that educate predominately children of color, many of whom struggle with poverty, and who have been traditionally underestimated, underserved, and underrated in science classrooms. In all these ways, this volume is a significant contribution to a critically under-researched area of science education.

Maria Varelas is Professor of Science Education, Department of Curriculum and Instruction, University of Illinois at Chicago.

Christine C. Pappas is Professor Emerita of Literacy and Language Education, Department of Curriculum and Instruction, University of Illinois at Chicago.

EDUCATION LIBRARY
UNIVERSITY OF KENTUCKY

CHILDREN'S WAYS WITH SCIENCE AND LITERACY

Integrated Multimodal Enactments in Urban Elementary Classrooms

Maria Varelas and Christine C. Pappas

WITH

AMY ARSENAULT, JUSTINE M. KANE, ELI TUCKER-RAYMOND, ANNE BARRY,
BEGOÑA MARNOTES COWAN, SHARON GILL, JENNIFER HANKES,
NEVEEN KEBLAWE-SHAMAH, IBETT ORTIZ, TAMARA CIESLA,
HONGMEI DONG, SOFIA KOKKINO PATTON, LYNNE PIEPER, LI YE

Routledge
Taylor & Francis Group

NEW YORK AND LONDON

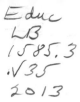

Educ
LB
1585.3
.V35
2013

First published 2013
by Routledge
711 Third Avenue, New York, NY 10017

Simultaneously published in the UK
by Routledge
2 Park Square, Milton Park, Abingdon, Oxon OX14 4RN

Routledge is an imprint of the Taylor & Francis Group, an informa business

© 2013 Taylor & Francis

The right of Maria Varelas and Christine C. Pappas to be identified as author of this work has been asserted by him/her in accordance with sections 77 and 78 of the Copyright, Designs and Patents Act 1988.

All rights reserved. No part of this book may be reprinted or reproduced or utilized in any form or by any electronic, mechanical, or other means, now known or hereafter invented, including photocopying and recording, or in any information storage or retrieval system, without permission in writing from the publishers.

Trademark notice: Product or corporate names may be trademarks or registered trademarks, and are used only for identification and explanation without intent to infringe.

Library of Congress Cataloging in Publication Data
Varelas, Maria.
  Children's ways with science and literacy: integrated multimodal
  enactments in urban elementary classrooms/Maria Carelas and
  Christine C. Pappas with Amy Arsenault . . . [et al.].
       p. cm.
    Includes bibliographical references and index.
  1. Science–Study and teaching (Elementary)–United States.   2. Language
  arts–Correlation with content subjects–United States. 3. Education,
  Urban–United States. I. Pappas, Christine, C. II. Arsenault, Amy.
  III. Title.
  LB1585.3.V352 2012
  372.35′044–dc23   2012025135

ISBN: 978-0-415-89784-6 (hbk)
ISBN: 978-0-415-89785-3 (pbk)
ISBN: 978-0-203-07691-0 (ebk)

Typeset in Bembo
by Swales & Willis Ltd, Exeter, Devon

We dedicate this book to all the children in the ISLE classrooms who allowed us to capture the beauty of their thinking and engagement in science and literacy.

I also dedicate this book to my family, Nikos—my soul-mate for life, Eleni—my witty kid who makes me laugh when I need it most, and Antonios—my easy-going college kid, and my mom whose caring and compassion nurtured my love for teaching and learning.

–Maria

I also dedicate this book to my family, all of whom have or are writing books: George, a book on philosophy, Christina, a hybrid realistic fiction fantasy, and Sara, a book on 19th-century art and literature.

–Chris

We hope this book always reminds all of us of what children, often positioned as facing challenges, can achieve in school when offered opportunities.

CONTENTS

PREFACE

In this book, we present research on primary-grade children's learning in urban school classrooms where teachers enacted integrated science-literacy curriculum and instruction. This was a collaborative university-school project entitled "Integrated Science-Literacy Enactments" (ISLE). There has been a call for approaches that connect science learning with language and literacy (Holliday, Yore, & Alvermann, 1994; Palincsar & Magusson, 2001; Romance & Vitale, 2012; Saul, 2004; Yerrick & Roth, 2005; Yore, Bisanz, & Hand, 2003). This book offers insights into how young children from diverse ethno-linguistic, racial, and socio-economic backgrounds, many of them Latino/a or African American, and living in challenging economic conditions, engaged in science and language/literacy and developed a wealth of complex understandings in their classrooms.

Each of the two integrated curricular units—*Matter* and *Forest*—enacted in the classrooms centered on a unifying theme that served as an organizing framework for students to anchor their science learning by forming connections among various sub-topics. In the *Matter* unit, children explored the three states of matter (solids, liquids, gases)—their characteristics and examples of everyday substances in each of these states—changes of state (such as freezing, melting, evaporation, and condensation), and the water cycle. In the *Forest* unit, children studied plants and animals living in a temperate forest community—underground, on the ground, and above the ground—their characteristics, classes they belong to, and relationships among them, including food webs. The unifying theme in each unit provided a "metaconceptual bonus–a 'powerful idea,' a cross-cutting idea, a perspective on perspective taking, a dimension of experience" (Ackerman, 1989, p. 29). This is particularly important for younger children who need a structure or "hub" to support and connect their many experiences in the natural world and the many topics that they encounter in school (Pappas, Kiefer, & Levstik, 2006).

Children participated in a range of classroom activities, which we call *curriculum genres*. They engaged in: hands-on explorations; whole-class read-alouds of children's literature information books that informed and extended these inquiries; small-group literature groups, whose responses/findings were shared with the class; activities in which they created class artifacts (ongoing semantic maps, murals, graphic organizers) and individual texts (illustrated journals and their own information books); drama experiences; and, home projects that they shared at school. These were multimodal opportunities for children to engage in at both levels of scientific activity: theorizing about the world around them *and* collecting, analyzing, and interpreting data from observations or experiments, or, in other words, constructing empirical evidence (Varelas, 1996). Because the information books employed in these units realized typical, multimodal, scientific communication (Lemke, 1998, 2004; Pappas, 2006), children were enculturated to both scientific thought and the ways in which it is expressed. Moreover, ISLE curricular and instructional practices promoted children's reasoning and sense making, both at the individual level and the collective level (in small groups and in whole-class discussions). Finally, the various curriculum genres promoted dialogic interactions (Bakhin, 1981; Wells, 1999) where children were offered spaces to contribute their comments and questions, which teachers and peers were able to build on and extend. In this way, children's lifeworld knowledge and emergent science understandings were shared together, explored, and further developed, as children and their teacher engaged in scientific practices.

Overview of the Book

The book is organized in four major sections. In Section I, Chapter 1 provides the theoretical perspective of the ISLE project, along with details about the two integrated curricular units (*Matter* and *Forest*) that were developed, enacted, and studied. It also shows the timelines of the curriculum-genre activities in each unit, and information on the six collaborating teachers' classrooms.

Section II consists of six chapters, focusing on different curriculum genres. These chapters discuss ways in which a genre was enacted and offer evidence and insights on pedagogical construct(s) essential for that genre. Chapter 2 is about the intertextual connections created during whole-class read-alouds of children's literature information books. Chapter 3 also focuses on these read-alouds exploring children's diverse forms of participation enacted through distinct language acts. Chapter 4 concentrates on a hands-on exploration in the *Matter* unit, studying scientific practices and reasoning that children used. Chapter 5 is about the illustrated information books that children created at the end of each unit; it examines content, text-picture relationships, linguistic registers, and audience awareness, as well as English language learners' use of various modes in expressing scientific ideas. Each unit included a drama activity; Chapter 6 explores the kinds of dramatizing and meaning making expressed in bodily-kinesthetic performances and talk. Chapter 7 covers home projects, which provided opportunities for children to engage in a science inquiry (and write/draw about it in a booklet) out of the classroom and with family members, and then share at school.

In Section III, consisting of two chapters, we present how learning in science-literacy enactments evolved over the course of the year. Chapter 8 focuses on content learning, and Chapter 9 on children's identities as scientists.

Finally, in Chapter 10 (Section IV), we synthesize ideas from the previous chapters highlighting what children do in urban early-grade classrooms when offered various integrated and dialogic opportunities. We use the construct of "ecology of learnerhoods" (Varelas, Kane, & Pappas, 2010) to orchestrate ideas that we deem important in envisioning classrooms where possibilities for learning science and multimodal literacy can flourish.

Who the Authors Are

The two co-Principal Investigators of the ISLE project were: Maria Varelas, Professor of Science Education at the University of Illinois at Chicago, and Christine C. Pappas, Professor of Language and Literacy Education at the University of Illinois at Chicago (currently an Emerita).

The six collaborating teachers, who taught in Chicago Public Schools, include: Anne Barry and Sharon Gill, who taught 1st grade; Marnotes Cowan and Ibett Ortiz, who taught 2nd grade; and Jennifer Hankes and Neveen Keblawe-Shamah, who taught 3rd grade.

The ISLE team also included a large number of graduate students who contributed to the many phases of the project. Some of them have co-authored the chapters in this book while at other institutions where they currently hold various positions. The co-authors are: Amy Arsenault, Justine M. Kane, Eli Tucker-Raymond, Hongmei Dong, Li Ye, Sofia Kokkino Patton, Lynne Pieper, and Tamara Ciesla. Other graduate students who worked on the ISLE project and offered invaluable contributions include: Alla Korzh, Della Levitt, Qian Fan, Jim Radebaugh, and Eric Cason.

Funding for the Project

The ISLE project was funded by a four-year (2004–2008) US National Science Foundation (NSF) Research On Learning and Education (ROLE) grant (REC-0411593) to Maria Varelas and Christine C. Pappas as Principal Investigators. The data presented, statements made, and views expressed in this book are solely the responsibilities of the authors and do not necessarily reflect NSF's views. The ISLE team is grateful for NSF's generous support of such a project focusing on young children and science in urban schools. The findings from this project, some of which we share in this book and others that we have shared in various articles and presentations, led to bringing the ISLE approach to many more Chicago Public

School classrooms by working with 30 additional teachers through funding from the Polk Bros. Foundation.

References

Ackerman, D. B. (1989). Intellectual and practical criteria for successful curriculum integration. In H. H. Jacobs (Ed.), *Interdisciplinary curriculum: Design and implementation* (pp. 25–37). Alexandria, VA: Association for Supervisor and Curriculum Development.

Bakhtin, M. M. (1981). *The dialogic imagination: Four essays by M. M. Bakhtin.* (M. Holquist, Ed., M. Holquist & C. Emerson, Trans.). Austin: University of Texas Press.

Holliday, W. G, Yore, L. D., & Alvermann, D. (1994). The reading-science learning-writing connection: Breakthroughs, barriers, and promises. *Journal of Research in Science Teaching, 31,* 877–893.

Lemke, J. L. (1998). Multiplying meaning: Visual and verbal semiotics in scientific text. In J. R. Martin & R. Veel (Eds.), *Reading science: Critical and functional perspectives on discourses of science* (pp. 87–113). London: Routledge.

Lemke, J. L. (2004). The literacies of science. In E. W. Saul (Eds.), *Crossing borders: Literacy and science instruction: Perspectives on theory and practice* (pp. 33–47). Newark, DE: International Reading Association.

Palincsar, A. S., & Magusson, S. (2001). The interplay of first-hand and second-hand investigations to model and support the development of scientific knowledge and reasoning. In S. M. Carver & D. Klahr (Eds.), *Cognition and instruction* (pp. 151–191). Mahwah, NJ: Erlbaum.

Pappas, C. C. (2006.). The information book genre: Its role in integrated science literacy research and practice. *Reading Research Quarterly, 41,* 226–250.

Pappas, C. C., Kiefer, B. Z., & Levstik, L. S. (2006). *An integrated language perspective in the elementary school: An action approach* (4th ed.). Boston: Pearson.

Romance, N. R., & Vitale, M. R. (2012). Interdisciplinary perspectives linking science and literacy in grades K-5: Implications for policy and practice. In B. J. Fraser, K. G. Tobin, & C. J. McRobbie (Eds.), *Second international handbook of science education* (Vol. 2, pp. 1351–1373). New York: Springer.

Saul, E. W. (Ed.). (2004). *Crossing borders in literacy and science instruction: Perspectives on theory and practice.* Newark, DE: International Reading Association.

Varelas, M. (1996). Between theory and data in a 7th grade science class. *Journal of Research in Science Teaching, 33,* 229–263.

Varelas, M., Kane, J. M., & Pappas, C. C. (2010). Concept development in urban classroom spaces: Dialectical relationships, power, and identity. In W.-M. Roth (Ed.), *Re/Structuring science education: ReUniting psychological and sociological perspectives* (pp. 275–297). Dordrecht, The Netherlands: Springer-Kluwer.

Wells, G. (1999). *Dialogic inquiry: Toward a sociocultural practice and theory of education.* Cambridge, England: Cambridge University Press.

Yerrick, R. K., & Roth, W.-M. (Eds.). (2005). *Establishing scientific classroom discourse communities: Multiple voices of teaching and learning research.* Mahwah, NJ: Erlbaum.

Yore, L. D., Bisanz, G. L., & Hand, B. M. (2003). Examining the literacy component of science literacy: 25 years of language arts and science research. *International Journal of Science Education, 25,* 689–725.

SECTION I

Theoretical Perspectives and ISLE Curricular and Instructional Features

1

INTEGRATING SCIENCE AND LITERACY

Forms and Functions

Maria Varelas and Christine C. Pappas

How may we support young racially, ethno-linguistically, and socio-economically diverse children's learning of science in urban schools? What kinds of curricular and instructional opportunities may be useful? How may we help children make sense of, think about, use, and communicate scientific concepts and practices, and positively identify themselves with science? These are some of the questions that the ISLE (Integrated Science-Literacy Enactments) project attempted to address and that we share in this book.

The ISLE project aimed at designing, enacting, and studying integrated science-literacy possibilities in six urban 1st–3rd grade classrooms in Chicago Public Schools (CPS). The curriculum that was co-designed between UIC-based and CPS-based educators and researchers consisted of two extended integrated units, *Matter* and *Forest*, which provided the basis of science instruction for one school year. In this chapter, we present the overarching theoretical perspective of the project, and then provide overviews of the curricular units and details on the six classroom settings.

Science and Young Children in Urban Classrooms

Sociocultural Theory of Learning

The theoretical framework of our project is based on a sociocultural approach combining Vygotsky's (1978, 1987/1934) view of development and learning with Bakhtin's (1981) emphasis on social languages. We embrace a constructivist approach to science education distinct from transmission learning on the one hand, and Piagetian-inspired discovery learning on the other (Driver, Asoko, Leach, Mortimer, & Scott, 1994), that emphasizes the role of cultural tools, including language, in the learning process (Wertsch, 1998). In such a view, children do not learn science by reinventing scientific inquiry all by themselves. Instead, they learn by encountering concepts, processes, practices, and language that have been established over the course of time. Children use their own reasoning to make sense of these sociocultural achievements, and at the same time, they are influenced by them to reorganize their understandings. "Bring[ing] together the social-interactive and personal-sense-making parts of the learning process" (Leach & Scott, 2003, p. 103) is critical to science learning. Children come to school with a plethora of experiences around scientific concepts and practices—they wonder, ask questions, want to discover, build on, and share their ideas with others. In school, the teacher is essential in facilitating the children's bridging of their own lifeworld knowledge with scientific concepts and language (Becker & Varelas, 1995; Pappas & Zecker, 2001; Roth & Tobin, 2007; Varelas, 1996; Varelas, Luster, & Wenzel, 1999; Wells, 1999).

Such a sociocultural, constructivist view is also relevant for language and literacy learning. Children, in their day-to-day interactions, create and recreate the contexts in which texts (oral, written, and multimodal) are used (Kress, 1997); moreover, these interactions influence and are influenced by these texts (Green & Dixon, 1993; Reder, 1994; Rex, 2006). That is, children interpret and give meaning to texts and actions in these contexts—they construct their understandings as social and cultural acts. Such a view, then, represents a movement away from transmission-oriented teaching-learning literacy practices to ones that allow for children's increasing control of texts and their meaning (Cazden, 2001; Rex & Schiller, 2009; Sipe, 2008; Willinsky, 1990). It involves redefining literacy by *building on* the diversity of students, valuing and incorporating students' local and cultural varied understandings in the curriculum. Similarly to science learning, the role of the teacher in literacy learning is critical (Pappas, 1999; Pappas, Kiefer, & Levstik, 2006; Pappas & Zecker, 2001).

Enacting Dialogic Classroom Discourse

For children from various ethno-linguistic and racial backgrounds to be able to use their "ways with words" (Heath, 1983) to express their ideas so that teachers can build on and extend them, a certain type of classroom discourse needs to be enacted in the classroom. Discourse, here, denotes both the language and the actions of a community of people, and, in our case, the community formed by the students and the teacher in a classroom (Bakhtin, 1986; Fairclough, 1992; Gee, 2011; Gee & Green, 1998; Rex & Schiller, 2009; Wells, 1999). Discourse represents the socially situated practices that are constructed in the varied moment-to-moment interactions, and as such is a major semiotic tool to mediate intellectual activity and knowledge building (Halliday, 1993; Halliday & Hasan, 1985; Pappas & Zecker, 2001; Vygotsky, 1987/1934; Wells, 1999; Wertsch, 1991).

For children's current understandings to be shared, explored, and developed in the classroom, "creative discourse agency" (Bayham, 2006) and "navigational space" (Moje, Ciechanowski, Kramer, Elis, Carrilo, & Collazo, 2004) are needed. This implies moving away from traditional classroom discourse where the teacher controls the talk through the characteristic initiate-response-evaluate (IRE) talk structures (Cazden, 1988, 2001; Edwards & Mercer, 1987; Young, 1992). Such discourse structures allow for few opportunities for students' culturally and linguistically different knowledge bases and interactional styles to be instrumental in their learning (McCollum, 1991). Thus, the aim of the ISLE project was to develop and study collaborative, or what we call dialogic interactions classroom discourse as alternatives to teacher-dominated IRE patterns. Teachers in ISLE classrooms attempted to create experiences and routines where both teacher and student voices are privileged in collaborative transactions (Bakhtin, 1981; Nystrand, 1997; Nystrand, Wu, Gamoran, Zeiser, & Long, 2003: Pappas & Varelas, 2004; Pappas & Zecker, 2001; Sawyer, 2004; Varelas & Pappas, 2006; Wells, 1999).

Children of Color and Science Education

Bryan and Atwater (2002) warn us that children of color (African American or Latino/a) are often portrayed in science education in ways that emphasize or echo deficit views. In science, and other subjects too, students of color have been identified as lacking knowledge, preparation, and achievement, and not pursuing science-related careers (National Science Board, 2010). However, increasingly, science education researchers working in urban classrooms have found that when we expand the repertoire of tools and outcomes associated with learning, we can see more of the strengths and successes that students of color can experience in classrooms, thereby problematizing the deficit-oriented rhetoric (for a review of studies, see Varelas, Kane, Tucker-Raymond, & Pappas, 2012).

Like William Tate (2001), we consider science education to be a civil rights issue. That is, children in low-income families, who are members of ethno-linguistic and racial groups who have faced discrimination in various forms, need to have similar opportunities to those that usually "executive class" students enjoys (Anyon, 1981). Such opportunities embrace various important dimensions of what Freire (1994/1992) called "pedagogy of hope," including access, participation, and achievement. For an urban classroom to become a place where liberatory education (Freire, 1990/1970) is enacted, a delicate dialectic is required. Individual children need to maintain their distinct voices (Wertsch, 1998), as the class produces common language, understandings, and modes of engagement.

Integrating Science and Literacy as a Vehicle for Science Learning

Science as a discipline represents particular ways of thinking, and communicating scientific ideas is realized by particular linguistic registers (Halliday, 1978; Halliday

& Martin, 1993; Lemke, 1990; Pappas et al., 2006; Schleppegrell, 2004). In fact, Wellington and Osborne (2001) argue that because "every science lesson is a language lesson . . . paying more attention to language is one of the most important acts that can be done to improve the quality of science of education" (pp. 1–2). Moreover, science ideas are not expressed solely through language; instead, science is a *multimodal* discipline that also uses other modes of meaning—visual, gestural, spatial, and so forth (Kress, Jewett, Osborn, & Tsatsarelis, 2001; Lemke, 1998, 2004; Roth, 2009; Unsworth, 2001). Different modes of communication offer different affordances, different ways to represent, and different aspects of meaning making (Kress, 2000; 2003; Kress et al., 2001; Kress & van Leeuwen, 2006). Thus, it was essential to create ways for students to engage in multimodal science experiences in the classroom, which are also part of scientific practice; scientists talk, read, write, use visual images, do hands-on laboratory work (Goldman & Bisanz, 2002; Norris & Phillips, 2003; Yore, Bisanz, & Hand, 2003; Yore, Hand, & Florence, 2004).

Curriculum Genres

From a social-semiotic perspective, communication is understood only as it relates to social structure—systems of *meanings* are related to a *social* system or culture (Halliday, 1978; Halliday & Hasan, 1985; Lemke, 1990; Pappas & Zecker, 2001). Thus, different social-semiotic relationships are seen to occur in the classroom through the shifts of the various teaching-learning activities that transpire during a school day. These recurring-interaction events or routines are encoded in particular behavioral patterns, which have corresponding communicative patterns that express particular types of meaning (Bakhtin, 1986; Bloome & Bailey, 1992; Christie, 1987a, 1987b; Lindfors, 1999; Pappas & Zecker, 2001). We call these demarcated event and participant structures or routines *curriculum genres*.

Both integrated science-literacy units, *Matter* and *Forest*, incorporated a range of curriculum genres—socially recognizable sequences of actions that realized particular meanings or purposes for teachers and students. As such, each curriculum genre provided particular multimodal affordances that represented "structures of expectations" (Tannen, 1993) where classroom participants came to know how to interact and mean. Curriculum genres were distinctive *frames or forms* in which teacher and children shared particular expectations about how to construct scientific understandings and discourse together (Lindfors, 1999), and, thus, had particular *functions* in terms of teaching and learning science.

Both units included the following curriculum genres:

- **Dialogic read-alouds**: Whole-class sharing of illustrated children's literature information books that served as vehicles of thinking about science ideas that informed and extended hands-on explorations and exposed children to typical scientific communication.

- **Hands–on explorations**: Opportunities to engage children in collecting, analyzing, and interpreting data, or, in other words, empirical evidence in the context of either observations or experiments.
- **Journaling**: Ways for children to individually write and draw about scientific ideas presented in hands-on, read-aloud, and other curriculum-genre experiences.
- **Semantic mapping**: Whole-class use of graphic organizers to depict and synthesize ideas being explored in a unit.
- **Literature circles**: Small-group reading and discussing of an illustrated children's literature information book, whose ideas are then shared with the whole class, thus, offering children opportunities to be positioned as "experts" on topic(s) related to the one(s) explored in the unit.
- **Drama**: Bodily-kinesthetic ways to enact scientific phenomena through action and talk.
- **Class mural**: A way to represent and synthesize, via a variety of art-based materials, major scientific ideas and relationships.
- **Home project**: An at-home inquiry (which includes materials to do a hands-on inquiry, a children's literature book on the topic, and a blank booklet to document the inquiry), which is then shared in class, thus offering children opportunities to both interact with family members around science and communicate to peers and teacher about their exploring at home.
- **Individual multimodal information book-making**: Children creating their own multimodal information books on a topic of their own choice to act as authors and present their science understandings that have been developed throughout a unit.

As children engaged with texts, material objects, dialogue, ideas, and symbols in the various curriculum genres enacted in their classroom community, they were supported, bridging their own understandings and ways of multimodal communication with those of the scientific community. In doing so, children became learners of *both* science and literacy. Below we provide a brief overview of each unit.

The ISLE Curricular Units

Brief Overview of the Matter Unit

In the *Matter* unit, children explore the three states of matter (solids, liquids, gases)—their characteristics and examples of everyday substances in each of these states—changes of state, such as freezing, melting, evaporation, and condensation, and the water cycle. Figure 1.1 shows the various unit activities by lesson. The unit consists of 20 lessons of about 45 minutes to one hour each. The number of days each lesson took to implement varied by classroom, as teachers enacted the unit according to their schedules, their students' abilities and grade levels, and their practice.

ISLE: Matter Unit

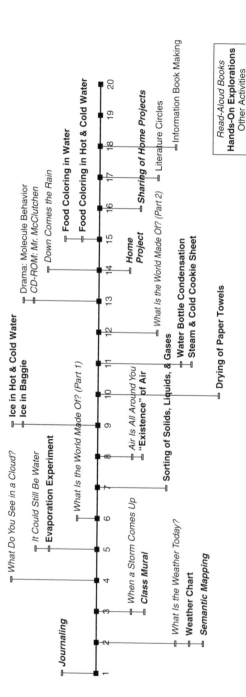

FIGURE 1.1 *Matter* unit timeline of approximately 20 lessons varying in duration.

The *Matter* unit begins with children exploring weather phenomena. In between read-alouds of the books *What Is the Weather Today?* (Fowler, 1991) and *When a Storm Comes Up* (Fowler, 1995), the class creates a weather word bank and each child starts a weather chart (with pictures and words) that is kept for about 10 days (or 5 non-consecutive days).

The unit moves in to beginning to explore ideas about the water cycle with the read-aloud of the books *What Do You See in a Cloud?* (Fowler, 1996) and *It Could Still Be Water* (Fowler, 1992). Children start working in groups to conduct an evaporation experiment where they observe, measure, and record how the water level changes in graduated cylinders over a period of time at various locations in the classroom.

As the unit continues, children explore properties of solids, liquids, and gases through the read-aloud of the first part of the book *What Is the World Made Of?* (Zoehfeld, 1998), and an exploration where they sort everyday objects into different states of matter and discuss reasons. Children then study further the gaseous state of air through the read-aloud of *Air Is All Around You* (Branley, 1986), and they engage in the exploration presented in the book where they submerge a cup, with a paper towel stuffed in its bottom, upside down in a bowl of water and notice that it does not get wet due to the existence of air that takes up space.

Next students engage in a read-aloud of the second part of *What Is the World Made Of?* after they participate in a number of explorations that involve changes of state of matter—children melt an ice cube in a baggie as fast as they can; they observe ice cubes melting in hot and cold water and compare the times it takes for ice cubes to melt; they observe wet paper towels drying in different formations (flat on a surface, hanging down, and crumpled up in a ball) and consider reasons why different amounts of time are needed to dry; they observe and explain why a frozen and sealed water bottle "sweats"; and they describe and explain how the teacher makes rain by holding a cold cookie sheet on top of boiling water. Next, students explore the idea that matter is made of molecules that behave differently at different states through a drama activity where they act as molecules within solids, liquids, and gases, and then examine the CD-ROM *States of Matter* (1997).

The unit then returns to the water cycle and how rain is made through the read-aloud *Down Comes the Rain* (Branley, 1983), which is also the book that is sent home as part of a home project that also includes an exploration of drying up paper towels in different configurations and at different places in their homes. Another exploration, where students observe and draw a drop of food coloring spreading through a cup of water in different temperatures, offers them an opportunity to think about how molecules "wiggle" faster in higher temperatures.

Toward the end of the unit, students participate in literature circles with the books: *Snow Is Falling* (Branley, 1986), *What Will the Weather Be?* (DeWitt, 1991), *Feel the Wind* (Dorros, 1989), *Weather Words and What They Mean* (Gibbons, 1990), *Water Cycle* (Hughes, 2004), and *Rain* (Miles, 2005). Each small group then shares highlights of its book discussion.

In addition, children write and draw in their own science journals throughout the unit; create a class mural of their evolving ideas about matter; keep track of their ideas on an ongoing class semantic map; and at the end of the unit, create their own illustrated information book on a topic of their choice.

Brief Overview of the Forest Unit

In the *Forest* unit, children explore plants and animals living in a temperate forest community—underground, on the ground, and above the ground—their characteristics, classes they belong to, and relationships among them, including food webs. Figure 1.2 shows the various unit activities by lesson. The unit consists of approximately 26 lessons of about 45 minutes to one hour each. The number of days each lesson took to implement varied by classroom, as teachers enacted the unit according to their schedules, their students' abilities and grade levels, and their practice.

The *Forest* unit begins with children sharing their images of what is found under, on, and above the ground in a forest (which they have documented in their journals), and participating in read-alouds of the books *In the Forest* (First Discovery Book, 2002), and *A Forest Community* (Massie, 2000). They then zoom into the underground world with the read-alouds of *Animals Under the Ground* (Fowler, 1997), *Earthworms* (Llewellyn, 2000) and *An Earthworm's Life* (Himmelman, 2000).

In between the read-alouds of *Earthworms* and *An Earthworm's Life*, children observe worms and study worm behavior (in light vs. dark and wet vs. dry environments), and engage with the electronic text *The Adventures of Herman* (University of Illinois Extension, 2004a). Children then move to studying seeds and plants through read-alouds of *Seeds* (Saunders-Smith, 1998) and *From Seed to Plant* (Gibbons, 1991), and several hands-on explorations. Children observe a lima bean, and plant and observe its growth into a lima bean plant; they study the effects of light and water on plants over a period of time; and they investigate ways in which various seeds travel. The home project starts—children read and discuss the book *From Seed to Plant* with their families, and plant and observe lentils, and record their growth.

The unit continues with the study of trees through the electronic text *Trees Are Terrific* (University of Illinois Extension, 2004b) and the read-aloud of *A Log's Life* (Pfeffer, 1997). Read-alouds of parts of *A Forest Community* focusing on owls, chipmunks, and termites give children opportunities to learn about features, behaviors, needs, and enemies of these animals. The electronic text *Let's Talk About Insects* (University of Illinois Extension, 2004c) supplements the read-aloud focusing on termites. Next, a hands-on exploration on camouflage, where children pick up different-color dots spread on differently-patterned fabrics, helps them discuss camouflage relative to prey–predator relationships.

ISLE: Forest Unit

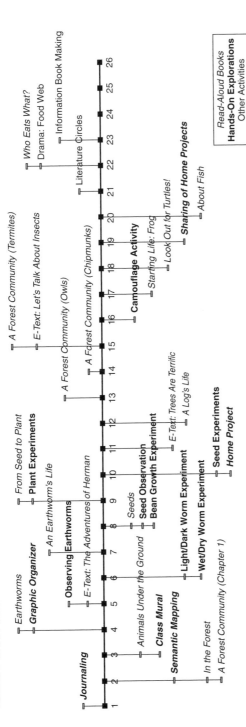

FIGURE 1.2 *Forest* unit timeline of approximately 25 lessons varying in duration.

Read-alouds of *Starting Life: Frog* (Llewellyn, 2003), *Look Out For Turtles!* (Berger, 1992), and *About Fish* (Sill, 2002) follow. The class then conducts literature-circle activities with the books: *Tunneling Earthworms* (Dell'Oro, 2001), *Inside an Ant Colony* (Fowler, 1998), *From Seed to Plant* (Fowler, 2001), *Snakes Are Hunters* (Lauber, 1988), *Chipmunks* (Whitehouse, 2004), and *Quiet Owls* (Riley, 2001). Each small group then shares with the class highlights from its book discussion.

Before the end of the unit, children explore food chains and webs through the read-aloud of *Who Eats What?* (Lauber, 1995) and a drama activity where each student is assigned to be a particular animal or plant in the forest, and the class acts out interdependency in a forest community.

Similarly to the *Matter* unit, in addition to the above activities, children write and draw in their own science journals throughout the unit; create a class mural of their evolving ideas about forest and its inhabitants; keep track of their ideas on an ongoing class semantic map; and at the end of the unit, create their own illustrated information book on a topic of their choice.

Classroom Settings

Six classrooms (two classrooms of each grade level, 1st through 3rd) were the focus of the project, and it was the study of their enactments that helped us develop the understandings shared in this book. The teachers and students in these classrooms will come alive as we present data from them in the subsequent chapters, but we provide here general profiles so that the reader starts building images of these classrooms. Although the teachers and university-based educators have worked together for several years, extensive and systematic data collection happened during one school year. We use these data in the chapters that follow to both show ways in which integrated science-literacy enactments can take place and provide evidence of the opportunities they create.

The classrooms were part of the Chicago Public School system. The demographics of the classrooms for the year of the full data collection are shown in Table 1.1. In each classroom, 10 children (five girls and five boys) were selected as *focal* students, representing the ethno-linguistic and racial make-up of the classroom. Although several types of data were collected on all the students, more extensive data collection took place with the focal students. Below we offer a brief introduction of each teacher and her classroom.

Anne Barry, a European American teacher, had been teaching for 35 years and for 22 years in the school where ISLE was enacted. This school was in the lower west side of the city in a neighborhood that is the heart of the Mexican American community and home of the National Museum of Mexican Art. The school's student population had begun to shrink as the neighborhood had started being gentrified and the low-income residents forced to leave. Most of the students in this K-8 school were Latino/a (97%), some more recent immigrants than others. During the first half of the year, desks in Anne's 1st-grade class were organized in

TABLE 1.1 Demographics of ISLE Classrooms

Grade	Teacher	Student Ethnicity	Student % w.Reduced Lunch	No of Girls	No of Boys	Total No of Students
1	Anne Barry	Latino/a	94	6	15	21
1	Sharon Gill	Diverse	40	14	16	30
2	Ibett Ortiz	Latino/a	95	13	8	21
2	Begoña Marnotes Cowan	Diverse	60	14	13	27
3	Neveen Keblawe-Shamah	Latino/a	95	15	14	29
3	Jennifer Hankes	African American	98	14	7	21

four groups of between four and six students each sitting at desks facing each other. In the second half of the year, Anne slightly changed the layout of her room. The groups were combined to form two long rows of 10 or 11 students each facing each other. When Anne was reading aloud, the children moved their chairs to a reading section of the room arranging them into four rows facing her. Hands-on explorations and journaling were done at their desks.

Sharon Gill, an African American teacher, had been teaching for 32 years and all at the school where ISLE was enacted, teaching 1st grade. This school was just west of the heart of downtown, close to a university campus and medical district, educating a diverse student body, including White, Latino/a, African American, and Asian children. It was a magnet school focusing on language instruction, drawing students from across the city and offering them opportunities to develop proficiency in various languages in addition to English. When Sharon was conducting a read-aloud in her 1st-grade classroom, the students sat on the floor in front of her in a semi-circle. During hands-on explorations and journaling, students were arranged in five groups with each group consisting of six students sitting in two rows of three facing each other.

Ibett Ortiz, a Mexican American teacher from Chicago, had been teaching for 8 years and for 5 years at the school where ISLE was enacted. This school was in the same neighborhood of the city as Anne's school—lower west side of the city where predominately Mexican families have lived since the 1950s. Although gentrification had threatened to change the population of the immediate school neighborhood, the school continued to serve predominately Mexican students. The school was over 95% Latino/a, with the majority being of Mexican descent. Over 35% of the students were identified as English language learners, and the majority of all families also spoke Spanish at home. In Ibett's 2nd-grade bilingual classroom, desks were usually arranged facing each other in groups of four or five. Students conducted their hands-on explorations and small-group work at these desks. Read-alouds were conducted on a rug in the front of the room, and demonstrations on a table in the rear of the classroom.

Begoña Marnotes Cowan, a Cuban American teacher, had been teaching for 13 years. Her school was in the city's north side, and had undergone gentrification—whereas before the school had served predominately Latino/a students, it was now serving a diverse student body consisting of mostly White (48%) and Latino/a (35%) students with a small percentage of African American students. Over the last few years, the school had been changing from serving almost all Latino/a students to serving a diverse student body as a new subdivision had been added where once was a factory. When the science read-alouds were enacted in her 2nd-grade class, Begoña had her students sit in an area on the floor she had designated as the "nonfiction rug." When students took part in hands-on explorations and journaling, the room was set up into five round tables with four, five, or six students each.

Neveen Keblawe-Shamah, a Palestinian American teacher from Chicago, had been teaching for 5 years, all in 3rd grade at the school where ISLE was enacted, the same school at which Ibett was teaching. Desks in Neveen's 3rd-grade class were usually arranged facing each other in groups of four or five. She conducted the read-alouds on a rug in the rear of her room, and her students conducted their hands-on explorations and small-group work at their desks.

Jennifer Hankes, a European American teacher, had been teaching for seven years, all at the school where ISLE was enacted. This school was located on the west side of the city in a predominantly African American neighborhood enduring a high level of crime, street gangs, and shootings even near the school. In most of the families, females were the head of the household (fathers were mostly not present) and the only resources available in the neighborhood were a few convenience stores and fast-food restaurants. Jennifer had looped with her students from 2nd grade. Her 3rd-grade classroom was organized into five teams of four students. Teams consisted of four desks that faced each other. The teams were relatively stable throughout the year, with minor adjustments to facilitate changing student relationships. For read-alouds, students sat on a rug that was situated in the library section of the classroom. For all other science-literacy engagements, students sat at their desks.

In their classrooms, these teachers enacted ISLE curricular and pedagogical approaches and offered their students opportunities to engage in scientific practices that have been part of the existing science education standards (National Research Council, 1996), and are highly emphasized in the recently released new *Framework for K-12 Science Education* (National Research Council, 2012) and the upcoming Next Generation Science Standards. The teachers also helped their young students, many of whom were students of color living in challenging economic conditions, develop scientific understandings around two topics, matter and forest, and communicate them via a range of multimodal means. The children not only did and learned science, but also positioned themselves as scientists by the end of the year. The nature of their achievements is presented in the following chapters. Conventions of transcription for discourse excerpts, which are provided to support our findings in various chapters, are shown in the Appendix.

Appendix: Conventions of Transcription for Discourse Excerpts

//	False start, repetition, or abandoned language replaced by new language structures
|	Break in a speaker's turn due to next speaker
< >	Uncertain words
==	Speaker's pause at the end of uncompleted utterance, seemingly to encourage another speaker to talk
(★★★)	Inaudible, or impossible to transcribe, word
(★★★ ★★★)	Inaudible, or impossible to transcribe, stretches of language
<u>Underscore</u>	Emphasis
# #	Overlapping language spoken by two or more speakers at a time
CAPS	Reading of text in a book
{ }	Speaker's miscue or modification of text read
[ ]	Non-spoken contextual information
. . .	Omitted part of transcript

References

Anyon, J. (1981). Social class and school knowledge. *Curriculum Inquiry, 11*, 3–42.

Bakhtin, M. M. (1981). *The dialogic imagination: Four essays by M. M. Bakhtin.* (M. Holquist, Ed., M. Holquist & C. Emerson, Trans.). Austin: University of Texas Press.

Bakhtin, M. M. (1986). *Speech genres and other late essays.* (C. Emerson & M. Holquist, Eds., V. W. McGee, Trans.). Austin: University of Texas Press.

Bayham, M. (2006). Agency and contingency in the language learning of refugee and asylum seekers. *Linguistics and Education, 17*, 24–39.

Becker, J., & Varelas, M. (1995). Assisting construction: The role of the teacher in assisting the learner's construction of pre-existing cultural knowledge. In L. Steffe (Ed.), *Constructivism in education* (pp. 433–446). Hillsdale, NJ: Erlbaum.

Bloome, D., & Bailey, F. (1992). Studying language and literacy through events, particularity, and intertextuality. In R. Beach, J. L. Green, M. L. Kamil, & T. Shanahan (Eds.), *Multidisciplinary perspectives on literacy research* (pp. 181–210). Urbana, IL: National Conference on Research in English.

Bryan, L. A., & Atwater, M. M. (2002). Teacher beliefs and cultural models: A challenge for science teacher preparation programs. *Science Education, 86*, 821–839.

Cazden, C. B. (1988). *Classroom discourse: The language of teaching and learning.* Portsmouth, NJ: Heinemann.

Cazden, C. B. (2001). *Classroom discourse: The language of teaching and learning.* Portsmouth, NJ: Heinemann.

Christie, F. (1987a). The morning news genre: Using functional grammar to illuminate educational issues. *Australian Review of Applied Linguistics, 10*, 182–198.

Christie, F. (1987b). Learning to mean in writing. In N. Stewart-Dore (Ed.), *Writing and reading to learn* (pp. 21–34). Rozelle, Australia: Primary English Teaching Association.

Driver, R., Asoko, H., Leach, J., Mortimer, E., & Scott, P. (1994). Constructing scientific knowledge in the classroom. *Educational Researcher, 23*, 5–12.

Edwards, A. D., & Mercer, N. (1987). *Common knowledge: The development of understanding in the classroom.* London: Methuen.

Fairclough, N. (1992). *Discourse and social change*. Cambridge, England: Polity Press.

Freire, P. (1990). *Pedagogy of the oppressed*. New York: Continuum. (Original work published in 1970.)

Freire, P. (1994). *Pedagogy of hope: Reliving pedagogy of the oppressed*. New York: Continuum. (Original work published in 1992.)

Gee, J. P. (2011). *Social linguistics and literacies: Ideology in discourses* (4th ed.). New York: Routledge.

Gee, J. P., & Green, J. L. (1998). Discourse analysis, learning, and social practice: A methodological study. In P. D. Pearson & A. Iran-Nejad (Eds.), *Review of Research in Education, Vol. 23* (pp. 119–169). Washington, DC: AERA.

Goldman, S. R., & Bisanz, G. L. (2002). Toward a functional analysis of scientific genres: Implications for understanding and learning processes. In J. Otero, J. A. Leon, & A. C. Graesser (Eds.), *The psychology of science text comprehension* (pp. 19–50). Mahwah, NJ: Erlbuam.

Green, J. L., & Dixon, C. N. (1993). Talking into being: Discursive and social practices in the classroom. *Linguistics and Education, 5*, 231–239.

Halliday, M. A. K. (1978). *Language as a social semiotic: The social interpretation of language and meaning*. London: Longman.

Halliday, M. A. K. (1993). Towards a language-based theory of learning. *Linguistics and Education, 5*, 93–126.

Halliday, M. A. K., & Hasan, R. (1985). *Language, context, and text: Aspects of language in a social-semiotic perspective*. Victoria, Australia: Deakin University Press.

Halliday, M. A. K., & Martin, J. R. (1993). *Writing science: Literacy and discursive power*. Pittsburgh, PA: University of Pittsburgh Press.

Heath, S. B. (1983). *Ways with words: Language, life, and work in communities and classrooms*. Cambridge, England: Cambridge University Press.

Kress, G. (1997). *Before writing: Rethinking the paths to literacy*. London: Routledge.

Kress, G. (2000). Design and transformation: New theories of meaning. In B. Cope & M. Kalantzis (Eds.), *Multiliteracies: Literacy learning and the design of social futures* (pp. 153–161). London: Routledge.

Kress, G. (2003). *Literacy in a new media age*. London: Routledge.

Kress, G., Jewitt, C., Ogborn, J., & Tsatsarelis, C. (2001). *Multimodal teaching and learning: The rhetorics of the science classroom*. London: Continuum.

Kress, G., & van Leeuwen, T. (2006). *Reading images: The grammar of visual design*. London: Routledge.

Leach, J., & Scott, P. (2003). Individual and sociocultural views of learning in science education. *Science & Education, 12*, 91–113.

Lemke, J. L. (1990). *Talking science: Language, learning, and values*. Norwood, NJ: Ablex.

Lemke, J. L. (1998). Multiplying meaning: Visual and verbal semiotics in scientific text. In J. R. Martin & R. Veel (Eds.), *Reading science: Critical and functional perspectives on discourses of science* (pp. 87–113). London: Routledge.

Lemke, J. L. (2004). The literacies of science. In E. W. Saul (Eds.), *Crossing borders: Literacy and science instruction: Perspectives on theory and practice* (pp. 33–47). Newark, DE: International Reading Association.

Lindfors, J. W. (1999). *Children's inquiry: Using language to make sense of the world*. New York: Teachers College Press.

McCollum, P. (1991). Cross-cultural perspectives on classroom discourse and literacy. In E. H. Hiebert (Ed.), *Literacy for a diverse society: Perspectives, practices, and policies* (pp. 108–121). New York: Teachers College Press.

Moje, E., Ciechanowski, K. M., Kramer, K., Elis, L., Carrilo, R., & Collazo, T. (2004). Working toward third space in content area literacy: An examination of everyday funds and knowledge and discourse. *Reading Research Quarterly, 39*, 38–70.

National Research Council. (1996). *National science education standards*. Washington, DC: National Academy Press.

National Research Council. (2012). *A framework for K-12 science education: Practices, crosscutting concepts, and core ideas*. Washington, DC: National Academies Press.

National Science Board. (2010). *Science and engineering indicators 2010*. Arlington, VA: National Science Foundation.

Norris, S. P., & Phillips, L. M. (2003). How literacy in its fundamental sense is central to scientific literacy. *Science Education, 87*, 224–240.

Nystrand, M. (1997). *Opening dialogue: Understanding the dynamics of language and learning in the English classroom*. New York: Teachers College Press.

Nystrand, M., Wu., L. L., Gamoran, A., Zeiser, S., & Long, D. A. (2003). Questions in time: Investigating the structure and dynamics of unfolding classroom discourse. *Discourse Processes, 35*, 135–198.

Pappas, C. C. (1999). Becoming literate in the borderlands. In A. Göncü (Ed.), *Children's engagement in the world: Sociocultural perspectives* (pp. 228–260). Cambridge, England: Cambridge University Press.

Pappas, C. C., Kiefer, B. Z., & Levstik, L. S. (2006). *An integrated language perspective in the elementary school: An action approach* (4th ed.). New York: Pearson.

Pappas, C. C., & Varelas, M., with Barry, A., & Rife, A. (2004). Promoting dialogic inquiry information book read-alouds: Young urban children's ways of making sense of science. In E. W. Saul (Eds.), *Crossing borders: Literacy and science instruction: Perspectives on theory and practice* (pp. 161–189). Newark, DE: International Reading Association.

Pappas, C. C., & Zecker, L. B. (Eds.). (2001). *Working with teacher researchers in urban classrooms: Transforming literacy curriculum genres*. Mahwah, NJ: Erlbaum.

Reder, S. (1994). Practice-engagement theory: A sociocultural approach to literacy across languages and cultures. In B. M. Ferdman, R.-M. Weber, & A. G. Ramierz (Eds.), *Literacy across languages and cultures* (pp. 33–74). Albany: State of University of New York Press.

Rex, L. A. (Ed.). (2006). *Discourse of opportunity: How talk in learning situations creates and constrains*. Cresskill, NJ: Hampton Press.

Rex, L. A., & Schiller, L. (2009). *Using discourse analysis to improve classroom interaction*. New York: Routledge.

Roth, W.-M. (2009). *Dialogism: A Bakhtinian perspective on science and learning*. Rotterdam, The Netherlands: Sense Publishers.

Roth, W.-M., & Tobin, K. (Eds.). (2007). *Science, learning, identity: Sociocultural and cultural-historical perspectives*. Rotterdam, The Netherlands: Sense Publishers.

Sawyer, R. K. (2004). Creative teaching: Collaborative discussion as disciplined improvisation. *Educational Researcher, 33*, 12–20.

Schleppegrell, M. J. (2004). *The language or schooling: A functional linguistic perspective*. Mahwah, NJ: Erlbaum.

Sipe, L. R. (2008). *Storytime: Young children's literary understanding in the classroom*. New York: Teachers College Press.

Tannen, D. (1993). What's in a frame: Surface evidence for underlying expectations. In D. Tannen (Ed.), *Framing in discourse* (pp. 14–56). New York: Oxford University Press.

Tate, W. (2001). Science education as a civil right: Urban schools and opportunity-to-learn considerations. *Journal of Research in Science Teaching, 38*, 1015–1028.

Unsworth, L. (2001). *Teaching multiliteracies across the curriculum: Changing contexts of text and image in classroom practices.* Buckingham, England: Open University Press.

Varelas, M. (1996). Between theory and data in a 7th grade science class. *Journal of Research in Science Teaching, 33,* 229–263.

Varelas, M., Kane, J. M., Tucker-Raymond, E., & Pappas, C. C. (2012). Science learning in urban elementary school classrooms: Liberatory education and issues of access, participation, and achievement. In B. J. Fraser, K. Tobin, & C. McRobbie (Eds.), *Second international handbook of science education* (pp. 91–103). Dordrecht, The Netherlands: Springer-Kluwer.

Varelas, M., Luster, B., & Wenzel, S. (1999). Meaning making in a community of learners: Struggles and possibilities in an urban science class. *Research in Science Education, 29,* 227–245.

Varelas, M., & Pappas, C. C. (2006). Intertextuality in read-alouds of integrated science-literacy units in urban primary classrooms: Opportunities for the development of thought and language. *Cognition & Instruction, 24,* 211–259.

Vygotsky, L. S. (1978). *Mind in society.* Cambridge, MA: Harvard University Press.

Vygotsky, L. S. (1987). *Thinking and speech.* In R. W. Rieber & A. S. Carton (Eds.), *The collected works of L. S. Vygotsky* (Vol. 1): *Problems of general psychology.* (N. Minick, Trans.). New York: Plenum Press (original work published 1934).

Wells, G. (1999). *Dialogic inquiry: Toward a sociocultural practice and theory of education.* Cambridge, England: Cambridge University Press.

Wellington, J., & Osborne, J. (2001). *Language and literacy in science education.* Philadelphia, PA: Open University Press.

Wertsch, J. V. (1991). *Voices of the mind: A sociocultural approach to mediated action.* Cambridge, MA: Harvard University Press.

Wertsch, J. V. (1998). *Mind as action.* New York: Oxford University Press.

Willinsky, J. (1990). *The New Literacy: Redefining reading and writing in schools.* New York: Routledge.

Yore, L. D., Bisanz, G. L., & Hand, B. M. (2003). Examining the literacy component of science literacy: 25 years of language arts and science research. *International Journal of Science Education, 25,* 689–725.

Yore, L. D., Hand, B. M., & Florence, M. K. (2004). Scientists' views of science, models of writing, and science writing practices. *Journal of Research in Science Teaching, 41,* 338–369.

Young, R. (1992). *Critical theory and classroom talk.* Clevedon, England: Multilingual Matters.

Matter Unit Resources

Branley, F. M. (1983). *Down comes the rain.* New York: HarperCollins.

Branley, F. M. (1986). *Air is all around you.* New York: HarperCollins.

Branley, F. M. (1986). *Snow is falling.* New York: HarperCollins.

DeWitt, L. (1991). *What will the weather be?* New York: HarperCollins.

Dorros, A. (1989). *Feel the wind.* New York: HarperCollins.

Fowler, A. (1991). *What's the weather today?* New York: Children's Press.

Fowler, A. (1992). *It could still be water.* New York: Children's Press.

Fowler, A. (1995). *When a storm comes up?* New York: Children's Press.

Fowler, A. (1996). *What do you see in a cloud?* New York: Children's Press.

Gibbons, G. (1990). *Weather words and what they mean*. New York: Holiday House.

Hughes, M. (2004). *Water cycle*. Chicago: Heinemann Library.

Miles, E. (2005). *Rain*. Chicago: Heinemann Library.

New Media. (1997). *States of matter*, multimedia CD-ROM for PC and Macintosh. New York: Facts on File.

Zoehfeld, K. W. (1998). *What is the world made of? All about solids, liquids, and gases*. New York: HarperCollins.

Forest Unit Resources

Berger, M. (1992). *Look out for turtles!* New York: HarperCollins.

Dell'Oro, S.P. (2001). *Tunneling earthworms*. Minneapolis, MN: Lerner.

First Discovery Book. (2002). *In the forest*. New York: Scholastic.

Fowler, A. (1997). *Animals under the ground*. New York: Children's Press.

Fowler, A. (1998). *Inside an ant colony*. New York: Children's Press.

Fowler, A. (2001). *From seed to plant*. New York: Children's Press.

Gibbons, B. (1991). *From seed to plant*. New York: Holiday House.

Himmelman, J. (2000). *An earthworm's life*. New York: Children's Press.

Lauber, P. (1988). *Snakes are hunters*. New York: HarperCollins.

Lauber, P. (1995). *Who eats what?: Food chains and food webs*. New York: HarperCollins.

Llewellyn, C. (2000). *Earthworms*. New York: Franklin Watts.

Llewellyn, C. (2003). *Starting life: Frog*. Chanhassen, MN: Northword.

Massie, E. (2000). *A forest community*. Austin, TX: Streck-Vaughn.

Pfeffer, W. (1997). *A log's life*. New York: Simon & Schuster.

Riley, J. (2001). *Quiet owls*. Minneapolis, MN: Lerner.

Saunders-Smith, G. (1998). *Seeds*. Mankato, MN: Pebble Books.

Sill, C. (2002). *About fish: A guide for children*. Atlanta, GA: Peachtree.

University of Illinois Extension. (2004a). *The adventures of Herman: Schools Online www. urbanext.uiuc.edu/schools/* Urbana, IL: University of Illinois Board of Trustees.

University of Illinois Extension. (2004b). *Trees are terrific: Schools Online www.urbanext.uiuc. edu/schools/* Urbana, IL: University of Illinois Board of Trustees.

University of Illinois Extension. (2004c). *Let's talk about insects: Schools Online www.urban ext.uiuc.edu/schools/* Urbana, IL: University of Illinois Board of Trustees.

Whitehouse, P. (2004). *Chipmunks*. Chicago: Heinemann Library.

SECTION II

Exploring ISLE Curriculum Genres

2

READ-ALOUDS OF CHILDREN'S LITERATURE INFORMATION BOOKS

Dialogic Sharing and Intertextuality

Amy Arsenault, Maria Varelas, Christine C. Pappas, Anne Barry, and Neveen Keblawe-Shamah

Children do not reinvent scientific inquiry, ideas, and language all by themselves; instead, children learn from more knowledgeable others by engaging in collaborative discourse in the context of various artifacts jointly constructing scientific understandings and linguistic registers. This is at the heart of Vygotsky's (1978, 1987) sociocultural, constructivist framework of learning. One of the artifacts that can promote children's learning of science is children's information books, which are available on many science topics, but whose use in science instruction has been limited (Duke 2000; Pappas, 2006; Purcell-Gates, Duke, & Martineau, 2007). Such texts provide ongoing sources for prototypical explanations of scientific concepts (Ogborn, Kress, Martins, & McGillicuddy, 1996), explain scientific phenomena, and provide a tool that helps children link empirical evidence and theorizing (Varelas & Pappas, 2006). Moreover, such books also provide the kind of language that scientists use as they read, write, and talk, modeling the linguistic registers and genres of the science discipline (Halliday & Martin, 1993; Lemke, 1990; Wellington & Osborne, 2001). Thus, as children and teacher engage with the words and pictures of informational texts, they make sense and talk science (Varelas & Pappas, 2006).

Classroom learning environments are complex physical and symbolic settings where social and cognitive relationships intertwine. Students use familiar concepts and resources to make sense of new ideas and integrate them in their cognitive structures. They "draw on multiple resources or funds to make sense of the world" (Moje, Ciechanowski, Kramer, Ellis, Carrillo, & Collazo, 2004, p. 42). One tool that can be useful to them in this endeavor is intertextuality. People textualize their experiences and the world in which they live, making those phenomena part of their language resources (Bloome & Egan-Robertson, 2004). Intertextuality is the act of referencing other texts, the juxtaposition of other texts to any current text being considered, read, or discussed. We use "text" in an expansive way that includes written texts, but also recounts of events and experiences, oral discourse, pictures, diagrams, charts, musical notes, algebraic equations, scientific formulae (Pappas, Varelas, Barry, & Rife, 2003; Wells, 1990; Wells & Chang-Wells, 1992). In earlier research, we have identified four main categories of intertextual links that include connections to: written texts, other texts that are orally shared, other media, and prior classroom discourse (Category I); recounting of hands-on explorations (Category II); recounting of events (Category III); and referencing "implicit" generalized events (Category IV). (See Pappas et al., 2003, for more details.)

Intertextuality is a social construction (Bloome & Egan-Robertson, 1993; Egan-Robertson, 1998; Fairclough, 1992; Lemke, 1985, 1992; Varelas, Pappas, & Rife, 2004). It hinges on the mutual recognition of the speaker and the addressee(s), not only because to make an intertextual link both have to recognize it, but also because it identifies, and implicitly or explicitly evaluates, ways of being in the world. Thus, in order to be recognized as such, intertextual connections need to meet the criteria of social recognition, acknowledgement, and social significance (Bloome & Egan-Robertson, 1993). Intertextuality can be a transformative agent in the collective production of knowledge supporting the development of hybrid, third spaces (Barton, 2008) that help "learners see connections, as well as contradictions, between the ways they know the world and the ways others know the world" (Moje et al., 2004, p. 44).

Intertextuality is especially powerful in read-alouds of informational texts that are shared dialogically in a classroom. Initiating or taking up intertextual connections during information text read-alouds provide children with the opportunity to co-construct meaning with their peers by voicing their thoughts, reorganizing their ideas, and creating new concepts together as a community of learners—this is the epistemic function of intertextuality (Wells, 1999). However, there is only now a small, but growing research base about young children's engagement with science information books (e.g., Duke, 2003; Smolkin & Donovan, 2001), and there is an even smaller pool of studies that explore specifically children's responses to these books, and more specifically, their use of intertextuality in the context of such read-alouds.

Furthermore, over the years, research has shown that girls are especially marginalized when it comes to science learning, engagement, and enjoyment (Barton, 2008; Brickhouse & Potter, 2001; Ford, Brickhouse, Lottero-Perdue, & Kittleson, 2006). Social interaction is particularly important for learning science, as the practice of science is a discursive activity involving the collective use of science-related terms and methods of argumentation to construct concepts (Olitsky, 2007). A variety of studies, though, have shown that young women may refuse to participate in scientific activities if taking part in such activities is incongruent with their gendered identities (Carlone, 2004). Girls do participate in activities that center on science and understanding the world scientifically, if given appropriate opportunities and social spaces (Lefebvre, 1974) to co-construct science knowledge with each other and their teacher. Having interactions in which students receive mutual support and are included leads to successful experiences and increased participation in science instruction (Olitsky, 2007). Furthermore, in such contexts, girls are more likely to appropriate scientific meanings (Brickhouse, Lowery, & Schultz, 2000).

Therefore, in this chapter, we explore how intertextuality may contribute to developing a classroom environment that nurtures girls' and boys' involvement, offering them many, multiple, and varied opportunities to do, talk, think, and share science. To that goal, we examined intertextual links across the two units, *Matter* and *Forest*, how children and teachers in the six ISLE classrooms made these links, and how these links were taken up to help children explore science concepts and make meaning in the classroom during the read-aloud sessions of 12 children's literature information books. (See Chapter 1 for details about the two integrated units and demographic make-up of the six classrooms.)

Engagement and Intertextuality

The second read-aloud of the *Matter* unit, the read-aloud of the book *When a Storm Comes Up* (Fowler, 1995), took place in late September and was the read-aloud with the highest number of intertextual links in this unit across all classes. Children showed their fascination with storms through intertextual links with other written texts, movies, television, and events. In Excerpt 1 below, Begoña Cowan's 2nd grade class is discussing ideas such as sleet, hailstorms, hail, and hailstones at about midway through the read-aloud. Conventions of transcription for classroom discourse are explained in the Appendix at the end of Chapter 1. In the excerpts, the intertextual links are in bold.

> Excerpt 1:
>
> 1   Ms. Cowan: It is one of our storm words. You got it. Check this out. This is hail [pointing to first picture in book]. IN A HAILSTORM, RAINDROPS FREEZE INTO ICE BEFORE THEY REACH THE GROUND. HAIL {COULD} BE AS BIG AS THIS. BUT DON'T WORRY, most of them are only that big [pointing to second picture with smaller hail], HAILSTONES ARE ALMOST ALWAYS MUCH SMALLER. Hail is usually about the size of a penny. All right?
>
> 2   Caitlyn: But it can be as big as a baseball.
>
> 3   Ms. Cowan: But it can be as big as this [teacher holding up picture on page 18 representing hail in various sizes ranging from 3/4 of an inch to 1/4 of an inch].
>
> 4   Caitlyn: Or a baseball.

5	Ingrid:	Or as big as a golf ball.
6	Ms. Cowan:	Well I don't think it can be as big as a baseball, but it can be // yeah, there is something called golf ball sized hail. Cassandra?
7	Cassandra:	**Hail, if it is that big in the other picture, it will break your car window in the front. If it is that big.**
8	Ms. Cowan:	Yes it can. It can hurt you. Fall on your head. Hit a window at home.
9	Cassandra:	**It's on *The Day After Tomorrow*. It's a movie.**
10	Ms. Cowan:	Oh the movie, *The Day After Tomorrow*...AMONG THE WORST KINDS OF STORMS ARE HURRICANES AND TORNADOS. A HURRICANE |

The book *When a Storm Comes Up* discusses various types of storms, including hailstorms, and how rain freezes into ice before it reaches the ground (changing from a liquid to a solid). The topic of hail comes up in the middle of the read-aloud and leads to three children bridging their own spontaneous concepts and understandings with scientific concepts introduced by the information book. Begoña points out that hail are usually the size of a penny, or it can be the size of hail shown in the book on page 18 (about 1/4″ to 3/4″ in diameter). In a dialogically-oriented classroom, authority is shared, and this allows two girls to challenge the range of size of hail, not accepting hail only being the size of a penny or smaller as shown in the book and described by their teacher. Caitlyn and Ingrid believe hail can be bigger than a penny and refer to sports balls for size comparison (baseball and golf ball, units 2, 4–5). Begoña challenges Caitlyn's description of hail being the size of a baseball, but supports Ingrid's description of hail being the size of a golf ball—"there is something called golf ball sized hail" (unit 6). Although Caitlyn and Ingrid focus on the form (and specifically the size) of hail, Cassandra takes the discussion further by accepting the size of hail presented in the book, which is also reinforced by the teacher (unit 7), and moving to the function of hail. Ingrid and Caitlyn's discussion is a catalyst for Cassandra's intertextual link that pushes the discussion forward and highlights an association between form and function, a fundamental science concept (National Science Council, 1996, 2012). Cassandra makes an intertextual connection (units 7 and 9, Category I—reference to other media, a movie) to *The Day After Tomorrow*, and how it destroyed a car windshield. The teacher takes up and validates Cassandra's reference by acknowledging the movie, and then the read-aloud continues.

Toward the end of the read-aloud, after several storms had been discussed (hail, rain, snow, hurricanes), the topic of tornadoes fascinated the children who had many questions and ideas. Caitlyn had already tried to bring up the idea of tornadoes prior to Begoña's reading about that topic in the book, but Begoña had asked Caitlyn and the rest of the class to wait and share their ideas later when they came to this topic in the book. Such instructional decisions may be necessary to support the flow of a read-aloud, keeping related ideas together, but they can also discourage children's interest and engagement, if they happen repeatedly. When tornadoes were finally covered in the book, Caitlyn's hand shot up and Begoña remembered her promise to the class and gave Caitlyn the floor to share her idea, and, as it turned out to make an intertextual connection as well. In the discourse below (Excerpt 2), Caitlyn and Natasha discuss with the class additional scientific information on tornadoes via intertextual connections with other books.

Excerpt 2:

1	Ms. Cowan:	Okay. A TORNADO FORMS OVER LAND. THE WINDS WHIRL AROUND IN A TALL, FUNNEL-SHAPED COLUMN. CARS, ROOFS, EVEN ENTIRE HOUSES CAN BE SUCKED UP OFF THE GROUND BY A TORNADO. THE GOVERNMENT // Okay we got to the tornado part. Tell them.
2	Caitlyn:	Tornadoes can hop and twist around or wiggly-waggly. Or just around and around and around in a great circle. **And I have a book of tornadoes that has this picture where there is a damaged one house right here and a house that hasn't even been touched on the other side.**
3	Ms. Cowan:	Umhm. A tornado could go down on the same street and you could have one side totally damaged and the other side fine. I am going to pick Daniel and Natasha because they have not had a turn and Anna, all right? Daniel.
4	Daniel:	What do you mean by tornadoes can hop?
5	Caitlyn:	**Well in the book called *Tornado Turbo* that I read the magic school bus |**
6	Ms. Cowan:	Is it one of the books we have?
7	Caitlyn:	Yeah.
8	Ms. Cowan:	Well there you go. **We do have *Twister on Tuesday* and *The Magic School Bus.*** Wait back to her.
9	Caitlyn:	It can hop. It can go up for a little while then go back down and skip a house very easily.
10	Ms. Cowan:	Okay, so guys just think of it this way. **If you are walking down the street and you guys are playing a game or something and there is a twig or a tree // how many of you guys // oh you know what David [Ms. Cowan's son] does?**

He loves hopping on the tiles // you know if there is red and black tiles, he will hop on all the black ones. That is kind of what a tornado can do. Daniel good question. Natasha?

11 Natasha: **In a book I have at home |**
12 Ms. Cowan: Talk to them.
13 Natasha: **It says sometimes by Florida a lot of tornadoes come out of the water and they are called waterspouts.**
14 Ms. Cowan: All right. And Anna.

The text that the teacher reads from the book presents information about a tornado, its shape, formation, and damage capabilities. Caitlyn introduces supportive scientific information that tornadoes can progress by irregular movements and that you cannot predict what direction they are going or what will be damaged. Caitlyn makes an intertextual link (units 2 & 5, Category I: Reference to written text), a connection with another book, the *Magic School Bus*: *Twister Trouble* (Cole, 2001), which she refers to as "Tornado Turbo." Caitlyn seems to have gathered information about the destruction capabilities of a tornado from the written text and the pictures in that book which she presented to the class. The teacher acknowledges and validates Caitlyn's contribution and conveys to the class that the *Magic School Bus* book is available in the classroom, as well as another book, *Twister on Tuesday* (Osborne, 2001). In this exchange, Caitlyn's intertextual connection provided a valuable opportunity for other students to become aware of classroom resources, and promoted discussion on the properties and potential impact of tornadoes.

Then another 2nd-grader, Daniel, asks for clarification of Caitlyn's intertextual link and physically turns his body to ask her directly about her reference to tornadoes hopping (unit 4). Daniel's quest for understanding emerged as a result of Caitlyn's contribution. In a supportive, collaborative, dialogic classroom, where authority and expertise are shared, children feel free to question and make sense of each other's ideas. Caitlyn answers Daniel's question by describing what she means by "hop," providing a well-crafted description of a tornado's movement that justifies how a tornado can skip houses (unit 9). Read-alouds of children's informational texts enacted in a dialogic manner offer various opportunities for children to think about scientific concepts in their own *lifeworld* languages (Gee, 1999).

Next, Natasha uses Caitlyn's intertextual connection as a catalyst to make her own intertextual connection (Category I: Reference to written text) by offering her knowledge about what she learned from another book at home (unit 13). Natasha also gives additional scientific information by introducing the term "waterspout." If children are given the space to share and contribute, one intertextual connection can often lead to other children making intertextual connections to the ideas presented in a read-aloud, thus furthering understanding and learning.

In both Excerpts 1 and 2, children brought up Category I links (connections to written text or other media), which is the second most frequent intertextuality type after Category III links (connections to recounting events) that we identified in all ISLE classrooms. The discourse excerpts above illustrate some of the possibilities that emerge when children use such type of intertextuality to share and discuss salient scientific ideas and make meaning.

In ISLE classrooms, intertextuality also offered children other ways to wonder and make sense of ideas. Excerpt 3 below took place in Sharon Gill's 1st-grade class during the read-aloud of the book *Down Comes the Rain* (Branley, 1983). The children just finished listening about water changing to water vapor, then condensing into water droplets that together make a cloud, from which eventually drops fall to the earth as it rains. Especially salient in this discourse excerpt is the space offered to several students to contribute intertextual connections and make sense of the properties of hail.

Excerpt 3:

1	Olivia:	**Um . . . Oh yeah, heavy rain is also called raining cats and dogs because it is a really heavy rain.**
2	Ms. Gill:	Yeah we just say that. That doesn't really mean that it is really raining cats and dogs.
3	Olivia:	Yeah I know it is like a metaphor.
4	Ms. Gill:	It is a metaphor, right. John?
5	John:	Has is ever hailed in Chicago?
6	Alam:	**Yeah, I felt it too when I came back from a soccer game I think.**
7	Ms. Gill:	**Yeah, sometimes you can hear it hitting your house.** [She makes noises like the hail hitting your house] **Toot, toot, toot. Like someone is throwing rocks.**
8	John:	I have never heard it.
9	Ms. Gill:	You might one day.
10	John:	**I have heard rain hitting my house.**
11	Ms. Gill:	Well listen for it someday.
12	Child:	**One time raindrops blasted through my house it was so heavy.**
13	Ms. Gill:	Umhm, Lauren.
14	Lauren:	If you throw rocks is it like hail?
15	Ms. Gill:	Why did you say that?
16	Lauren:	Because rocks are kinda of like hail.
17	Ms. Gill:	Why?

18	Lauren:	Because hail is hard.
19	Ms. Gill:	Because it is hard. So how is hail // how is hail // what is inside? Who remembers? What is hail made out of? Hailstones are made out of what?
20	Lauren:	Rubble.
21	Ms. Gill:	Not rubble. The hailstones that come out of the clouds.
22	Lauren:	Water.
23	Ms. Gill:	I can't hear you.
24	Lauren:	Water.
25	Ms. Gill:	What kind of water? How does it feel when we go higher and higher and higher?
26	Children:	Cold.
27	Ms. Gill:	So if we go higher and higher and higher and we have water what are we going to get?
28	Lauren:	Cold water.
29	Alam:	Hail.
30	Ms. Gill:	Cold water and if we get cold and we keep going up. [Points with one finger up in the air.]
31	Alam:	Freeze.
32	Ms. Gill:	Shh.
33	Lauren:	Freezing.
34	Ms. Gill:	And when it is freezing it turns into?
35	Lauren:	Hail.
36	Ms. Gill:	And how would hail // what do we have down here that feels like hail. We have something in the room. What do you call that stuff? We put it in the freezer.
37	Class:	Ice.

Down Comes the Rain was the final read-aloud book in the *Matter* unit and at this point in the year the children had extensively discussed states of matter and their changes (freezing, melting, evaporation, condensation), and the water cycle. The book presents different types of rain (drizzling, pouring), and Olivia describes heavy rain with a common euphemism—"raining cats and dogs" (unit 1, Category I: Reference to other text, a rhyme or saying). John asks whether it has ever hailed in Chicago, prompting Alam to describe a personal event (Category III) at a soccer game in Chicago where he felt hail. Another boy described an event where raindrops were so heavy they blasted through his house (unit 12, Category III), building upon John's comment that he has heard rain, but not hail, hitting his house. The children seem interested in talking and thinking about the severity of this form of precipitation.

Moreover, the class picks up on the teacher's analogy of hail to rocks hitting a house (unit 7, Category IV: Implicit generalized event), and her intertextual link brings her, along with John, Alam, and Lauren, to discuss the properties of hail, including hardness, composition, and formation related to the water cycle. Lauren is confused by her teacher's intertextual link of hail and rocks and asks a clarifying question, "if you throw rocks is it like hail?" (unit 14). Sharon helps Lauren understand by pushing her to explain "why," leading to the notion of the hardness of both rocks and hail. Next the teacher and children construct the idea of "coldness" that is needed for hail to be formed. This classroom discussion and the social space given to Lauren to share, discuss, and learn, provided the entire class with meaning making opportunities, as the class listened in on how and where hail is formed.

Intertextuality unfolded differently in the *Matter* and *Forest* units and in the different ISLE classrooms. Whereas the two 1st-grade classes had about the same number of links in both units, the links in the two 3rd-grade classes increased at different rates from the *Matter* unit to the *Forest* unit. The *Forest* unit took place much later in the year, and by that time, children may have been more used to the dialogic practices of their classrooms that nurtured connection making, sharing, exploration of ideas, and discussion.

The read-aloud of the book *Seeds* (Saunders-Smith, 1998), in the *Forest* unit, had the highest density of intertextual connections across all read-alouds in both units. Ibett Ortiz's 2nd-grade bilingual class had the highest number of intertextual links for that read-aloud (30 links during a 43-minute read-aloud). Excerpt 4 took place close to the end of the read-aloud, and again shows Category III personal-event connections. [Discourse in Spanish is followed by the English translation in brackets and italics.]

Excerpt 4:

1   Ms. Ortiz: Vamos a ver aqui, este se llama sunflower seed, el girasol. Wow! Uno a la vez. *[Let's see here, this is called a sunflower seed (points to book). Wow! One at a time.]*

2   Mateo: **En primer grado Mrs. Garcia nos daba en un vaso, las flores y las llevabammos a la casa y crecian. [*In the first grade Mrs. Garcia used to give us a glass some flowers and we would take them home to grow.]***

3   Girl: Pero eran de calabaza esas semillas. *[But they were pumpkin seeds.]*

4   Boy: A mi si me crecio. *[Mine did grow.]*

5   Girl: A mi tambien. *[Mine too!]*

6   Boy: Ami se me murio por tanta agua. *[Mine died because of too much water.]*

7   Ms. Ortiz: Se te murio porque le echaste mucha agua? Uno a la vez no puedo escuchar a todos a la misma vez. *[The plant died because you overwatered it? One at a time because I cannot hear everyone at the same time.]*

8	Boy:	Que es un girasol? [*What is a sunflower?*]
9	Girl:	Es una flor. [*It is a flower.*]
10	Bernardo:	**En primer ano, Mrs. V. me dio una flor en un vaso com mi nombre y me la lleve a mi casa y entonces ya iba creciendo se iba haciendo grande y grande y luego se murio.** [*In the first grade, Mrs. V. gave me a flower in a cup with my name on it and I took it home and it started to grow. It grew and grew taller and then it died.*]
11	Ms. Ortiz:	Porque crees que se murio? [*Why do you think it died?*]
12	Boy:	Su hermano a lo mejor le echo algo. [*His brother probably put something in it that made it die.*]
13	Bernardo:	**Mi hermano le estaba quitando la tierra y estaba com agua.** [*My brother was taking the soil off but it had water.*]
14	Soledad:	**Cuando yo me lleve la planta crecio muy chiquita.** [*When I took the plant it didn't grow that much.*]
15	Ms. Ortiz:	Crecio chiquita, no se hizo grande! Vamos a seguir despues van a tener tiempo para escribir sus comentarios. [*It grew small, it didn't get big! We are going to continue, after you will get the opportunity and time to write down your comments.*] SEEDS NEED AIR, WATER, {WARMTH IN THE SOIL} TO GROW. Entonces las semillas necesitan aire, agua y tambien el calor para crecer. Tambien necesitan comida que se encuentra en la tierra. [*Then the SEEDS NEED AIR, WATER, AND {ALSO} WARMTH TO GROW. THEY ALSO NEED FOOD {THAT IS} FOUND IN THE SOIL.*]

Children in Ibett's 2nd-grade class recounted several specific personal events and events that involved their family members. Mateo, Bernardo, Soledad, and other students told about experiences they had in 1st grade with growing flowers and pumpkin seeds at home. Although some children were successful in growing these plants, others were not. Some children's plants died (units 6 and 10), and this offered the class an opportunity to suggest explanations about why that happened. One boy (unit 6) spontaneously offered a reason (overwatering), but since Bernardo did not offer a reason when he added that his plant had died too (unit 10), Ibett encouraged him to offer an explanation by asking, "*Why do you think it died?*" (unit 11). Two different reasons emerged—the presence of a harmful substance (unit 12) and taking away the soil (unit 13). Contemplating these possible reasons nuanced further what the children were learning regarding what seeds need to grow, which Ibett reiterated (unit 15) as a way of offering Soledad ideas to consider in order to construct an explanation for her outcome.

Everyday Experiences and Explorations as Contexts for Intertextuality

As indicated above, the most frequent type of intertextual links made in all classrooms and across the two units were Category III—connections to recounts of events in children's everyday lives (57% of all links were of this type). Children's experiences carried knowledge that was incorporated in the classroom talk as the teachers made space for such sharing. As children brought in their funds of knowledge (González & Moll, 2002) by making intertextual connections to personal (or personally-related) and specific or habitual events in their lives, they engaged further with scientific ideas and processes. Additionally, children referred to hands-on explorations, those done in class during the units, but also explorations elsewhere, to make sense of ideas presented in the information book read-alouds.

Excerpt 5 took place in Neveen's 3rd-grade class during the beginning of the final read-aloud in the *Matter* unit, *Down Comes the Rain*. Neveen has just read about putting water into a saucer and seeing what happens to the water (i.e., evaporation), when Adalia offers an intertextual link.

Excerpt 5:

1	Adalia:	**It's like when you wash dishes and you put them through the #dryer. And# the next morning the water's gone.**
2	Child:	#Yeah. They dry.#
3	Ms. Shamah:	That's true! [turns to class] Does that happen?
4	Class:	Yes.
5	Ms. Shamah:	[turns back to Adalia] So what does that // where does that water go?
6	Adalia:	It turns to droplets and goes up to the clouds.
7	Ms. Shamah:	What is the droplets?
8	Adalia:	Um, air and water vapor?
9	Ms. Shamah:	Water vapor.
10	Christopher:	**It is like in the summer, when one day it rains and the next day when we didn't see the // the puddle no more. It's not there.**
11	Ms. Shamah:	Right. So what happened to the puddle?
12	Class:	It evaporated.
13	Ms. Shamah:	Evaporated. Go ahead Danita.
14	Danita:	**I'm gonna see // I'm gonna see // I'm gonna see // I'm gonna try to be like a scientist and see how the water evaporates.**

Adalia (unit 1) and Christopher (unit 10) bring up two different events (drying dishes and summer puddles that dry up) that they must have experienced in their lives and that they accurately associate with evaporation. In these events—generalized ones—no particular people are involved and there is no reference to a specific time. Intertextuality in the form of connections to implicit generalized events (Category IV) represents an important linguistic tool where children do not use narrative autobiographical accounts, recounting stories of events they or identified others have experienced, but rather share impersonal accounts of scientific phenomena (Pappas & Varelas, 2004).

In unit 14, Danita makes a different type of connection regarding a future hands-on exploration having to do with studying at home how a body of water evaporates (Category II: Recounting of hands-on explorations). She associates herself with a scientist, repeating several times that she is "gonna see" how the water evaporates and that this is being "like a scientist." Although Neveen's class, like the other ISLE classes, has already completed an evaporation experiment where the students took measurements of water evaporating in various graduated cylinders at different locations in the classroom, Danita makes sense of the text that Neveen has just read by wanting to do her own investigation at home. Maybe the information text motivated her to conduct her own exploration in a different setting than that of her classroom, where she can observe again the change.

Excerpt 6 below provides another example of a student, Sergio, in a different class, Anne Barry's 1st grade, making an intertextual connection during the read-aloud of the book *Down Comes the Rain*, which refers to a home experience involving water in the freezer.

Excerpt 6:

1	Sergio:	**One time I had this bag of water and I put it in the refrigerator and it freezed.**
2	Ms. Barry:	Did you put it in the freezer part?
3	Sergio:	[shakes head yes]
4	Ms. Barry:	Okay, what happened when you did that?
5	Sergio:	It freezed.
6	Ms. Barry:	It freezed. Why did it freeze?
7	Girl:	Cause it's cold in there.
8	Ms. Barry:	Okay, what happens to the molecules?
9	Francisco:	It moves a little.
10	Ms. Barry:	Moves a little, then what?
11	Francisco:	When you take it out, it moves faster.
12	Ms. Barry:	Why does it move a little faster when you // okay, it got frozen and then // why does it move a little faster?

Sergio recounts an event (Category III) of putting water into the refrigerator, which, as a result, "freezed" (unit 1). Anne takes up Sergio's intertextual link and asks for an explanation (unit 6), which a classmate provides referring to the low temperature of the freezer (unit 7). Anne advances the discussion even further (units 8 and 10), encouraging the students to apply what they had discussed about molecules and how they behave in different states of matter (see Chapter 6 for more details on this) to the event that Sergio recounted. Responding to Anne's request to connect freezing to molecular movement, Francisco offers an accurate scientific understanding (unit 9) which he further articulates (unit 11) after Anne's continuous probing (unit 10) to describe how molecules move when frozen water is taken out of the freezer, and therefore, melts.

In Excerpt 7, Mary in Jennifer's 3rd-grade class recounted a personal specific event (Category III) at the end of the read-aloud of the book *Animals under the Ground* (Fowler, 1997) in the *Forest* unit. The book describes relationships among animals under the ground, and the importance of worms and ants in providing food for moles and other burrowing mammals. This led to the discussion of food chain ideas and who eats what. Kenny asked the question, "What do ants eat?" and several children replied with answers: "they can eat other insects"; "they eat anything"; "maybe other insects"; "maybe leaves"; and "crackers." Mary was sitting in the back corner of the room, but she raised her hand high because she wanted to share.

Excerpt 7:

1 Mary: **When I was at a pet store, my aunt and my mom, we were goin' to get some food for our fish and our fish // they eat little goldfish. And then they eat those little goldfish and they is called feeders. And next to the feeders was some insect and they real tiny and then I talked to the pet store manager and he told me about those animals and they said they go out and they dangerous because they poisonous if they go out and get a hold of somethin' it will turn them a different color.**

2 Ms. Hankes: So we do know some animals are poisonous, aren't they? There might even be some poisonous animals in the forest.

Mary is touching upon important scientific concepts through her intertextual connection (Category III), building on the answers she has heard that referred to insects. Mary is also sharing her knowledge about the food chain and how some fish eat other fish for food, associating the name for these types of fish (feeders) with their purpose. Mary's link offers a caution (danger and poisonous) and nuances the idea that all insects can be food for other animals. Jennifer not only re-voices Mary's idea ("we do know some animals are poisonous"), but she also positions Mary as knowledge provider. As a result of Mary's contribution, Jennifer suggests to the class that there may be poisonous animals in the forest, the environment that they are currently thinking about.

Another example is shown in Excerpt 8, where midway through the read–aloud of the book *What Do You See in a Cloud?* (Fowler, 1996), three girls in Begoña's 2nd-grade class are recounting personal generalized, habitual events involving clouds, and Begoña takes this opportunity to reinforce scientific concepts about properties of clouds. Begoña has just read about being able to see your breath on a winter day and how you actually form a small cloud when your warm, moist breath reaches the cold air.

> Excerpt 8:
>
> 1   Carolina: **Because when you open your freezer, like the freezer is real cold, so it makes a cloud [swirling motion with her hands] but, you don't know it but some people do. So, it goes up to the sky** [making a swirling motion with her hands].
>
> 2   Ms. Cowan: But, that cloud is water.
>
> 3   Carolina: Yes.
>
> 4   Gabriella: **And sometimes when you are in your car, when you are looking out the window your breath comes out and then it smudges the window.**
>
> 5   Ms. Cowan: Umhm. And that smudge is because your breath is hot and the air is cold, the window is cold. And the moist air, because you've got saliva in your mouth, you got water.
>
> 6   Cassandra: So, it's the winter and water.
>
> 7   Ms. Cowan: Right. Indira is the last one right now. Can you guys listen to Indira?
>
> 8   Indira: **Well, when you are in the winter, like your mouth is really warm and the air outside is freezing, and when you do it [she exhales] it comes together and it makes this little [making box shape with her hands], it makes cloud kind of and then it disappears.**
>
> 9   Ms. Cowan: You got it!

In Excerpt 8, we find three examples of intertextual connections to recounting everyday experiences. Carolina describes how you can create a cloud with a freezer. She is implying that a cloud is made when it is really cold around (as is the case in a freezer). The teacher takes up Carolina's link and reinforces the idea that clouds are made of water. Gabriella offers another example, but she does not even imply "coldness." Thus, the teacher validates her contribution and highlights the difference in temperatures, along with the need for moisture (unit 5), which another child, Cassandra, echoes ("So, it's the winter and water," unit 6). Finally, Indira's intertextual link reinforces several main ideas and correctly describes in detail (reflecting closely the book's and teacher's description) how a cloud is formed (unit 8). These intertextual connections provided these children (and the rest of the class) the opportunity to co-construct meaning with their peers and the teacher by voicing their thoughts, organizing their ideas, and creating new concepts together as a *community of learners* (Wells, 1999).

Concluding Thoughts

We explored in this chapter how a particular discourse tool, intertextuality, was enacted in the ISLE classrooms and offered children opportunities for participation and meaning making in read-alouds of informational texts. Children, both girls and boys, and teachers engaged with science ideas and attempted to make sense of them by relating them with resources available to them in their lives in and out of the classroom. Each classroom enacted intertextuality in particular ways, since it was a unique community of learners governed by particular norms and influenced by the dynamics of that particular group of students and by the ways in which the teacher orchestrated that community.

The dialogic classroom provides spaces for intertextual connections to arise and it also offers sites for discussion between the children and the teacher and among the children themselves, each of whom is seen as a potential source of knowledge and expertise. Moreover, intertextuality is a lens through which children can see themselves and be seen by others as scientists.

Although intertextuality offers opportunities, it may also lead to tensions for a classroom community. It is possible that some intertextual links, especially children's recounts of lifeworld events, could take the classroom discourse into unintended directions, making it difficult for teachers (and other children) to reinforce or develop ideas. As a result, teachers need to be on guard and create strategies to cope with such occasions. Finally, it is important to note that intertextuality can have a very idiosyncratic flavor, marked by individuals' experiences, cultural ways of being, and socialization patterns. There is no common pattern for enacting intertextuality for all classrooms, but when participants hear, acknowledge, validate, and take up connections, intertextuality becomes a powerful tool to nurture meaning making.

Despite the above challenges, the various examples that we highlighted in this chapter point to the many and varied possibilities that intertextuality affords a classroom community. Intertextuality functions in such a way that gives children, of various ethno-linguistic backgrounds in urban schools, the opportunity to share their rich experiences, their *funds of knowledge* (González & Moll, 2001), and draw on multiple resources to make sense of the world (Moje et al., 2004) and establish connections with science. As links are created and shared in classroom discourse, intertextuality materializes as a social construction (Bloome & Egan-Robertson, 1993; Egan-Robertson, 1998; Fairclough, 1992; Lemke, 1985, 1992; Varelas et al., 2004) where children along with their teacher co-construct meaning of new and old ideas presented in informational texts. In this way, intertextuality is a communal phenomenon where people interact with each other and with texts (broadly defined) to provide the strands in the rich tapestry of classroom meaning making.

References

Barton, A. C. (2008). Creating hybrid spaces for engaging in school science among urban middle school girls. *American Educational Research Journal, 45,* 68–103.

Bloome, D., & Egan-Robertson, A. (1993). The social construction of intertextuality in classroom reading and writing lessons. *Reading Research Quarterly, 28,* 304–333.

Bloome, D., & Egan-Robertson, A. (2004). The social construction of intertextuality in classroom reading and writing lessons. In N. Shuart-Faris & D. Bloome (Eds.), *Uses of intertextuality in classroom and educational research* (pp. 17–64). Greenwich, CT: Information Age Publishing.

Branley, F. (1983). *Down comes the rain.* New York: HarperCollins.

Brickhouse, N., Lowery, P., & Schultz, K. (2000). What kind of girl does science? The construction of school science identities. *Journal of Research in Science Teaching, 37,* 441–458.

Brickhouse, N. W., & Potter, J. T. (2001). Young women's scientific identity formation in an urban context. *Journal of Research in Science Teaching, 38,* 965–980.

Carlone, H. B. (2004). The cultural production of science in reform-based physics: Girls' access, participation, and resistance. *Journal of Research in Science Teaching, 41,* 392–414.

Cole, J. (2001). *The magic school bus, a science chapter book: Twister trouble.* New York: Scholastic.

Duke, N. K. (2000). 3.6 minutes per day: The scarcity of informational texts in first grade. *Reading Research Quarterly, 35,* 202–224.

Duke, N. K. (2003). Reading to learn from the very beginning: Information books in early childhood. *Young Children, 58*(2), 14–20.

Egan-Robertson, A. (1998). Learning about culture, language, and power: Understanding relationships among personhood, literacy practices, and intertextuality. *Journal of Literacy Research, 30,* 449–487.

Fairclough, N. (1992). Discourse and text: Linguistic and intertextual analysis within discourse analysis. *Discourse and Society, 3,* 193–218.

Ford, D. J., Brickhouse, N. W., Lottero-Perdue, P., & Kittleson, J. (2006). Elementary girls' science reading at home and school. *Science Education, 90,* 270–288.

Fowler, A. (1995). *When a storm comes up.* New York: Children's Press.

Fowler, A. (1996). *What do you see in a cloud?* New York: Children's Press.

Fowler, A. (1997). *Animals under the ground.* New York: Children's Press.

Gee, J. P. (1999). *An introduction to discourse analysis: Theory and method* (2nd ed.). New York: Routledge.

González, N., & Moll, L. C. (2001). *Cruzando El Puente*: Building bridges to funds of knowledge. *Educational Policy, 16,* 623–641.

Halliday, M. A. K., & Martin, J. R. (1993). *Writing science: Literacy and discursive power.* Pittsburgh, PA: University of Pittsburgh Press.

Lefebvre, H. (1974). *The production of space* (E. Nicholson Smith, Trans.). Oxford, England: Blackwell.

Lemke, J. L. (1985). Ideology, intertextuality, and the notion of register. In J. D. Benson & W. S. Greaves (Eds.), *Systemic perspectives on discourse: Selected theoretical papers from the Ninth International Systemic Workshop* (Vol. 1, pp. 275–294). Norwood, NJ: Ablex.

Lemke, J. L. (1990). *Talking science: Language, learning, and values.* Norwood, NJ: Ablex Publishing.

Lemke, J. L. (1992). Intertextuality and educational research. *Linguistic and Education, 4,* 257–267.

Moje, E. B., Ciechanowski, K. M., Kramer, K., Ellis, L., Carrillo, R., & Collazo, T. (2004). Working toward third space in content area literacy: An examination of everyday funds of knowledge and discourse. *Reading Research Quarterly, 39,* 38–70.

National Research Council. (1996). *National science education standards.* Washington, DC: National Academy Press.

National Research Council. (2012). *A framework for K-12 science education: Practices, crosscutting concepts, and core ideas.* Washington, DC: National Academies Press.

Ogborn, J., Kress, G., Martins, I., & McGillicuddy, K. (1996). *Explaining science in the classroom.* Buckingham, England: Open University Press.

Olitsky, S. (2007). Promoting student engagement in science: Interaction rituals and the pursuit of a community of practice. *Journal of Research in Science Teaching, 44,* 33–56.

Osborne, M. P. (2001). *Twister on Tuesday.* New York: Random House.

Pappas, C. C. (2006). The information book genre: Its role in integrated science literacy research and practice. *Reading Research Quarterly, 41,* 226–250.

Pappas, C. C., & Varelas, M. (with Barry, A., & Rife, A.) (2004). Promoting dialogic inquiry in information book read-alouds: Young urban children's ways of making sense in science. In W. Saul (Ed.), *Crossing borders in literacy and science instruction: Perspectives on theory and practice* (pp. 161–189). Newark, NJ: International Reading Association.

Pappas, C., Varelas, M., Barry, A., & Rife, A. (2003). Dialogic inquiry around information texts: The role of intertextuality in constructing scientific understandings in urban primary classrooms. *Linguistics and Education, 13,* 435–482.

Purcell-Gates, V., Duke, N. K., & Martineau, J. A. (2007). Learning to read and write genre specific text: Roles of authentic experience and explicit teaching. *Reading Research Quarterly, 42,* 8–45.

Saunders-Smith, G. (1998). *Seeds.* Mankato, MN: Pebble Books.

Smolkin, L. B., & Donovan, C. A. (2001). The information book read aloud, comprehension acquisition, and comprehension instruction. *Elementary School Journal, 102,* 97–122.

Varelas, M., & Pappas, C. (2006). Intertextuality in read-alouds of integrated science-literacy units in urban primary classrooms: Opportunities for the development of thought and language. *Cognition and Instruction, 24,* 211–259.

Varelas, M., Pappas, C. C., & Rife, A. (2004). Dialogic inquiry in an urban 2nd grade classroom: How intertextuality shapes and is shaped by social interactions and conceptual understandings. In R. Yerrick & W.-M. Roth (Eds.), *Establishing scientific classroom discourse communities: Multiple voices of research on teaching and learning* (pp. 139–168). Mahwah, NJ: Erlbaum.

Vygotsky, L. S. (1978). *Mind in society.* Cambridge, MA: Harvard University Press.

Vygotsky, L. S. (1987). *Thinking and speech*. In R.W. Rieber & A.S. Carton (Eds.), *The collected works of L.S. Vygotsky (vol. 1): Problems of general psychology* (N. Minick, Trans.). New York: Plenum Press (original work published 1934).

Wellington, J., & Osborne, J. (2001). *Language and literacy in science education*. Buckingham, England: Open University Press.

Wells, G. (1990). Talk about text: Where literacy is learned and taught. *Curriculum Inquiry, 20*, 369–405.

Wells, G. (1999). *Dialogic inquiry: Towards a sociocultural practice and theory in education*. Cambridge, England: Cambridge University Press.

Wells, G., & Chang-Wells, G. L. (1992). *Constructing knowledge together: Classroom as centers of inquiry and literacy*. Portsmouth, NH: Heinemann.

3

CHILDREN'S LANGUAGE ACTS

Diverse Forms of Participation in Read-Alouds

Eli Tucker-Raymond, Maria Varelas, Christine C. Pappas, and Ibett Ortiz

In this chapter, we explore young children's distinctive ways of participating in whole-class read-alouds of children's literature information books as part of integrated science-literacy enactments. Through examination of 24 children's participation (four from each of the six ISLE classrooms), we sought to understand how the children used language over time and across read-alouds in idiosyncratic, yet similar, ways. To provide in-depth examples of various forms of participation, we present here three case studies to illustrate individual students' language use as it unfolded in three different classrooms. Children's language use interacts dynamically with classroom norms for science learning, thinking, talking, and doing. In describing and analyzing children's participation, we build on research that considers young children as capable wonderers, theorizers, and meaning-makers and as active constructors of science knowledge-in-process (e.g., Gallas, 1995; Metz, 2011; Warren, Ballenger, Ogonowski, Rosebery, & Hudicourt-Barnes, 2001).

Science is about understanding the world around us. It involves a "theory-data dance" between observing-experimenting and explaining various phenomena (Varelas, 1996). Literacy practices, such as reading, writing, drawing, and talking, are critical aspects of scientific activity. Information text read-alouds and hands-on explorations complement each other in that they offer different opportunities for engagement in, and expression of, the theory-data dance. Moreover, in dialogically-oriented instruction, a tenuous balance is enacted between creating spaces for children to offer, test, and develop their own ideas in the midst of the classroom community *and* guiding them toward more articulated science understandings. A dialogic approach allows students to use language in their own meaningful ways and, thus, participate in the classroom community.

Participation in Classroom Communities

In the six ISLE classrooms, every student participated in the same activities and in the same curriculum as other students. (See Chapter 1 for details about the curricular units, *Matter* and *Forest*, and demographic make-up of each classroom.) Yet every child is unique. What, then, is the relationship among ways in which individual children participate in the classroom, especially when they are allowed and encouraged to make sense of science ideas presented to them via children's literature science informational texts? In part, how students engage in the class-room, if they want their contributions to be seen as legitimate, largely depends on what is sanctioned behavior in their classroom. Thus, what has been previously sanctioned and privileged in a classroom mediates what students subsequently do. Such sanctions, privileges, and engagements involve navigating tensions among individual children's beliefs about school and science, teachers' enactments of science instruction, and science practices that are emphasized in classroom instruction (Jurow & Creighton, 2005).

As students participate in a learning community, their experiences are mediated by the goals, values, tools, and relationships within that community (Wenger, 1998). To operate successfully in a classroom, students must be able to recognize and utilize the affordances of their classrooms—the particular configurations of goals, values, tools, and relationships as manifested through teacher and student talk and action. As students learn what is acceptable in science class, how the teacher teaches science, what is expected of them, and what the stance toward science is in the classroom (see Chapter 9), children are able to participate in science class in more nuanced and strategic ways. The ways in which they take part in activities help to construct future interactions in their classroom community of learners.

Children's Talk in Dialogic Classrooms

We use the term curriculum genres to denote the major, regular, and recognizable activities that were routinely found in the classrooms we studied (Christie, 1991; Pappas & Zecker, 2001). The ISLE curricular units included a range of curriculum genres—for example, whole-class dialogic read-alouds of information books, small-group hands-on explorations, individual journal writing, and so forth (see Chapter 1 for a complete list). Curriculum genres serve as resources for classroom participants, helping to delineate what is expected of them. The types and range of language acts (Lindfors, 1999) that students employ are partly influenced by the features of each curriculum genre. Moreover, different curriculum genres constrain or encourage different forms of participation, providing a wider or narrower range of choices for participants in an interaction (Bakhtin, 1986). In this chapter we focus on read-alouds as the curriculum genre under study.

An essential pedagogical principle in the ISLE classrooms was dialogic instruc-tion. Dialogic instruction, as a part of the larger construct of dialogic discourse and action, is marked by an exchange of ideas and the inclusion of multiple participants' goals in a way that authority for learning is shared among participants (Nystrand, 1997). In dialogic discourse, the focus of a conversation or action may shift in ways that meet both the goals of individuals and the goals of the community (Wells, 1999). The dialogic read-alouds we report on in this chapter provide the space in which children make choices whether to speak up, ask a question, or remain quiet. In this study, we are interested in the children's instantiation of choices, but only as choices that are manifested over time, as recurring paths of participation for individual children. In describing and analyzing these choices, we work toward a fuller understanding of the meaning and learning potential of participants in integrated science-literacy enactments.

Different students take advantage of different resources, both those that come from their experiences outside the activity they are participating in and legitimate ways of participating in that particular activity. Such resources may include different topics of discussion, and even within particular topics, students may pay attention to different nuanced aspects of these topics. As we attempt to understand young children's types and range of speech, differences also include *ways* of drawing on those resources. Such individual ways of participating—what children pay attention to and how, as well as with whom—mediate differentially the ways in which they experience the curriculum and how their teacher (and peers) respond to them (O'Connor & Michaels, 1993).

Individual language acts that children articulate are *utterances*. We conceptualize an utterance as a meaningful turn in dialogue—that is, an uninterrupted stretch of speech that is bounded by the speech of others and that makes sense to others. Utterances are language acts, or types of speech that serve different functions and denote different kinds of relationships between speakers. As an example of language acts in dialogic read-alouds, the students learn that they may make connections from the texts to their personal lives, if they are relevant. These utterances are *intertextual connections to personal events*. (See Chapter 2 for an analysis of intertextuality in read-alouds.) Children also learn that there are other ways to participate in read-alouds, such as by describing a picture, or reasoning about the causes of natural phenomena discussed. Each of these ways of participating, *making a personal connection, reasoning*, or *describing*, is a language act. Science language acts take different forms and can be identified in a number of different ways: tentativeness; imaginative, dramatic, and visual talk; reaching devices; and the use of specific words (Lindfors, 1999). As is noted in sections below, in describing children's distinctive patterns of language use, we focus on three students who employed unique, but recognizable configurations of language acts to participate in class: (1) reasoning and hedging; (2) using reaching devices including intertextual connections and analogies; and (3) questioning.

- *Reasoning and Hedging*: Reasoning can be defined broadly as making connections among ideas, allowing children to make sense of how and why things happen. Reasoning may specify a mechanism or steps in which something happens or include causal accounts of phenomena and events—the more advanced form of reasoning (Wilson & Keil, 2000). In dialogic discourse, markers of hedging, such as, *I think, maybe, if*, that denote tentativeness, or qualification of an idea, may offer opportunities for reasoning.

- *Reaching Devices*: Reaching devices are ways in which children connect new content to what they already know. They are language acts that include intertextual references to events, other texts, students' own lives, and previous talk (see Chapter 2 for further details). They also include "analogy, comparison, metaphor–devices that help [students] go beyond by stretching what they know . . . These types of rhetorical devices allow one to stand with one foot in the known, while placing the other in the unknown. They carry creative thinking forward" (Lindfors, 1999, p. 171).

- *Questioning*: Questions are another way in which children participate in dialogic read-alouds. Children ask many different types of questions, some based directly on the ideas in the book, others that seem to be based on the book ideas but are extended, and still others that sometimes seem to come from nowhere. Questions can broaden or narrow the conversation. They are another way in which children extend what they already know to the new information they are learning and beyond.

Analyzing Diverse Forms of Participation

We asked: What are some of children's diverse forms of participation, enacted through language acts, within and across the read-aloud curriculum genre? We selected four of the focal students in each of the six ISLE classrooms, as representatives. The 24 children (similar numbers of girls and boys) we focused on included: three African American boys and three African American girls; nine Latina and five Latino students; one Asian-American girl and one Asian-American boy; and two European-American boys.

Descriptive fieldnotes (Wolcott, 1994) of all read-alouds in both units were the main source of data for this study. We also examined artifacts that children produced in activities, such as ongoing semantic mapping and journaling, and any other texts that were produced either individually or as a class. These artifacts served as additional information that helped to triangulate findings about ways in which children interacted in read-alouds.

We employed both quantitative and qualitative descriptive methods of data analysis. Quantitative methods allowed us to determine the relative incidence of different language acts in read-alouds and helped us determine those that were most relevant for qualitative analysis. Qualitative analysis allowed us to focus on meaning in children's talk (Mercer, 2004). Analysis focused on children's individual utterances. However, we believe that all language use is grounded in social context. As such, when deciding how to categorize a specific utterance, we took into account the sequence of utterances that preceded and followed children's individual contributions.

In our analysis, we included every recorded utterance in read-alouds for each of the 24 focal students during the course of the year. This resulted in a combined total of 1,861 utterances for the year. We created and refined a list of types of language acts as we read and reread the fieldnotes of classroom discourse. We used a multi-case approach to qualitatively study children's forms of participation via language acts: rather than build each case individually and then try to compare children, we compared children *as* we built their cases. We compared each child with the other three children in that classroom, the children in the other classroom in the same grade, and children in the other grades as well. We also compared the types of language acts found in each classroom with those found in the others at the same grade and across grades.

Language Acts across Classrooms

Children interacted with the curriculum, each other, and the teacher in different ways. They attended to different aspects of the curricular topic and the read-aloud genre through a variety of forms. To set some context for the case studies below, we first discuss the language acts used the most by the 24 focal students across classrooms and by grade level. Table 3.1 shows the language acts across all 24 children in each of the two units (*Matter* and *Forest*), including only the language acts that constituted at least 5% of all utterances in at least one unit. This accounts for 86% of utterances in the *Matter* unit (which included eight read-alouds) and 80% of utterances in the *Forest* unit (which included 15 read-alouds).

TABLE 3.1 Prevalent Types of Language Acts in Read-Alouds for All 24 Children

Language Acts	Mean Percentages	
	Matter Unit	Forest Unit
Telling	30.1	25.5
Naming	11.0	8.8
Reasoning	8.3	7.6
Intertextual Connections	11.6	8.8
Comparing	4.5	6.7
Questioning	9.2	16.2
Describing	6.1	5.0
Predicting	5.4	1.9

Note: Number of utterances made by all 24 children in read-aloud sessions: *Matter*: *n* = 426, *Forest*: *n* = 1435.

Telling the teacher or other classmates what one knows was the most common language act in read-alouds. However, the mean for the telling language act dropped from 30.1% in the *Matter* unit to 25.5% in the *Forest* unit, the biggest drop among language acts. The rest of the language acts were evident at the same level in the two units, with the exception of *questioning* language acts that increased 7%, which represents the largest change across units.

Looking across grade levels, we found differences in the language acts that children used in read-alouds in each of the two units. Table 3.2 and Table 3.3 show the percentages of the *most prevalent* language acts in each of two units, *Matter* and *Forest*, respectively. Because we do not include all of the language acts, numbers do not add up to 100%.

In the *Matter* unit, the percent of *telling* language acts dropped for each grade level by about 8%, although *naming* specific entities increased as the children got older. Other language acts that increased with each grade level were *intertextual connections* and *questioning*. However, *reasoning* was higher in the 2nd-grade classrooms than in any of the other classrooms. This was mostly due to the repeated invitations of the 2nd-grade teachers for children to think about "how" and "why" in the *Matter* unit. *Predicting* was a major way of participating in read-alouds for 1st-graders, mostly because their teachers asked them outright to say what would happen next in the text. This was barely evident in the 2nd and 3rd-grade classrooms.

In the *Forest* unit, *reasoning* language acts increased by grade level, but *questioning* and *intertextual connections* appeared more in the 2nd-grade classrooms than in the 3rd-grade classrooms. Moreover, *predicting* dipped sharply for the 1st-grade classrooms between the *Matter* and *Forest* units. Sharon, the teacher in one of the two 1st-grade classrooms, constantly asked for predictions in the *Matter* read-alouds, where 30% of her four children's utterances were predicting language acts. In the *Forest* unit, she stopped asking for predictions. Also, in the *Forest* unit, Anne, the

TABLE 3.2 Most Prevalent Language Acts in the *Matter* Read-Alouds by Grade

Language Acts	Mean Percentages		
	1st grade	*2nd grade*	*3rd grade*
Telling	38.0	30.0	22.4
Naming	6.8	10.8	15.4
Reasoning	3.5	13.5	7.9
Intertextual Connections	7.9	9.8	11.6
Comparing	5.8	2.4	5.3
Questioning	1.1	11.0	15.5
Describing	9.1	4.6	4.5
Predicting	15.9	0.0	0.4

Note: Total number of utterances of the 8 children in each grade level: 1st grade: $n = 113$, 2nd grade: $n = 176$, and 3rd grade: $n = 137$.

TABLE 3.3 Most Prevalent Language Acts in the *Forest* Unit Read-Alouds by Grade

Language Acts	Mean Percentages		
	1st grade	*2nd grade*	*3rd grade*
Telling	34.4	20.4	21.8
Naming	9.1	14.0	3.1
Reasoning	3.1	7.5	12.3
Intertextual Connections	6.5	10.4	9.5
Comparing	4.1	6.1	9.9
Questioning	11.6	21.9	15.1
Describing	7.3	4.0	3.5
Predicting	3.0	0.3	2.5

Note: Total number of utterances of the 8 children in each grade level: 1st grade: $n = 291$, 2nd grade: $n = 505$, and 3rd grade: $n = 639$.

teacher in the other 1st-grade classroom, began asking her students for their "wonderings" about the topic of the book they were about to read and thus, *questioning* became almost 20% of the utterances that her four students used to participate in the read-alouds.

The kinds of questions, directions, and goals the teacher set, as well as the opportunities she gave each of the students, mediated how individual students in each class participated. In the *Matter* unit, there were a few language acts that stood out for some of the classrooms. For instance, in Neveen's 3rd-grade classroom, 30% of her four students' utterances in the *Matter* unit were *naming* language acts. No other classroom came close. In Jennifer's 3rd-grade class in the *Matter* unit, *questioning* constituted 26% of her four students' utterances. No *questioning acts* were offered by the four students in Anne's 1st-grade class in the *Matter* unit, but these four students did *describe* entities presented in the read aloud books in 18% of their utterances—much more than any other class. As stated above, the four students in Sharon's 1st-grade class *predicted* in 30% of their utterances in the *Matter* unit.

In the *Forest* unit, Anne's four students continued to participate by *telling* (about 40% of utterances) while students, who we focused on for this analysis, in the rest of the classrooms either stayed relatively stable or dropped in the percentage of *telling* language acts. In 2nd grade, whereas Begoña's four students *named* entities in about 27% of their utterances, Ibett's four students did so only in less than 1% of their utterances. But Ibett's students made *intertextual connections* (about 16%) in a greater percentage of utterances, as well as asked *questions* more often (34%) than students in other classrooms. *Questions* for Anne's 1st-grade students jumped to 19% of all their utterances in the *Forest* unit. In Sharon's 1st grade, although the *predicting* language acts that her four students offered in the read-alouds of the two units dropped to 6% in the *Forest* unit, her students still offered by far the most of such language acts.

Such differences in children's language acts from class to class suggest that teachers conducted their read-alouds in different ways, such as asking for predictions or not, encouraging questions or not, or asking students to give explanations for scientific phenomena. However, there are also enough similarities among the classrooms in terms of which language acts were most prevalent, as well as how prevalent each was, to suggest that there were significant similarities between the different enactments of the read-alouds. The ways in which students individually participated were a result of their teachers' read-aloud styles (Ciesla, Gill, & Hankes, 2007), the content of the books, and their own attentions and intentions within the curriculum. In this way, students "revoiced" the intentions of others through their very personal ways of participation (Bakhtin, 1981). It is to these personal ways of participation that we now turn.

Case Studies of Children's Forms of Classroom Participation

Reasoning and Hedging: Sally

Sally, a Latina 3rd-grader in Neveen Keblawe-Shamah's class, was a leader among her classmates. Not only was she socially popular, but she was also someone to whom the students consistently looked for approval in academic matters as well, especially during small-group work. Even other leaders and strong personalities in the classroom deferred to Sally. She rarely ceded control of small-group work to others, and then, only when *everyone* else in the group adamantly opposed her. Sally was not afraid to offer her ideas about the world in small groups or whole class.

As she engaged in the read-alouds, Sally *reasoned* to support her own contributions and to make sense of those of her classmates. She both spontaneously provided reasons for phenomena under discussion and responded to her teacher's prompts for elaboration. More often than anyone else, her talk included hedging words, such as "might," "maybe," and "kind of" (Lindfors, 1999). In the *Earthworms* (Llewellyn, 2000) read-aloud in Lesson 4 of the *Forest* unit (see Chapter 1 for details on this curriculum genre [and others] and the position of this lesson in the curricular timeline of the unit), Sally reiterated that worms did not like dry soil after her teacher had read about this idea in the book. (Conventions of transcription are given on p. 15.)

Excerpt 1:
1   Ms. Shamah: . . . THERE ARE VERY FEW WORMS IN
{THE} SANDY SOIL. THIS IS BECAUSE
RAINWATER DRAINS AWAY QUICKLY, AND
THE SOIL BECOMES TOO DRY FOR THEM.
So what do we know so far about worms?
2   Sally: That they don't like dry soil.
3   Ms. Shamah: They don't like dry soil. Okay.

4	Christopher:	They like it wet.
5	Yadira:	They like the wet because it's smooth.
6	Ms. Shamah:	Okay. That might be why, but we'll find out some more. Yes.
7	Sally:	Maybe they like wet water, but they don't like um wet water // wet // too much soil that's wet.
8	Ms. Shamah:	Okay. Maybe they // Sally said maybe they like wet // you said "wet water"?
9	Sally:	Soil.

In Excerpt 1, Sally first reiterated an idea from the book (unit 2), but then refined her statement to guess that the soil they like is wet, but not too wet (unit 7). Sally in this case used a modifier in the beginning of the sentence, placing a high modal ("maybe") character on the utterance. A little later, Sally used "maybe" again when the class was talking about worms' lack of skeletons and she reasoned that "Maybe that's why they could go in all those shapes," and "Maybe that's why they don't stand // they don't stand like us . . . cause they might just fall."

In many of her other contributions she used such modal terms, namely, "if," "might," or "maybe." Her emergent language act—reasoning—which was expressed in this hedging manner—was different from many of her classmates who participated by naming entities in a forest or telling about what they knew. One interpretation might be that Sally was tentative in her answers. However, if we consider Sally's otherwise confident ability to navigate school and social situations, it is more probable that Sally was employing a scientific practice in which hedging allows for scientific ideas to accommodate further study; providing such loopholes, by limiting the scope of claims, makes scientific theorizing and discoveries more acceptable to the larger scientific community. In this way, Sally was able to get many of her contributions included and accepted in the ongoing classroom discourse because they were presented as possibilities, and not necessarily as irrefutable truths.

Sally was heavily involved in Lesson 4. At one point, she reasoned that if a worm's air pockets get filled with water, they would die, and that the worms would try not to die by going above ground. Then Neveen asked her to explain her thinking.

Excerpt 2:

1	Ms. Shamah:	Why do they do that?
2	Andres:	#To let some of the water.#
3	Child:	#So they could get air.#
4	Ms. Shamah:	So they can get air. And why else? What else would happen on the surface? To the // to the water in their skin?
5	Andres:	It might come out.

6	Sally:	Some might evaporate from their skin.
7	Ms. Shamah:	Maybe some, Sally, might evaporate from your skin. And Andres said "Come out," right? So maybe that's // do you think that's possible? Juanita, do you think that's possible?
8	Sally:	I think what I said's possible.

In Excerpt 2, Sally guessed what *might* happen to the water (unit 6) based on what she had learned in the *Matter* unit. While Andres offered that some *might* come out, Sally reworded his reasoning to include the scientific term, "evaporate" (unit 6). Neveen acknowledged the possibility of Sally's contribution (unit 7) and then, perhaps because Sally and a few others had been dominating the conversation, she tried to elicit a response from a normally quiet child. Sally heard Juanita's name, but spoke anyway, asserting herself once again and *evaluating* her own statement. However, she did so without looking at the teacher, perhaps aware that it was not really her turn to answer. Sally quietly bumped up against the rules of participation that, when a teacher calls on a student, that student answers. Even though the teacher had positively responded to her reasoning, Sally wanted it known that what she said had some validity.

Making Connections to Content: Cassandra

Cassandra was an African American girl in Begoña Marnotes Cowan's 2nd-grade classroom. She was a regular contributor to classroom discussions both in large whole-class settings and in small groups. Her contributions were also often lengthier than other students'. By the end of the year, she was one of a few students whom Begoña would call on consistently yet also limit the length of her turns. Cassandra was recorded participating in read-alouds more than the other three students from her class whom we included in this study.

In read-alouds Cassandra's participation was fairly consistent; she was recorded saying something in all but one read-aloud across both units. Unlike many of the other students in all six classes, Cassandra used a broad range of forms to participate in both the *Matter* and the *Forest* read-alouds. Like Sally, Cassandra rarely asked questions. Instead, Cassandra employed reaching devices—intertextual connections and comparisons—in about 20% of her total utterances. In the *Matter* unit, like many of the other students, Cassandra connected to personal events, texts, and events in the world. She also was more inclined to compare phenomena or characteristics of animals. For the most part her shift from intertextual event connections to comparisons coincided with the shift in curricular units from *Matter* to *Forest*. However, the deeper into the *Forest* unit the class went, the percentage of her *comparing* language acts increased, indicating that Cassandra was still using connections to make sense of the read-alouds, but was changing the kinds of connections that she was making to participate in her science class.

In analyzing Cassandra's participation, we divided the read-aloud sessions across the two units into three equal parts of eight sessions. Some read-alouds lasted longer than one session, hence there were 24 sessions for 21 read-alouds. While our division does not capture differences between instructional units, it does help to see how Cassandra's interactional forms changed as she learned how to participate in her classroom's read-alouds over the course of the year. In the first eight read-aloud sessions, Cassandra used eight *intertextual connections* and one *comparing* language act. In the second eight read-aloud sessions, Cassandra used three *intertextual connections* and four *comparing* language acts. Finally, in the last eight read-aloud sessions, Cassandra used four *intertextual utterances* and nine *comparing* language acts.

Cassandra's early use of intertextual connections in the first eight read-alouds suggests that she was comfortable talking about her personal experiences related to weather as sources of data in the beginning of the class's science study. Cassandra's connections also served as connections for other students as they built on her contributions. For example, in Lesson 4 of the *Matter* unit, during the read-aloud of the book *What Do You See in a Cloud?* (Fowler, 1996), her teacher had just read about the place of evaporation in the water cycle and that when water vapor went up it became colder.

Excerpt 3:

1	Cassandra:	Like when you get steam on your bathroom mirror.
2	Daniel:	That is why it fogs up, warm water hits cold air.
3	Carolina:	The fog, taking a real hot shower. My cousin Samantha took a real hot shower and when she got out the mirror was all fogged up.

In Excerpt 3, children built on each other's talk in an exploratory way, led by Cassandra. Cassandra was the first in the read-aloud to make an intertextual connection—to a generalized event of getting "steam on your bathroom mirror." Daniel extended her response to reason about the cause of the "fog" as the encounter between warm water and cold air, and Carolina attempted to combine both of the previous responses. Students were trying out new ideas in discussion with one another and they were using their experiences and what they knew to support their positions on these new ideas. Cassandra's intertextual connection allowed other students to build on what she said and reason.

In Lesson 12 of the *Matter* unit, during the read-aloud of *What Is the World Made Of? All about Solids, Liquids, and Gases* (Zoehfeld, 1998), Cassandra referenced the same topic, steam, as in Excerpt 3, except here she personalized it. In the dialogic read-alouds, students were allowed to respond to the book in a variety of ways, including telling personal stories. Cassandra's personal stories also allowed the class to articulate scientific ideas.

Excerpt 4:

1	Cassandra:	This morning after my mom took a shower, there was steam on my shower and I said all this is water vapor.
2	Ms. Cowan:	Be careful when the steam is on the mirror and running down. Is it |
3	Alicia:	That is called condensation.
4	Ms. Cowan:	Yes!
5	Alicia:	The gas turned back into the liquid.
6	Ms. Cowan:	The gas is warm and the mirror is cold and that is called ==
7	Class:	Condensation.
8	Cassandra:	It was wet.

In Excerpt 4, Cassandra recounted a personal event. She related a story of an event that took place at home, and used science language. Cassandra called what formed on the mirror "water vapor," water in the gaseous state. Begoña cautioned her, attempting to discuss further whether what was on the mirror was a gas or liquid, offering a clue in support of the latter as she referred to the steam "running down," a property of liquids. With Alicia's contribution, the class discussed condensation, its definition and causes, and eventually Cassandra emphasized the property of the state of matter that was formed on the mirror—"it was wet."

As Cassandra participated in more read-alouds, she did not change much in terms of the number of connections she made, however, the types of connections that she made *did* change. Cassandra's participation in Begoña's 2nd-grade class was distinctive partly because of the amount of *comparing* language acts that she used in the *Forest* read-alouds. These comparisons employed "like-examples" of other entities or metaphoric expressions. Most of her comparing examples were to animals, especially earthworms, suggesting that the kinds of connections she was making later in the year had less to do with life outside of school and more to do with ideas and relationships between ideas in the unit. That is, as she participated in the classroom, she drew more often on the classroom discourse and curricular resources of the unit.

As the *Forest* unit progressed, Cassandra made more and more connections between animals the class was learning about in the current lesson and those they had learned about in previous lessons. In many of these cases, she used earthworms as a comparison to the animal under study. This is not surprising considering there were a number of instructional activities related to earthworms early in the unit including: (1) two read-alouds of children's information books; (2) a read-aloud of an electronic text specifically about earthworms; (3) the appearance of earthworms in other books (*Animals under the Ground* (Fowler, 1997), for instance); and (4) two hands-on explorations with earthworms. Earthworms served as an anchor animal for the *Forest* unit, in part because of their central role in the forest ecosystem.

Cassandra made connections to worms more than any other animal. This was the case in Lesson 15 in the *Forest* unit, during a read-aloud on termites from the book *A Forest Community* (Massie, 2000).

Excerpt 5:

1	Ms. Cowan:	They have little germs in their body to help them digest the wood.
2	Cassandra:	I have two things. It is just like a bird.
3	Ms. Cowan:	Can you explain?
4	Cassandra:	The bird needs to crush up the food and eat stones with it. Also, it is like an earthworm, it needs moisture to keep it alive.

Cassandra used two *comparing* language acts relating termites to birds and earthworms (unit 4), bringing up different ideas regarding each one. Although the connection between the two ideas is not clear, Cassandra's *comparing* language acts offered her and the class a chance to consider animal behaviors and their relationships to animal survival.

Asking Questions: Lawrence

The ISLE units were an opening onto a new world of schooling for Lawrence, an African American boy in Jennifer Hankes' 3rd-grade classroom. It was as if Lawrence finally had a forum to ask all the questions he had ever wanted to (Kane, 2009). He asked so many questions that his teacher periodically had to tell him to write them down because she could not answer them all. He asked questions about the science topics the class was studying, but more often than not, he extended what the class was working on to other ideas he was wondering about. In this way, Lawrence made connections between domains of science and thought about natural phenomena in a connected, systemic manner.

Lawrence was often slower than his classmates in answering teacher questions and so did not get to contribute to classroom discourse in that way as often as some others. Moreover, when he did reason or attempt to explain ideas, his line of thinking was sometimes hard to follow for the teacher in the moment. But in asking his own questions, Lawrence excelled. He asked more questions and more complex types of questions than his classmates—Lawrence was recorded asking 55 questions in read-alouds over both units, compared to an average of 22 for his other three classmates whom we focused on this study. Jennifer also supported question asking in general by providing time and space for it. She set up a trifold board to which she attached Post-Its filled with student questions. She then referred to the questions on Post-Its in subsequent read-alouds. These and other interactions helped to positively reinforce Lawrence's behavior. He believed that he was a good student because he asked questions and he often made sense of science through his questions.

In Excerpt 6 from Lesson 14 of the *Matter* unit, during the read-aloud of the book *Down Comes the Rain* (Branley, 1997), Lawrence asked how air from the sun makes snow melt after Jennifer had read about water vapor turning to water droplets.

> Excerpt 6:
> 1   Ms. Hankes: So because we know that those clouds are moving with the air. Sometimes they join other clouds, don't they? Tia, I need you over here. If we're that sick, we gotta go home. Come on. Move closer, you're part of our group. So over here it says, WHEN {HORSES}, COWS, DOGS, AND CATS BREATHE OUT, THEY PUT WATER {VAPOR} {IN} THE // WATER VAPOR {IN} THE AIR, TOO. ON A COLD DAY, THE WATER VAPOR CHANGES TO DROPLETS AND {IT} MAKES LITTLE CLOUDS {that} YOU CAN SEE. Lawrence.
> 2   Lawrence: Um, how could the um air be coming out to the sun to make the um snow melt?
> 3   Ms. Hankes: Okay, I am going to get to that as soon as we are done with the story // um with the book, okay, and I will talk to you about the sun cause I know you had a question about what is the sun made out of.
> 4   Tasha: It's heat.
> 5   Ms. Hankes: Okay, we are going to come back to that.

In Excerpt 6, Lawrence's question (unit 2) seemed unrelated to what Jennifer had just read. Jennifer had read about condensation, a process involving water vapor changing to liquid water as it cools down, but Lawrence's question was about melting, a process involving solid water, snow, changing to liquid water as it warms up. However, earlier Jennifer had read the book pages referring to melting and to evaporation where the sun's heat was brought up. Lawrence needed to understand how the sun's heat leads to these changes, but the class had not engaged yet with his quest for understanding. Jennifer acknowledged his repeated question (unit 3) and promised to come back to it (unit 4).

Later in the read-aloud, Jennifer returned to Lawrence's question and told the class that the sun "is a gas . . . It's a star. Stars are big giant [makes a great big ball by spreading her arms apart and holding her hands up like it is holding a big ball] balls of gas . . . [The sun] produces a lot of heat or energy." At the end of the read-aloud, Lawrence had a new question that he wrote on a Post-It note that he affixed on the class's "Scientists Ask Questions" poster board. Accepting that the sun produces a lot of heat, as Jennifer told the class, he needed to figure out how this heat escapes the sun. He wrote: "How can heat or energy come out of sun?"

Lawrence incorporated what he learned, yet still continued to participate in much the same way: he asked analytic questions in order to make sense of how and why things happen. As a matter of fact, not only did Lawrence put that question on the "Scientists Ask Questions" poster board, but he also added three more: "Can water vapor come from the ocean?"; "When you [spray] perfume how can it escape?"; "How [does] ice stick together when there's water?" All these questions were related to ideas that were brought up in the book, and would be addressed as the unit unfolded.

Final Thoughts

In dialogic read-alouds, teachers have to balance every child's right and desire to participate and respond to the text with their own goals, priorities, and concerns to complete the curriculum within the allotted time. At the same time, they have to make sure that students understand scientific concepts, and do it all in a manner that keeps everyone's attention. In the ISLE classrooms, as teachers and students wrestled with figuring out how to participate, they created their own ways of enacting the dialogic read-alouds. Teachers created expectations for children's participation by inviting them to contribute when they had something to say, by asking them to raise their hands, or by cutting them off when they felt children's stories or other contributions went too far afield.

The findings we report in this chapter shows that even in conforming to the expectations of the read-alouds in their classrooms, the three children we presented as case studies were able to creatively carve their own forms of participation through repeated patterns of different language acts—reasoning and hedging, making intertextual connections and comparisons, and asking questions. In doing so, they each enriched their classmates' learning as well. In this way, students' different kinds of participation became resources for the class to experience different dimensions of learning. They brought their individual resources to bear on the collective construction of the whole by directing attention to one dimension or another—reasons for events, phenomena, features; similarities and differences; and the unknown. Students, and their individual idiosyncrasies, played a critical role in the read-aloud conversations.

Evidence from Sally, Cassandra, and Lawrence suggests that students participated uniquely—connected the science ideas to their own experiences, connected ideas together in their own ways, and asked different questions from one another. The kinds of participation we have described also suggest that children moved toward more canonical scientific discourse as the year progressed. They did so by moving from more "centrifugal" personal connections and won-derings in the first read-alouds to more "centripetal" questions and comparisons as the year progressed (Bakhtin, 1981). That is, toward the end of the units, as

Cassandra did, children asked questions about, and made connections to, the content of the unit more often than they did to their personal lives. It is important to recognize that students did not abandon personal connections or imaginative wonderings in order to adopt scientific discourse, but as individuals, they did learn about ways of participating in the science classroom that drew on the material they were learning and their own lives in legitimate, and legitimated, ways.

Moreover, children's contributions led to the development of scientific ideas in the class. As Sally reasoned, she opened up hypothetical situations for consideration by the group. "If," "might," and "maybe" served as ways for Sally to take risks in expressing her ideas in scientific discourse. As Lawrence asked questions, other students responded with their own reasoning and ways of making sense. Cassandra's connections to personal events and content from the curriculum opened up spaces for other students to make their own meanings from what Cassandra had said and what they were learning about from the books.

It may be that teachers have to set up specific times and places for students to ask questions or make connections such as Jennifer's "Scientists Ask Questions" board. But then, those questions have to be revisited. Students' ideas, their ways of conveying them, and their participation in dialogic curricular and instructional enactments should be seen as emergent. Children do not receive and accumulate knowledge; they make and remake meaning constantly. Children zig and zag through curricular ideas (see also Chapter 8). They focus their attention on bits and pieces at a time and they come back to those bits and pieces, connecting them in their own individual ways, drawing on collective resources for participating.

References

Bakhtin, M. M. (1981). *The dialogic imagination: Four essays by M. M. Bakhtin.* (M. Holquist, Ed., M. Holquist & C. Emerson, Trans.). Austin: University of Texas Press.

Bakhtin, M. M. (1986). *Speech genres and other late essays.* (C. Emerson & M. Holquist, Eds., V. W. McGee, Trans.). Austin: University of Texas Press.

Branley, F. M. (1997). *Down comes the rain.* New York: HarperCollins.

Christie, F. (1991). Pedagogical and content registers in a writing lesson. *Linguistics and Education, 2*, 203–224.

Ciesla, T. L., Gill, S., & Hankes, J. (2007, April). *Exploring teaching styles of dialogic information book read-alouds.* Paper presented at the Annual Meeting of the American Education Research Association. Chicago.

Fowler, A. (1996). *What do you see in a cloud?* New York: Children's Press.

Fowler, A. (1997). *Animals under the ground.* New York: Children's Press.

Gallas, K. (1995). *Talking their way into science: Hearing children's questions and theories, responding with curricula.* New York: Teachers College.

Jurow, A. S. & Creighton, L. (2005). Improvisational science discourse: Teaching science in two K-1 classrooms. *Linguistics and Education, 16*, 275–297.

Kane, J. (2009). *Young African American children constructing identities in an urban integrated science-literacy classroom.* Unpublished doctoral dissertation, University of Illinois at Chicago.

Lindfors, J.W. (1999). *Children's inquiry: Using language to make sense of the world.* New York: Teachers College Press.

Llewellyn, C. (2000). *Earthworms.* New York: Franklin Watts.

Massie, E. (2000). *A forest community.* Austin, TX: Steck-Vaughn.

Mercer, N. (2004). Sociocultural discourse analysis: Analyzing classroom talk as a social mode of thinking. *Journal of Applied Linguistics, 1,* 137–168.

Metz, K. E. (2011). Disentangling robust developmental constraints from the instructionally mutable: Young children's epistemic reasoning about a study of their own design. *Journal of the Learning Sciences, 20,* 50–110.

Nystrand, M. (1997). *Opening dialogue: Understanding the dynamics of language and learning in the English classroom.* New York: Teachers College Press.

O'Connor, M. C., & Michaels, S. (1993). Aligning academic task and participation status through revoicing: Analysis of a classroom discourse strategy. *Anthropology and Education Quarterly, 24,* 318–355.

Pappas, C. C., & Zecker, L. B. (2001). *Transforming literacy curriculum genres: Working with teacher researchers in urban elementary classrooms.* Mahwah, NJ: Erlbaum.

Varelas, M. (1996). Between theory and data in a 7th grade science class. *Journal of Research in Science Teaching, 33,* 229–263.

Warren, B., Ballenger, C., Ogonowski, M., Rosebery, A. S., & Hudicourt-Barnes, J. (2001). Rethinking diversity in learning science: The logic of everyday sense-making. *Journal of Research in Science Teaching, 38,* 529–552.

Wells, G. (1999). *Dialogic inquiry: Toward a sociocultural practice and theory of education.* Cambridge, UK: Cambridge University Press.

Wenger, E. (1998). *Communities of practice.* Cambridge, UK: Cambridge University Press.

Wilson, R. A., & Keil, F. C. (2000). The shadows and shallows of explanation. In F. C. Keil & R. A. Wilson (Eds.), *Explanation and cognition* (pp. 87–114). Cambridge, MA: MIT Press.

Wolcott, H. (1994). *Transforming qualitative data: Description, analysis, & interpretation.* London: Sage.

Zoehfeld, K. W. (1998). *What is the world made of? All about solids, liquids, and gases.* New York: HarperCollins.

4

HANDS-ON EXPLORATIONS THAT NURTURE SCIENTIFIC PRACTICES*

Linking Doing with Thinking and Talking

Maria Varelas, Christine C. Pappas, Justine M. Kane, Amy Arsenault, Jennifer Hankes, and Begoña Marnotes Cowan

Hands-on explorations constitute a critical part of science learning and, as such, have been the focus of both pedagogical practices and research undertakings in science education. Observations, experiments, designing and building of objects and systems offer learners ample opportunities to engage with scientific practices that have been part of the "old" science education standards (National Research Council, 1996), but are also highly emphasized in the recently released new *Framework for K-12 Science Education* (National Research Council, 2012) and the upcoming Next Generation of Science Standards. Developing models and explanations, engaging in critique and evaluation of ideas, communicating understandings, and asking questions are some of the practices that are used as people develop scientific knowledge. Supporting children in engaging in scientific practices enables them to both construct knowledge and to see themselves (and be seen by others) as "doers" of science. Such engagement is *not* enabled *only* during hands-on activities as we abundantly demonstrate throughout this book, since reading, writing, illustrating, and performing are also contexts in which students have the opportunity to use scientific practices. Nevertheless, activities such as ones where children organize physical objects and develop a model of matter, or conduct an experiment to find out whether earthworms prefer light or dark, or observe a plant grow, are contexts in which they can try out and develop a range of scientific practices.

As we engage children in hands-on explorations, we need to be concerned with their meaning making that unfolds as they interact with materials, with each other and their teacher, and with language (everyday and scientific). Gee (2004) argues

* The chapter is an abridged version of the following journal article: Varelas, M., Pappas, C.C., Kane, J., & Arsenault, A. with Hankes, J., & Cowan, B.M. (2008). Urban primary-grade children think and talk science: Curricular and instructional practices that nurture participation and argumentation. *Science Education*, 92, 65–95.

that what he calls "lifeworld language," the everyday, informal language that children bring in the classroom from their out-of-school life, is very different from academic language, the language of each of the disciplines (e.g., science) that students need to learn. According to Gee, lifeworld language limits children's access to the knowledge of the discipline. Although Gee acknowledges that everyday language is sufficient for expressing the human experience ("the deepest insights into the human condition" [p. 27]), he notes that "everyday language is not how the Discourses of the sciences operate; in fact, although these [academic] Discourses most certainly grew out of this method of sense making, they developed in overt opposition to it . . . From the perspective of scientific Discourse, it [everyday language] can create a symmetry that is misleading and obscures important underlying differences" (p. 27), and in science it is these underlying differences that are most crucial. Thus, Gee claims that that we would do well to "marry scientific activities with scientific ways of using words rather than with lifeworld languages" (p. 25). Like Dewey (1902), though, we believe that this is not an "either-or" issue. Learners need to be introduced to academic Discourse (language, ideas, ways of being, acting, and thinking) (Gee, 1991), but they need to use it in ways that allow them to bridge this Discourse with their lifeworld Discourse and everyday experience if they are to "own" science. Thus, we tend not to view lifeworld language as a liability, a danger that needs to be avoided as soon as it establishes a way to academic languages. Instead, we see lifeworld language as an asset that needs to be continually made use of in classrooms and in learning, but also to be studied, explored, and analyzed in terms of its possibilities and its limitations. The ultimate goal is the meaning making that learners enact as they move back and forth "between the ways they know the world and the ways others know the world" (Moje, Ciechanowski, Kramer, Ellis, Carrillo, & Collazo, 2004, p. 44).

Moreoover, according to Southerland and her colleagues (Southerland, Kittleson, Settlage, & Lanier, 2005), meaning making is a complex phenomenon:

> Understanding any instance of meaning-making is complicated by the contextual nature of the meaning-making process itself. Said differently, to robustly portray meaning-making, one must take into account the nuances of the context and the ways in which these nuances shape the process.
>
> *(p. 1034)*

Meaning making takes place within the social actions, discourse processes, and cultural practices of a classroom community. In this way, the intellectual-thematic dimension of teaching is integrally intertwined with the socio-organizational dimension (Lemke, 1990; Varelas, Luster, & Wenzel, 1999). As a community of learners engages with ideas, they also engage with each other. They communicate and share meanings and ideas under particular norms that have been set and evolved in that classroom—norms about ways of conduct, of engagement with the subject matter, of talking, of moving, of being in the classroom. Thus, meaning making is "a social construction created through the moment-to-moment actions and interactions of the actors" (Kelly & Crawford, 1997, p. 536) and takes place at two levels, individual and collective. At the collective level, meaning making shapes and is shaped by the ways individual children make sense of ideas and engage in transactions with each other and the teacher. The discourse that unfolds during these transactions is a critical semiotic tool for meaning making. Bakhtin's (1981) dialogism emphasizes the notion of discourse as a social activity with continual weaving and reweaving of responsive utterances among discourse participants. In addition to many other factors, these transactions are influenced by the status and the power that each of the discourse participants has. Furthermore, students' status and power are influenced by their gender (Bianchini, 1997) and by the conceptions of themselves, of their teachers, and of their peers in terms of their social and academic standing. Students of higher academic or social status are privileged in-group interactions (Moje & Shepardson, 1998). They speak more frequently, and their ideas are more likely to be taken up by other students or their teacher.

In this chapter, we focus on one hands-on exploration from the *Matter* unit and explore how young children engage in various scientific practices and bridge their own spontaneous concepts and everyday experiences with scientific concepts that were introduced to them by children's literature information books and by their teacher. In this activity, children engaged in developing a model about the way in which matter is organized in solids, liquids, and gases. Studies on children's understandings of states of matter have not yet explored how children make meaning in classroom contexts as they participate in instructional discourse. Krnel, Glazar, and Watson (2003) examined the development of the concept of matter by children 3–13 years of age from a Piagetian perspective using clinical interviews. They found that only children older than nine years of age tended to use intensive properties (properties of the substances that the objects are made of, which are the same throughout and do not change with respect to amount, size, or shape) most of the time, whereas younger children did use a mixture of extensive (properties associated with the objects themselves—and thus change—and not the substances) and intensive properties. In the words of the authors: "the study, however, has not explored the role of social experience in the development of the concept of matter. This is an area for future research, i.e., to explore how social mediation interacts with learning through action" (p. 638). We consider the study reported on here as a step toward this direction.

Therefore, we looked closely at the thinking that unfolded in the midst of social transactions among children and between children and their teacher. We examined the intermingling of cognitive, intellectual relationships with social relationships within an activity that was designed and implemented to create discursive spaces for children to explore what makes something a solid, or a liquid, or a gas. The thinking and the language that we analyzed did not "belong" to individual children; they were collective constructions shaped by the moment-to-moment interactions of the discourse participants who were using particular objects for particular purposes.

Using and Supporting Scientific Practices during Hands-on Explorations

The sorting activity that is the focus of this analysis took place in Lesson 7 of the *Matter* unit (see Chapter 1 for details and timeline of the *Matter* unit). In the previous lesson, the teacher had read aloud the first part of the book *What Is the World Made Of? All About Solids, Liquids, and Gases* (Zoehfeld, 1998). This part (pp. 1–17) focuses on the definition and properties of the three states of matter, solids, liquids, and gases—e.g., "All liquids take on the shape of whatever they are in" (p. 13). The properties of the three states of matter presented in the book are summarized below:

- Solids: Can be hard or soft; keep their shape unless you do something to them.
- Liquids: Have no shape, take the shape of their container; can be thick, thin, slippery, sticky; can flow or be poured.
- Gases: Have no shape, fill up the container they are in; most gases are invisible, but you can feel and sometimes smell them.

The hands-on exploration was done in small groups, followed by a whole-class discussion based on the small-group work. Students were to sort several everyday objects in solids, liquids, and gases; record their decisions on a data sheet (organized in three columns—solids, liquids, and gases—and rows so that children write the name of, or draw, the object *and* write an explanation that supports their decision to place the object in that particular column); share, discuss, and record the reasoning behind their choices; and discuss their sorting in a whole-class discussion producing a whole-class chart. While in small groups, students were to put each of the objects on top of one of three construction papers (about 16–18 inches long) that had different colors and were labeled with one of the three states of matter ("Solids," "Liquids," "Gases"). The objects were a bottle with liquid soap, a bar of soap, shaving cream in a baggie, a can of chicken noodle soup, a pencil, a drinking straw, a helium balloon, a non-inflated balloon, a piece of clay, a sponge, salt in a baggie, a baggie puffed up with air, a bottle of water, a piece of string, a tube of paint, and a rubber band. Many of these objects are considered "ambiguous" because they include different substances and depending on what part of the object one focuses on, the object may be categorized in different states. For example, the water in the contents of the can of chicken noodle soup is liquid, but the aluminum can is a solid. Furthermore, other objects, such as the baggie with salt and the baggie with the shaving cream, are also "ambiguous" in ways that we will discuss in the concluding section. Thus, the objects used in this activity evoked conflict and debate among children, therefore fostering opportunities for reasoning as they sorted these objects.

Below, we focus on two classrooms to present and discuss ways in which scientific practices were enacted during hands-on explorations. Jennifer Hankes'

3rd-grade class is used as an example of how students worked through this activity in small groups, negotiating meaning and power. Begoña Marnotes Cowan's 2nd-grade class is used as an example of how whole-class discussion created affordances for meaning making. (See Chapter 1 for details about the demographic make-up of the classrooms.)

Small-Group Explorations in Jennifer's 3rd-Grade Classroom

Jennifer Hankes' class had read the first part of the book *What Is the World Made Of? Solids, Liquids, and Gases*, an important semiotic tool for this sorting activity that provided children with both prototypes of the three states of matter and specific characteristics—macroscopic properties—of each state. During the sorting exploration, Jennifer first engaged the children in a conversation about ideas presented in the book. Then, she described the hands-on activity and modeled the process with three different objects than those students would sort in their groups as she elicited reasons from them. Jennifer demonstrated how she would sort an object, draw it on the datasheet, and write an explanation for her choice. She differentiated between an object's container and its contents, and she told children that they could sort an object in their own ways. After an extended whole-class conversation around those three objects, Jennifer distributed the materials to children so that they could work in their small groups. The children examined the objects, discussed how they should sort them into three groups designated by the three construction papers, each labeled by "Solids," "Liquids," and "Gases," and also completed their own datasheet.

In one group, there are two boys, Terrance and Joe, and one girl, Kimberly (the fourth member of the group, Tamara, is absent). Jennifer arrives at the group shortly after the children have begun to sort the objects—within four to five minutes from when the objects were given to all the groups. As Joe and Kimberly are sorting objects, Terrance calls Jennifer to the group to ask about the helium balloon. While Terrance is talking with Jennifer, we can see in the video what looks like Joe's hand placing the baggie with the shaving cream in the liquids group. Terrance looks at Joe in surprise, and then Terrance immediately picks up the shaving cream, and shifts the conversation with Jennifer from the balloon to the shaving cream. (Conventions of transcription are given on p. 15.)

1	Terrance:	[Looks at Joe's placement of shaving cream in the liquids group and then at Joe. He picks up the shaving cream from liquids and squeezes it in the fingers of both hands, and addresses Ms. Hankes] I gotta ask you something. Is this um |
2	Ms. Hankes:	It's shaving cream.
3	Joe:	It goes there. It's a liquid. [Off camera]
4	Ms. Hankes:	So what do you guys // what do you guys think about the shaving cream?

Jennifer assumes that Terrance's question is about the shaving cream he is holding in his hands and invites students to share their thinking about their categorization of the shaving cream (unit 2). Although she does not specify what she wants them to tell her about the shaving cream, it is understood by the nature of the activity that what she has in mind is whether the shaving cream is a solid, liquid, or gas. The context and the history of the activity (how Jennifer introduced it, modeled it, and what the groups have been doing so far) make this a "taken-as-shared" understanding, a mutual assumption.

5	Terrance:	I think // I │
6	Joe:	It's solid. [Off camera. Joe is possibly continuing to sort objects and naming the category in which he places them.]
7	Terrance:	We think it's [shaving cream] um gas.
8	Joe:	A solid [Off camera, possibly continuing to sort].
9	Kimberly:	Um I think it's [shaving cream] a liquid.
10	Ms. Hankes:	Okay, so you [Kimberly] think it's a liquid and you [Terrance] think it's a gas?
11	Terrance:	He [Joe] thinks it's a solid.
12	Ms. Hankes:	Well, hey listen just │
13	Joe:	I didn't say it's a solid.
14	Ms. Hankes:	Listen. We can // we can have different ideas, but you have to explain it. What did you [Joe] think it was?
15	Joe:	I think it was liquid.
16	Ms. Hankes:	Tell me why.
17	Joe:	Because it ain't solid or a gas.
18	Ms. Hankes:	So you don't think it's a solid or gas. What makes it a liquid?
19	Kimberly:	I think it's a liquid, too.
20	Ms. Hankes:	And tell me why. Maybe this can help Joe's thinking.
21	Kimberly:	[Takes shaving cream from Terrance] I think it's a liquid because it's like it doesn't hold its place either.
22	Ms. Hankes:	It doesn't hold its place?
23	Kimberly:	[Shakes her head to mean no.]
24	Ms. Hankes:	Okay.
25	Terrance:	[Picks up the baggie with salt that had been placed in the gases group and then picks up the baggie of air at the same time. Holds up the baggie of air.] This is air. [Places the baggie of air back in the gases and holds onto the baggie of salt and begins to feel the salt inside the baggie.]
26	Kimberly:	And it's most like watery kind of.

| 27 | Terrance: | [Holds bag of salt out for Joe who takes the baggie] Feel that. |
| 28 | Ms. Hankes: | And watery? Good discussions. Keep talking a few more minutes. It looks like you guys have almost everything sorted. |

Social and cognitive relationships are interwoven here. Terrance first changes his mind from "I think" (unit 5) to "we think" (unit 7) signaling group agreement, but quickly both Joe and Kimberly object to that (units 8 and 9). All three children categorize the shaving cream differently. In these exchanges, they do not bring up reasons for their choices. Jennifer's summary of what children are saying (unit 10) seems to be expanding the discursive space for the children. Terrance corrects Jennifer about Joe's choice (unit 11), but Joe disagrees (unit 13), saying that the shaving cream is a liquid (similarly to Kimberly, unit 15). As Jennifer attempts one more time to open up the discussion on various ways of categorizing and to encourage the children to think about the reasoning behind their choices (unit 14), Joe and Kimberly respond to her request for explanation (units 15 and 19). Joe uses the process of elimination as a reason for thinking of the shaving cream as a liquid (unit 17), but Kimberly uses two different types of reasoning—a macroscopic property of liquids ("doesn't hold its place," unit 21, meaning that liquids do not hold their shape), and prototypical reasoning, as she compares the shaving cream with a very well-known representative of the liquid state of matter, water ("it's watery," unit 26). For Kimberly, the attribute "watery" may be a synonym of "not holding its place." Here, it is important to realize that the English everyday word "watery" blends a macroscopic property of the liquid state with a particular and abundant substance that can be found in that state. Furthermore, in our everyday language by referring to "water," we mostly imply the substance water (H_2O) in the liquid state, as we have specific words for water in the solid state (that we call ice) and for water in the gaseous state (that we call either water vapor or steam). Kimberly eventually holds onto the macroscopic reasoning and puts it down in her datasheet, whereas Terrance ends up not giving any reason for categorizing the shaving cream as a liquid, and Joe does not include this item on his datasheet at all. However, from the actual sorting of the objects, we know that Joe put the baggie with the shaving cream in the liquids category. We also begin to see how Terrance involves Joe— but not Kimberly—in his manipulation of objects (unit 27). As children move to categorizing another object, more negotiation and reasoning unfolds.

29	Terrance:	What's this soap for?
30	Joe:	Ain't solids heavy? [He is holding baggie of salt.]
31	Terrance:	We don't know what soap is. Is it liquid, solid, or gas?
32	Ms. Hankes:	Open it up. [She takes and unwraps the bar of soap from where students have placed the solids.]
33	Joe:	Soap, that's soap.

34	Ms. Hankes:	[Hands the bar of soap to Terrance then leaves the group.]
35	Joe:	I told you it's solid.
36	Terrance:	[Taps the bar of soap against the palm of his hand.] Um. [To himself] It's not // it's not gas.
37	Joe:	It ain't gas or a liquid. It ain't liquid so it's solid.
38	Kimberly:	[Takes the bar of soap from Terrance, smells it, and seems to wonder about Joe's and Terrance's decisions, but does not say anything.]
39	Terrance:	[Takes the soap back from Kimberly and taps it on his palm again.] It doesn't matter if it smells!
40	Joe:	It's solid! It's solid.
41	Terrance:	It [soap] is gas.
42	Joe:	#It's solid.#
43	Terrance:	#Oh, no it isn't.# Yes it is gas. I can show you because when you um put this in the tub it turns to bubbles [holds the bar of soap out toward Joe] and gas is bubbles like when you fart.
44	Joe:	That's the only time it's gas. It's solid.
45	Terrance:	It's gas.
46	Joe:	It's solid.
47	Terrance:	When you put it in the tub it turns into bubbles.
48	Joe:	No it don't.
49	Terrance:	Yes #it does.#
50	Joe:	#It just# // it just spreads.
51	Terrance:	When you put it in the tub|
52	Joe:	It just spreads.
53	Alla:	Terrance, does it keep its shape?
54	Joe:	Yes.
55	Alla:	Does it break if you <throw> it?
56	Terrance:	Well, when it gets even smaller when you wash up, it breaks into little um [giving the soap karate chops] ==
57	Ms. Hankes:	[She begins to speak to the whole class and calls for silence, but the conversation between the two boys continues.] Okay, can I have another frozen body moment! #Freeze like a statue.# Freeze like statues, like sculpture.
58	Joe:	#So, it keeps it shape. It's solid.#
59	Terrance:	[Terrance makes a face at Joe.] But it's gas, too.
60	Joe:	No it ain't.

Joe keeps using the process of elimination for deciding about the bar of soap; that is, for him, it should be considered a solid because it is not a liquid or a gas (unit 37). But, Terrance disagrees, offering a quite "unconventional" way of thinking (unit 43). Terrance considers a potential function of the substance as he thinks of the everyday uses of soap. What is most salient for Terrance is the fact that soap bubbles get formed when soap is mixed with water, and Terrance knows that soap bubbles have gases trapped in them. Terrance also associates the gas inside the soap bubbles to the human-body process of passing gas that this class had talked about when discussing the read-aloud *What Is the World Made Of? All About Solids, Liquids, and Gases.* As Joe and Terrance negotiate and argue about their ideas, Joe agrees with the potential function of soap, but that is not a good enough reason to categorize the soap as a gas. He accepts Terrance's thinking ("it's the only time it's gas," unit 44), but he really sees soap as a solid. As he tries to argue about his position, he eventually contradicts himself, changing his mind about soap turning into bubbles ("no it don't," unit 48). As Alla (one of the research assistants) steers the children's conversation toward considering the macroscopic properties of the states of matter (unit 53), Joe now moves away of his process-of-elimination strategy, adopting the macroscopic-properties strategy to convince Terrance that he is right and that soap is a solid (unit 58). Terrance, though, stands by his decision to think of soap as a gas (unit 59), and the recording of this group's work ends. Both Terrance and Joe hold onto their reasoning as reflected in their datasheets.

As the recording of this group's sorting resumes, Joe, Kimberly, and Terrance are continuing to sort objects into solids, liquids, and gases. They take objects from each other as they think about the categories they would put them in. Manipulation of the objects in this activity is an important part of the children's engagement. We find the group arguing about liquid paint in a container.

61	Kimberly:	[Picks up the tube of paint from the center of the table. It has not yet been sorted.]
62	Joe:	[Tries to take hold of the paint tube from Kimberly, who refuses to give it to him.] That's solid. No, it's gas // gas.
63	Ms. Hankes:	[To Joe] You think that's a gas? [With no indication of surprise or disapproval in her tone of voice] Why is that a gas?
64	Joe:	[Joe looks unsure and doesn't respond.]
65	Ms. Hankes:	[Takes paint from Kimberly.]
66	Kimberly:	Inside of it.
67	Ms. Hankes:	So, you think this is a gas that's inside here?
68	Terrance:	[Puts down bar of soap. Picks up shaving cream and begins to squeeze it.] Shaving cream is gas.
69	Ms. Hankes:	Shake it. [Gives paint back to Kimberly who shakes it.]
70	Joe:	[Off camera] That's liquid.
71	Kimberly:	[To Joe] It [the paint] do got gas in it. [Squeezes the tube of paint.]

| 72 | Joe: | This [bar soap] is solid. [Holds the bar of soap up to his nose to smell it, then places it in the solids category. Puts the baggie of air in the gases category. Picks up the baggie of salt.] This [salt] is gas. [Puts the baggie of salt in the gases category.] |
| 73 | Kimberly: | [Puts the paint into the liquids category.] |

First, Joe changes his mind about the tube of paint from a solid to a gas (unit 62). What is not explicit here is what part of the tube Joe is considering for the sorting, namely, the container (which is solid) or the contents—the "inside of it" as Kimberly says in unit 66. Jennifer does not show any surprise as Joe changes his idea (unit 63). She has modeled for the children that they can sort either the container or the contents of an item but they need to have reasons for their decisions. As Joe is categorizing probably the content of the tube as gas instead of as a liquid, Jennifer asks Joe to explain why he thinks that would be a gas. As Joe looks unsure and he does not respond, Jennifer suggests an action (shaking) that is related to a macroscopic property of liquids—when liquids are shaken we can hear the "flowing" sound. As Kimberly shakes the tube, Joe proclaims that it is a liquid (unit 70), restates the category of the previous object (soap bar is a solid), and moves on to the baggie with salt that he classifies as a gas. Apparently, Kimberly is giving some thought to Joe's idea that paint is a gas. She knows that paint "do got gas in it" (unit 71). There is no elaboration on this, as Joe moves quickly to other objects, but one way of thinking about this is that Kimberly thinks that the tube of paint is inflated, much like the baggie of air is. Her action of squeezing the tube while thinking of its contents supports this interpretation. Eventually, though, Kimberly is convinced that paint is liquid and puts it in the liquids category. In their datasheets, all the children sorted paint as a liquid giving the same macroscopic reason of losing its shape. Next, Terrance steers the group's discussion to the baggie with salt that had been placed in the gases category by Joe.

74	Terrance:	[Takes the baggie of salt from the gases category.] Hold it. [He has a frown on his face.]
75	Joe:	What you doing?
76	Terrance:	I'm trying to see something! [He jiggles the bag of salt.] It doesn't keep its shape. That's one point for gas. But // but liquid is soft. [He looks at Alla, a research assistant, who is operating the camera.] Is liquid soft?
		. . .
77	Terrance:	[He holds the baggie over the center of the table to show Joe and then seems to be thinking while pouring the salt from one part of the baggie to another. He puts his finger to his chin and looks closely at the baggie.]

78	Alla:	Is it gas?
79	Kimberly:	[Off camera] I think it is because like |
80	Terrance:	It is gas because it doesn't keep its shape.

Terrance seems to be using a macroscopic property of a substance to help him determine what salt may be. We have heard his group associating this property of keeping its shape with being a solid, so Terrance started using this type of reasoning as he was examining the salt inside the baggie (unit 76). He does not focus at all on the baggie (the container), only its contents. He decides that salt does not keep its shape (unit 80). He knows that gases do not keep their shapes ("that's one point for gas," unit 76) and he also probably knows that liquids share this characteristic, too. Although he is not explicit about this, the linguistic structure he uses to bring up liquids ("but liquid is soft," unit 76) implies that. This also signifies that for Terrance, there is a qualifying difference between liquids and salt—in his mind, liquids are soft (although he is not sure about it as he asks for confirmation) and salt is hard. As he is trying to coordinate more than one property, he looks puzzled and attempts to engage Joe in the decision-making. Terrance seems to continue being more drawn to Joe as a group partner, both of whom leave Kimberly out of the group negotiation. After a short period of time, when we do not have a recording of this group's work, Jennifer comes back to this group again and focuses on another item that the children have to sort, a piece of yarn, that Joe thinks is a "scrunchy." Joe has categorized it as a solid but Terrance identifies it as a liquid. As Jennifer asks them to justify their choices, Joe does not answer, but Terrance changes from first telling Jennifer that it is a solid to telling her that it is a liquid after focusing on what he perceives to be a macroscopic property of the yarn (as he keeps wiggling it), namely, that it does not keep its shape.

We see here an example of how learners give up temporarily their "sense" as their "formal" thinking runs into another possibility. Terrance must have known that the yarn is a solid, but during his attempt to use one of the new ideas he has been learning about, namely, the properties of the different states of matter, he comes up with a "sense-less" conclusion—that the yarn is a liquid. What he does not consider is that, for a substance to be in the solid state, the criterion of keeping its shape comes with the assumption that the substance is "left alone" from external influences. Of course, by moving the yarn, Terrance does change its shape. But, if left alone, the yarn does keep its shape. And that is exactly why Joe emphatically objects to Terrance's thinking—"yes, it do [keep its shape, with emphatic tone of voice]," thus arguing that the yarn is a solid. As the conversation unfolds, Joe continues to argue that the yarn is a solid offering yet another reason: "liquids do make noises . . . when they fall down and splash." Kimberly does not get involved in this conversation, whereas Jennifer is trying to get the two boys to hear each other: addressing Terrance, she says at one point "I think that you need to talk to Joe a little bit more." In their datasheets, Kimberly did not sort the yarn, Terrance seemed to be persuaded by Joe adopting his thinking that it is a solid because it "does not lose the shape," and Joe reverted to his process of elimination strategy as a reason for categorizing the yarn as a solid.

The camera then moves to other groups and when it comes back to this group, Jennifer is visiting it once more, asking the children why they have categorized various objects in the ways they did. She notices that they have not given reasons for their sorting on their datasheets and encourages them to do so. The conversation eventually is directed to the baggie with salt.

81	Kimberly:	[To Ms. Hankes] Ain't this [salt] a solid because look, it's like // it's like real small but it holds its shape. [Kimberly singles out one grain of salt in the bag and looks closely at it.]
82	Ms. Hankes:	[She looks very closely at the grain of salt with Kimberly] Hmm. It's real small but it still holds its shape. [Points to her paper] I never knew that. You tell me that. You put that in solids and tell me that explanation, okay? I like how you're looking really closely at it.
83	Joe:	Solid? What you mean it's a solid?
84	Ms. Hankes:	Well [to Kimberly] tell Joe why you said it was a solid.
85	Kimberly:	[Holding up the bag of salt toward Joe] Because look [separates one small grain of salt in the bag]. If you look real close you can see // it's like real teeny teeny little rocks.
86	Ms. Hankes:	[To the whole class] Oh, I forgot there's rubber band in there, too. I'd better write that one up there. [This whole-class interruption makes it hard to hear Kimberly who then stops speaking.]
...		
87	Joe:	[Takes the bag of salt from Kimberly and looks closely at salt.] I sure can see them. [He places the bag of salt in the solids category.]

Kimberly focuses on the individual grains that make up the amount of salt in the baggie. Although she does not call them "grains" (she called them "teeny teeny little rocks," unit 85), she tells Jennifer and Joe (Terrance is not there at this moment) that they are hard and they keep their shape. Thus, using these macroscopic properties, Kimberly justifies that the baggie with salt should be in the solids category. Her thinking persuades Joe (unit 87). After some more time spent on this activity (for which we do not have a record as the camera records another group) and as the activity is coming to an end, the group has yet another conversation on the baggie of salt. This time Terrance is there and he calls the salt "sugar." Terrance turns first to Joe and eventually to both him and Kimberly when he does not get an answer to his question from Joe.

88	Terrance:	[To Joe] Where did you put sugar? [Pointing to the datasheet] Where did you put sugar? Where did you put sugar?
89	Joe:	[Whispering] Shut up.
90	Terrance:	[In a silly voice] He just told me to shut up.
91	Joe:	[Smiling] No I didn't.
92	Terrance:	You just did!
93	Joe:	[Laughs, then to Kimberly] I'm done!
94	Terrance:	Or a gas. Why did you put it under gas? #Oow!# [To Kimberly] You just hit me on my head!
95	Kimberly:	#[She accidentally hits Terrance's head.]# Sorry. That, that, that, that, that [as she taps the solids category construction paper with her pencil but it's not clear why].
96	Terrance:	Why did you put the sugar |
97	Joe:	Where I was supposed to put it.
98	Terrance:	Why did you put the sugar? [He is looking at Kimberly's paper.]
99	Joe:	Where I was supposed to put it.
100	Alla:	It's salt.
101	Terrance:	Oh.
102	Terrance:	It loses its shape! [He's smiling and writing on his datasheet.]
103	Kimberly:	No it doesn't.
104	Terrance:	[To Kimberly] Yes it does. See, where's the salt? Who's got the salt? [Takes the baggie with the salt presumably from the solids category where Joe has placed it during the conversation with Kimberly— see unit 87. The actual position of the baggie of salt is not captured in the video.] See? Look. It loses its shape.
105	Kimberly:	[Takes the baggie of salt from Terrance] Oh, but let me show you something. Look. [She takes a small grain of salt in between two fingers while it's inside the baggie while Terrance is watching.] See that little rock that just moved? See that? See that little rock that just moved. It still holds its shape.
106	Terrance:	But it still loses its shape.
107	Kimberly:	No it doesn't.
108	Terrance:	[Keeps writing] It loses its shape. It loses shape.
109	Kimberly:	(★★★ ★★★).
110	Terrance:	It's not a grain.

This is another example of the various ways social and cognitive relationships unfold in this group. Terrance is clearly looking for Joe's thinking (unit 88). Earlier Joe had put the baggie of salt in the gases category, and although in this exchange he is not explicitly telling Terrance where he thinks the baggie with salt goes, nor why, we understand from Terrance's talk that Joe thinks the baggie of salt belongs to the gases group (unit 94). Terrance constructs a reason for this sorting—"It loses its shape!" (unit 102). But Kimberly disagrees and repeats to Terrance the line of reasoning (a grain holds its shape) that she shared with Joe when Terrance was away from their group. Kimberly's thinking does not convince Terrance, who dismisses her point (unit 106). In contrast to Joe who did see Kimberly's point, Terrance refuses to do so. There may be social and/or cognitive factors contributing to this tension. Socially, Terrance is not ready to hear Kimberly, and Kimberly, after trying to reason with Terrance, gives up. Cognitively, for Terrance, the unit of reference for examining the properties of salt is all of the salt in the baggie, not the individual grains that make up the whole amount that are the unit of reference for Kimberly. The children cannot see each other's reasoning because their unit of reference is different. Furthermore, Joe does not get involved in the debate between Kimberly and Terrance. It may be that although he was able to see Kimberly's point when Terrance was not there, now that Terrance is arguing so strongly that salt does not keep its shape, Joe has lost his weakly owned idea. With Kimberly's help, Joe was able to hold on to a new idea. We can think of his knowledge as having elasticity, so that it can be stretched and changed when somebody is "pulling it." But as soon as the external force is over, his knowledge returns to its original shape. This is what Vygotsky (1978, 1987/1934) associated with an individual's zone of proximal development—the potential knowledge, learning, and development an individual can achieve with the help of a more capable and advanced other. The "size" of this zone and the nature of interactions within it are influenced by many factors including gender dynamics. Joe could be thinking that when Terrance is around he should "stick together" with him, against Kimberly's proposition. At the end, Joe did not sort in his datasheet the baggie with salt, whereas Kimberly and Terrance held on to their differing ways of reasoning about it.

Whole-Class Debriefing in Begoña's 2nd-Grade Classroom

As Begoña Cowan introduced the sorting activity to her class, she challenged her children to come up with reasons that would persuade her and them about the state of matter that an item belongs to. She told the class: "You need to give reasons for why it should go someplace. That is what really counts." Then, the class sorted one object together as an example—a pencil, followed by working in their groups to sort the various objects. After children in Begoña's class sorted their objects in their small groups, they discussed their categorizing and reasoning about each of the objects in a whole-class session. In this debriefing session, Begoña refers to the objects, as well as pictures that she has taken (via an instant camera) of each object that children have sorted. She also has a large piece of paper on the board, with the three states of matter as headings.

31	Ms. Cowan:	[She holds a zip-lock baggie filled with air and a picture of the baggie] How about the baggie? Is the baggie a solid, liquid or gas?
32	Rafael:	A gas.
33	Ms. Cowan:	Why would you say it is a gas? Why? Prove it to me.
34	Rafael:	When you open it, the gas comes out.
35	Ms. Cowan:	Did you guys hear that?
36	Class:	Yeah.
37	David:	I disagree.
38	Ms. Cowan:	[To David] Can you let him finish because I am not sure you heard what he said. Rafael, repeat it.
39	Rafael:	When you open it the gas comes out and then goes into the room.
40	Ms. Cowan:	How do you know there was gas in here to let out?
41	Caitlyn:	Squeeze it.
42	Ms. Cowan:	What about when I squeeze it?
43	Caitlyn:	The air comes out.
44	Ms. Cowan:	So, it was a gas because it was poofy until you open it. And what happens when you open it?
45	Class:	Air gets out.
46	David:	I disagree.
47	Ms. Cowan:	It was a gas because it was fluffy until you opened it, and then you said the gas got out and it was invisible. Alright, David, you tell where you think it should go and why.
48	David:	I think it should go in the solids.
49	Ms. Cowan:	Why?
50	David:	Because if you leave it, it keeps its shape.
51	Ms. Cowan:	What keeps its shape?
52	David:	The baggie.
53	Ms. Cowan:	Oh guys, what is he talking about?
54	Class:	The bag.
55	Ms. Cowan:	[Pointing to the bag] Is this a gas or a solid?
. . .		[Begoña puts a picture of the baggie under the gas heading and another picture of the baggie under the solid one.]
56	Ms. Cowan:	Because why again? David, tell me.
57	David:	Because if you leave it alone, it keeps its shape.
58	Ms. Cowan:	If you say air what are you talking about?

59	Class:	A gas.
60	Ms. Cowan:	So, when you are talking about the air, it goes in the gas [pointing to gas column]. This [baggie] is a plastic [pointing to solid column].

As she has also done during the introduction of the activity, Begoña challenges her children to explain their sorting ("Why? Prove it," unit 33). Rafael focuses on the content of the baggie (air), which he categorizes as a gas (unit 32). As he responds to Begoña's invitation to explain why it is a gas, he does not offer an explanation, but a description of what happens—"when you open it the gas comes out" (unit 34)—that also indicates that he has been focusing on the content in the baggie rather than the material that the baggie is made of. Begoña attempts to lead him closer to an explanation, pushing him toward considering evidence ("how do you know?" unit 30), to which another child Caitlyn responds—"squeeze it" (unit 41), on which Begoña elaborates further as she specifies how the "poofyness" (unit 44) is an indication that there is something in there that it is invisible, so it must be a gas. However, David has been contesting Rafael's categorization right from the start. David thinks the baggie is a solid and not a gas, and he offers his explanation for it by focusing on a macroscopic property of solids (i.e., keeping their shape, unit 50). David's disagreement was used by Begoña as an opportunity to clarify the part of the object that children focus on. It is clear to the children what David refers to as they answer in chorus "the bag" (unit 54). Ambiguity as to what part of a multi-substance item is sorted by the children offers them an opportunity to debate, argue, articulate descriptions, and develop explanations. Begoña eventually uses this ambiguity to establish a common framework with the children (unit 60). Before this session, all the children except David had sorted the baggie with air as a gas in their datasheets. The debate among the children as to what part of the object to categorize continues as the class moves to the straw.

61	Ms. Cowan:	We got a straw. Do you see this [holding up a picture of a drinking straw]? [To Rachel] Do you have a question?
62	Rachel:	No, it is an answer. I know where it [the straw] goes.
63	Ms. Cowan:	Well, tell them.
64	Rachel:	Since it is plastic and since you can break it, I think it goes in solids.
65	Ms. Cowan:	Is a solid something you can break?
66	Class:	No.
67	Ms. Cowan:	Well you can break it.
68	Daniel:	If you leave it alone, it will keep its shape.
69	Ms. Cowan:	If you leave it alone, it will keep its shape. You could change the shape.
70	Courtney:	You can bend it.

71   Children: (★★★ ★★★).

72   Ms. Cowan: So, we are going to put the straw with solids.
                       Cassandra, nobody heard you.

73   Cassandra: I think you should put it in the gases because gases go
                       through it.

74   Ms. Cowan: What do you guys think about that?

75   Rachel: Totally disagree.

76   Ms. Cowan: Guys, did you hear what she said?

77   Caitlyn: I heard what she said and I totally disagree.

78   Cassandra: I think you should put it in the gases because the gases
                       come out of it.

79   Ms. Cowan: She wants to put the straw with the gas because when
                       you blow through a straw you are putting gas through
                       it and when you suck air through a straw you are
                       putting gas through it.

80   Yolanda: But it is not made of gas.

81   Ms. Cowan: Neither is a baggie or balloon. But the balloon and
                       plastic baggie hold gas, so we are going to stick this in
                       here [on the gases category]. A plastic straw // the air
                       that goes through it. It goes through it.

This time, Rachel, the first child to offer her thinking about the drinking straw, focuses on the material that the straw is made of and sorts it as a solid, offering spontaneously her reasoning. She gives two different reasons (unit 64)—"it is plastic," which is a prototypical explanation, and "you can break it," which relates to a macroscopic property that Rachel associates with solids. This is not a scientifically accepted property of solids and, although the read-aloud book that the class has previously read mentions "breaking" when exploring solids, it refers to breaking in the context of the property that solids have of keeping their shapes ("If your baby brother pounds it [a wooden block/solid] with a toy truck, it may chip or break, but then the broken pieces will hold their shapes" [Zoehfeld, 1998, p. 9]). As the class discusses this further, Daniel makes explicit the critical assumption for one of the macroscopic properties of solids—"If you leave it alone, it will keep its shape" (unit 68). Such reasoning legitimizes some children's contributions of the responses "you can break" and "you can bend" regarding solids. Furthermore, although the idea of breaking and bending is not an "official" macroscopic property of solids, it is, nevertheless, a very meaningful idea. It does not make sense to talk and think about liquids and gases "breaking" or "bending," because they do not have a definite shape of their own but take the shape of the container they are in.

However, Begoña's announcement that they "are going to put the straw with solids" (unit 72) triggers Cassandra's suggestion to put the straw in the gases "because gases go through it" (unit 73). Like Rafael earlier in the session, Cassandra thinks of the content rather than the material the straw is made of. But, Caitlyn and Yolanda contest this determination. For them, the straw is the "plastic," as Rachel has said. Caitlyn has earlier explained why the bag with air should be in the gases category, but she now "totally disagree[s]" (unit 77). One way to justify some children's reluctance to accept the contents of the straw as a reasonable part of the "object" to sort, as opposed to the baggie with the air in it, is the fact that it is not a closed system. Air can go through the straw, but it is not *in* the straw in the same way that air is *in* the bag.

As the class moves into discussing the sorting of the shaving cream, it is important to note that Begoña had put the shaving cream on a plate instead of a bag, which is different from what Jennifer had done in her class. This led to an interesting discussion, because of the differences seen in the shaving cream during the two days of the sorting activity. In the first day of the activity, when the children were working in small groups, the shaving cream was moist and smooth, whereas during the second day, when the whole-class discussion took place, it had changed consistency as it had dried up. Although, as a group (the ISLE project team), we had decided to put the shaving cream in a baggie, Begoña diverted from these plans, not recalling this point, because putting it on a plate rather in a baggie seemed most "natural" to her. Because of this unintentional event, the changes in the shaving cream used in this activity opened up new rich and interesting spaces for children to explore states of matter and their characteristics.

82	Ms. Cowan:	This is a good one. The shaving cream.
83	Child:	It doesn't look like shaving cream.
84	Ms. Cowan:	What do you mean it doesn't look like shaving cream?
85	Alicia:	[Pushing her hands together in a flattening motion] It flattened like a pancake.
86	Ingrid:	It melted from yesterday.
87	Sean:	Or evaporated or had a meltdown.
88	Ms. Cowan:	Yesterday, the shaving cream looked really poofy. Yesterday // we left it out over night.
89	Sean:	I don't have a flat pancake.
90	Ms. Cowan:	It was poofy yesterday. What do you guys think? Solid, liquid, or gas?
91	Class:	Solid.
92	Ms. Cowan:	Why is it a solid?
93	Alicia:	I think it is a solid because it is sticking to the plate right now, it is not pouring off.
94	Ms. Cowan:	It is not pouring or running off.
95	Ingrid:	I thought it was a liquid but then I noticed it was all poofy, and liquids are not poofy, so I thought there was gas in it.
96	William:	Yes, that is right because there are air pockets that are holding up the structure.

97	Ms. Cowan:	So the air, the gas, was what was making it all poofy. William was saying there are air pockets, and air makes it poofy. The air went away and made it flat. Alicia says, "look, it is not pouring off."
98	Sean:	And it is not spreading.
99	Daniel:	I thought it was liquid because when it was all poofy and we touched it, it wasn't spreading out. Or so, it wasn't like air because |
		. . .
100	Ingrid:	It was a liquid. It is kinda like whip cream. When you whip up whip cream it gets poofy. It was a liquid but then, I think how you made it // you um // you stirred it up really, really fast and air into it and it got poofy. It was a liquid and got gas.
101	Ms. Cowan:	So if the gas left // the gas made it ==
102	Ingrid:	I think it dried out.
103	Ms. Cowan:	I think someone said evaporated.
104	Rachel:	I // something to tell William. William, do you think that the shaving cream is a // like snow? It has tiny, tiny air pockets in it. I learned that from a book I read.
105	William:	Well, I think it is like that but I think it is a solid. I think what happened is it was a liquid when it first poured out and then when it reached a certain time it turned into a solid. And once the air pockets exploded, they were holding up the structure and making it poofy and it collapsed. So, I think it is a solid.
106	David:	I disagree. The thing is, it had that shape at the bottom when it was all poofy. I don't know. It might have evaporated or something. Because in that time, the bottom was in that shape and then the top disappeared.
107	Ms. Cowan:	Let me sum this up. There was air in it and that was what made it poofy?
108	William:	And also most of it was air pockets and collapsed into that shape.
109	Yolanda:	To the people who think it is a liquid, why do you think it is liquid?
110	Ms. Cowan:	That is what they were just explaining. They thought the air, the gas left, the liquid evaporated and leaving behind the soapy solid.
111	Daniel:	So it was all three and now it is just solid.
112	Ms. Cowan:	Could be. I am not sure.

113	Indira:	Maybe it had more air at first when it was poofy and it was on the plate and maybe it lost some of its air and it went down.
114	Caitlyn:	A little is still left.
115	Ms. Cowan:	Go home and talk to your mom and dad about this.
116	David:	There is air all around us so how could it just disappear?
117	Ms. Cowan:	I don't think it did disappear.
118	Sean:	It is kinda like, you know how	
119	David:	Evaporate?
120	Sean:	No. You know how when you put a potato to a timer it melts down. It gets less and less.
121	David:	At the bottom it was the same shape. There is air all around us. None of the air could have been just away. The gas couldn't have gone away from the shaving cream.
122	Ms. Cowan:	We have run over time, so we will finish this tomorrow.

First, the class discusses the difference in appearance of the shaving cream, sprinkled with Ingrid's and Sean's explanations for the change ("melted" or "evaporated," units 86 and 87). Alicia is the first to offer her categorization of the shaving cream. She excludes a property of liquids (pouring off), that we have seen used in this class before, to claim that the shaving cream is a solid (unit 93). Ingrid then reveals her own thinking process about the shaving cream as it originally was the day before—changing from thinking it was a liquid to thinking that "there was gas in it" because it was "poofy" (unit 95). Ingrid's reference to "poofy" becomes the focal point of the next few exchanges. William explains the puffiness as "air pockets holding up the structure" (unit 96), and Begoña acknowledges and validates his thinking. However, it is Ingrid who first offered this idea to the whole class and it is she who elaborates on how the air may be trapped in the shaving cream as she brings up the analogy with whip cream. It is important here to note that William had the reputation of being the "genius" when it came to science. Rachel's and William's exchanges (units 104 and 105) fit exactly William's identity. William had a particular "power" in the classroom discourse that is manifested here by both Begoña's and Rachel's positionings. However, David states explicitly that he disagrees with William (unit 106). He has heard William claiming that the shaving cream was first liquid that also included gas and when "the air pockets exploded" (unit 105) it became a solid. Although we do not know exactly on what basis David disagrees with William, we get the sense that David is actively interested in making sense of what William is saying and his own observations seem contradictory to William's account of what happened. Yolanda is also wondering what makes her classmates think that the shaving cream was first a liquid (unit 109). Begoña, though, does not quite hear her question and the answer she gives Yolanda focuses on gases rather than liquids. As the conversation unfolds, we get a better understanding of what has been a confusing point for David. Begoña, repeating a child's contribution, highlighted "evaporation" as a relevant phenomenon since the class is talking about drying out (unit 110). But, at the same time, William continues to talk about air trapped in the shaving cream that eventually escaped. David cannot make sense of this (unit 121). He is probably thinking: If air is all around us, how can the air inside the shaving cream disappear?

There seems to be two lines of reasoning, which are not differentiated. One line has to do with evaporation and drying out so that what it remains is less similar to a liquid and more similar to a solid. Sean's analogy with a baked potato (unit 120) is an example of making meaning along this line. Although liquids do not "meltdown" (unit 87) to gases, but they "evaporate into" gases, children who start constructing their understanding of changes of state of matter usually use words that they are more familiar with and that describe changes via the same principles (Varelas, Pappas, & Rife, 2006; Varelas, Pappas, Barry, & O'Neil, 2001). The other line of reasoning has to do with air escaping from the shaving cream that William started. There are two problems associated with this—one that Yolanda struggles with, as she cannot see how this explains that the shaving cream was a liquid the day before; and the other that David is puzzled by, as he cannot understand how the air escapes from the shaving cream. This piece of discourse exemplifies the possibilities and the challenges that are opened up as students and teachers engage in doing, thinking, and talking science. Reasoning is nurtured and demonstrated in multiple ways as confusion is evident.

Concluding Thoughts

The material artifacts of this activity were an essential part of how the discourse, thinking, and transactions among children were shaped. The "ambiguous" objects, such as the baggie with air, or the shaving cream, or the baggie of salt, encouraged children to debate ideas about states of matter and to argue with each other. Rafael thought the baggie of air was a gas because he was referring to the air inside, whereas David thought it was a solid because he referred to the bag itself. Although these were ambiguous objects for the children, they are not ambiguous objects for scientists, for insiders of the practice of science. Scientists would take for granted that when a container with a substance inside it needs to be categorized, they should classify the "matter" inside the container and not the container itself. When samples are sent to laboratories to be examined, scientists assume they have to study the contents and not the container. However, children, as outsiders of this practice, do not make these assumptions, but bring in their everyday practices and discourses to their scientific work in the classroom. Thus, such not-strictly-defined tasks, situations, and objects become for them opportunities to debate, argue, think, and explore.

In a similar way, the yarn is also an "ambiguous" object, because of what it can do, namely, change shape when it is moved. When Terrance was arguing that the yarn was a liquid and not a solid, he was using an idea (i.e., solids do not change shape) that was at the cross-section of his spontaneous understandings and the scientific understandings that his teacher was mediating for him and the rest of the class. However, for scientists, the assumption *without human intervention* is embedded in the language of "solids do not change their shape"; it is part of the scientific discourse that they know and take for granted. In scientific discourse, it is a shared understanding that solids do not change their shape *if they are left alone*. Even seemingly simple statements contain assumptions, assumptions that are not taken-as-shared knowledge for Terrance and other young learners. Such assumptions are part of a system of scientific language that Terrance did not yet have access to. The yarn, as an object to be studied and categorized, and his transactions with others in his class, forced him in some ways to bring together his lifeworld language (Gee, 2004) and the scientific language, expose the assumption of the scientific statement, and contribute to the collective theorizing and meaning making.

Teacher guidance came in various shapes and forms. The teachers summarized what children were saying, repeated or paraphrased what a child shared, encouraged children to think of reasons behind their choices, urged children to debate and explain to each other, and sometimes manipulated objects in particular ways that opened up new ways of looking at them. Jennifer asked children what they thought and challenged their answers. She encouraged Terrance to talk to Joe about his ideas. She suggested to children to shake the tube of paint. Begoña demanded from her children to "prove" that something was a solid, or a liquid, or a gas, thus offering arguments for their decisions. She poured the liquid soap out of its container. She put the shaving cream on a plate instead of in a sealable baggie. All these various ways teachers interacted with children and the materials that they brought in the classrooms, and in the curriculum, stand in contrast to the transmission-oriented teaching that is still prevalent in our schools. As illustrated, Jennifer and Begoña shared the floor with their students. Together they co-constructed "spaces" (Kane, Hankes, Varelas, & Pappas, 2006; Varelas, Kane, & Pappas, 2010) to negotiate meanings and understandings.

Furthermore, as children, with their teacher's guidance at times, held, squeezed, shook, and poured the various objects or substances, they thought about a particular part of an object and its characteristics, bringing together their relatively more spontaneous concepts with the more scientific concepts that they had been introduced to. What they did with the objects was important. Terrance poured the salt within the baggie, thus thinking that the salt does not keep its shape. The unit of reference for Terrance was the whole amount of salt and not an individual grain, which was Kimberly's way of thinking about the salt.

In various ways, the material artifacts used in this activity became ideational tools—semiotic devices that promoted children's engagement with science. The reasoning children shared was in the context of their manipulation of these artifacts—ambiguous artifacts—that children needed to construct as entities for this particular activity. As children engaged with these objects and attempted to integrate scientific concepts that were informed by the book and their teacher, interesting "twists" of sense making took place. At times, the children abandoned their current sense as they tried to use new ideas in their thinking. Terrance was arguing that salt was a gas and the piece of yarn was a liquid because he was using, in incomplete ways, the properties of gases and liquids that were discussed in class. For other children, like David, the properties were more fully developed in their minds. For David something is a solid "because if you leave it alone, it keeps its shape." The children's emergent understandings, although not scientifically correct, should be seen as a resource rather than a liability (Warren, Ballenger, Ogonowski, Rosebery, & Hudicourt-Barnes, 2001). They spark discussion and attention to ideas, and they boost dialogic inquiry as children have something to argue about, to think about, and to debate.

This study also enabled us to see how meaning making is intertwined with various socio-organizational aspects of inquiry—the ways in which children negotiated their roles within their group and in the whole-class sessions, how children worked with each other, how their ideas were heard by the other classroom participants. We saw children challenging each other. Joe, hearing the teacher's affirmation of Kimberly's idea that salt is a solid, asked, "A solid? What you mean it's a solid?" This gave Kimberly an opportunity to share her thinking about the individual grain of salt that Joe accepted as reasonable. Terrance was absent from the group at the time when Joe was willing to consider Kimberly's idea, but later when Terrance was challenging her idea, Joe did not step in the discussion. Children's social positions (and gendered positions) within the classroom shape the communication of ideas and the ways in which they make meaning. William was known as the "smart" boy, and his ideas were readily heard and accepted by the teacher and classmates. In every classroom, in every community of learners, there is an unequal distribution of power both in social and cognitive terms. While some children are seen as "smart," others are seen as "popular," and their voice is heard in different ways. At times children are not willing to contradict each other; their ideas are weakly held together or the bonds of their friendship are stronger than the power of their ideas. Children may also act as mediators, creating spaces for other children with less power. Meaning making unfolds and evolves at the cross-section of children's and their teacher's ways with ideas, objects, words, and people.

References

Bakhtin, M. M. (1981). *The dialogic imagination: Four essays*. (C. Emerson & M. Holquist, Trans.). Austin: The University of Texas Press.

Bianchini, J. (1997). Where knowledge construction, equity, and context intersect: Student learning of science in small groups. *Journal of Research in Science Teaching, 34*, 1039–1065.

Dewey, J. (1902). *Child and the curriculum*. Chicago: University of Chicago Press.

Gee, J. P. (1991).What is literacy? In C. Mitchell & K.Weiler (Eds.), *Rewriting literacy: Culture and the discourse of the other* (pp. 3–12). New York: Bergin & Garvey.

Gee, J. P. (2004). Language in the science classroom: Academic social languages as the heart of school-based literacy. In E. W. Saul (Ed.), *Crossing borders in literacy and science instruction: Perspectives on theory and practice* (pp. 10–32). Newark, DE: International Reading Association.

Kane, J. M., Hankes, J., Varelas, M., & Pappas, C. C. (2006, October). *Constructing spaces for science and literacy in an urban 3rd grade classroom.* Paper presented at the annual conference of the Association for Constructivist Teaching, Lisle, IL.

Kelly, G. J., & Crawford, T. (1997). An ethnographic investigation of the discourse processes of school science. *Science Education, 81,* 533–559.

Krnel, D., Glazar, S. A., & Watson, R. (2003). The development of the concept of "matter": A cross-age study of how children classify materials. *Science Education, 87,* 621–639.

Lemke, J. L. (1990). *Talking science: Language, learning, and values.* Norwood, NJ: Ablex.

Moje, E. B., Ciechanowski, K. M., Kramer, K., Ellis, L., Carrillo, R., & Collazo, T. (2004). Working toward third space in content area literacy: An examination of everyday funds of knowledge and discourse. *Reading Research Quarterly, 39,* 38–70.

Moje, E. B., & Shepardson, D. P. (1998). Social interactions and children's changing understanding of electric circuits. In B. Guzzetti & C. Hynd (Eds.), *Perspectives on conceptual change* (pp. 17–26). Mahwah, NJ: Erlbaum.

National Research Council. (1996). *National science education standards.* Washington, DC: National Academy Press.

National Research Council. (2012). *A framework for K-12 science education: Practices, crosscutting concepts, and core ideas.* Washington, DC: National Academies Press.

Southerland, S., Kittleson, J., Settlage, J., & Lanier, K. (2005). Individual and group meaning-making in an urban third grade classroom: Red fog, cold cans, and seeping vapor. *Journal of Research in Science Teaching, 42,* 1032–1061.

Varelas, M., Kane, J. M., & Pappas, C. C. (2010). Concept development in urban classroom spaces: Dialectical relationships, power, and identity. In W.-M. Roth (Ed.), *Re/Structuring science education: ReUniting psychological and sociological perspectives* (pp. 275–297). Dordrecht, The Netherlands: Springer-Kluwer.

Varelas, M., Luster, B., & Wenzel, S. (1999). Meaning making in a community of learners: Struggles and possibilities in an urban science class. *Research in Science Education, 29,* 227–245.

Varelas, M., Pappas, C. C., & Rife, A. (2006). Exploring the role of intertextuality in concept construction: Urban second-graders make sense of evaporation, boiling, and condensation. *Journal of Research in Science Teaching, 43,* 637–666.

Varelas, M., Pappas, C. C., Barry, A., & O'Neill, A. (2001). Examining language to capture scientific understandings: The case of the water cycle. *Science and Children, 38,* 26–29.

Vygotsky, L. S. (1978). *Mind in society.* Cambridge, MA: Harvard University.

Vygotsky, L. S. (1987). Thinking and speech. In R.W. Rieber & A. S. Carton (Eds.), *The collected works of L. S. Vygotsky (Vol. 1): Problems of general psychology* (N. Minick, Trans.). New York: Plenum Press. (Original work published 1934.)

Warren, B., Ballenger, C., Ogonowski,M., Rosebery, A. S., & Hudicourt-Barnes, J. (2001). Rethinking diversity in learning science: The logic of everyday sense-making. *Journal of Research in Science Teaching, 38,* 529–552.

Zoehfeld, K. W. (1998). *What is the world made of? All about solids, liquids, and gases.* New York: HarperCollins.

EDUCATION LIBRARY
UNIVERSITY OF KENTUCKY

5

BOOK WRITING AND ILLUSTRATING

Ways with Text and Pictures

Christine C. Pappas, Maria Varelas,
Hongmei Dong, Li Ye, Sofia Kokkino Patton,
Tamara Ciesla, and Sharon Gill

The focus of this chapter is young children's own illustrated science books that they composed as part of the two integrated science-literacy units, *Matter* and *Forest*, in the six ISLE classrooms. These books represented a culminating activity (a summative assessment), where children chose their own topic to write and draw about (see Chapter 1 for details), and teachers did not explicitly scaffold children about the content, text, or pictures of their books. The children's information literature books that had been read during the unit were available, but students could not take them to their desk for reference while composing their own books. Moreover, the children were told:

- Write about a part of what we have studied in the unit—something that other 1st (or 2nd or 3rd) graders, who haven't studied this unit, would like to read.
- Your book should include both writing and drawing. That is, your book should be like the books we read that have print and pictures.
- You can look at our semantic map, your journals, and other things we created during the unit, but this book should be your own book on a topic that you are interested in, not something that that you have copied from books.
- You won't be able to write/draw about everything we studied, so *you* will decide what to include. In making your book, you should think about what ideas you want to explain in writing and what ideas you want to explain in pictures.

After the children finished their books, a research assistant had individual book conversations with them, which were videotaped. Children were asked to share their book, reading page by page and explaining their pictures (what the different elements of their pictures were, why they decided to draw these pictures, why they used particular sizes, colors, shapes, etc.).

Using the books of the 60 focal children in the six ISLE classrooms (see Chapter 1 for details about the demographic make-up of the classrooms), we first explored what children showed they knew related to the content of each of the units, as well as how they expressed it via linguistic registers and use of visual images. We also studied two other issues with different sets of students in the context of one of the units: (1) how all 46 3rd graders from the two classrooms demonstrated a sense of audience awareness of their multimodal books, and (2) how the nine English language learners from across all classrooms (except Ibett Ortiz's 2nd-grade bilingual class) used the three modes of talk, text, and pictures to express scientific ideas.

Although there has been research on young children's capabilities to write informational texts (e.g., Donovan, 2001; Honig, 2010; Kamberelis, 1999; Purcell-Gates, Duke, & Martineau, 2007; Wollman-Bonilla, 2000), most of these studies have concentrated only on how children might have appropriated science genres. That is, the scientific content per se has not been explored, nor the accompanying illustrations that these primary students might have incorporated in their texts. Thus, examining all three dimensions of children's compositions—content, visual images, and linguistic text—as well as their talk in terms of audience and ELLs' developing academic communication of scientific ideas, offers new insights into young children's scientific and literacy development.

A Multimodal View of Learning Science

As indicated in previous chapters, a critical aspect of learning science is learning its particular discourse (Bazerman, 2004; Halliday & Martin, 1993; Lemke, 1990). As Sutton (1992) argues, learning science involves a new way of seeing any scientific topic and a new way of talking about it. That is, it entails that young children move from their lifeworld, everyday languages to "buy into" scientific academic language (Gee, 2004). A major type of challenge in learning the subject matter of science is linguistic (Halliday, 1993; Schleppegrell, 2004). Wellington and Osborne (2001) contend that addressing language is one of the most important factors in improving science because "learning the language of science is a major part (if not *the* major part) of science education" (p. 2).

However, another important feature of science is its use of various visual designs. Lemke (1998, 2004) has argued that adult science texts are multimodal, incorporating both visual and verbal semiotics—that is, besides the linguistic message, figures, graphs, charts, diagrams, and so forth, along with their labels and captions, also communicate meanings. However, although it has been recommended that young children include illustrations in their written texts, children's pictures have been seen only as a "rehearsal" or an impetus for their early written messages (Pappas & Varelas, 2009). Once children become more agile in writing text, educators no longer consider visual images as that important in children's writing. As Kress (1997) states, young children's images "are not seen as being as much a part of *communication* as language is . . . Images of most kinds are thought of as being about *expression*, not *information*, *communication*" (p. 36, emphasis in the original).

Young children make meaning in various modes. Even preschoolers draw pictures to represent their ideas, which reflect different genres—for example narrative or expository ones (Newkirk, 1989). They have an "appetite for meaning making . . . [as they] assess the semiotic possibilities of the world around them" (Kress, 1997, p. 33). In addition, they actively explore how to use the resources of word and image and how they might employ them together: "Their drawings are not just illustrations of a verbal text, not just 'creative embellishment'; they are part of a 'multimodally' conceived text, a semiotic interplay in which each mode, the verbal and the visual, is given a defined and equal role to play" (Kress & van Leeuwen, 2006, p. 113). Different modes of communication offer different affordances, different ways to represent meanings (Kress 2000, 2003; Kress & van Leeuwen, 2006; Kress, Jewitt, Osborn, & Tsatsarelis, 2001).

Writing and using visual images, as well as reading, talking, and doing hands-on laboratory work, are integrated activities in which professional scientists engage as part of their practices (Goldman & Bisanz, 2002; Norris & Phillips, 2003; Yore, Bisanz, & Hand, 2003). They use and construct multimodal texts that are integral to their scientific inquiries. For this reason, Kress et al. (2001) emphasize the importance of creating multimodal classrooms to support scientific learning. Thus, because writing/drawing is an essential means of *doing* science, young children also need opportunities to employ these modes in order to inform and express concepts and ideas as part of learning science (Pappas, 2006; Varelas, Pappas, & the ISLE Team, 2006), which the two units (*Matter* and *Forest*) afforded them. Although the children's multimodal books were created at the end of the units in ISLE classrooms, these literacy practices were not just *ends* of inquiry, but instead another *means* for inquiry in the context of the units (Howes, Lim, & Campos, 2009). Thus, besides the scientific ideas that children included in their books, what is also important is how they combined the two modes of communication and thinking to represent these ideas and explain their choices about the use of these modes.

This is a social-semiotic perspective (Halliday, 1978; Halliday & Hasan, 1985; Kress & van Leeuwen, 2006; Pappas, Kiefer, & Levstik, 2006; Riley, 2004; Unsworth, 2001) that attends to: (1) the event in which children created their multimodal books (**field**); (2) the purpose the children had as authors/illustrators (**tenor**); and, (3) the particular linguistic and visual-design features and elements children chose to express and depict (**mode**). Thus, what is of interest in this chapter is how children exploited the expressive potential of the semiotic relationships between, and among, different co-present modes (Hull & Nelson, 2005) in the books they created at the end of the two units.

Content of Children's Multimodal Books

Choice of Themes

In the *Matter* unit, children explored the three states of matter (solids, liquids, gases)—their properties (both similarities and differences among them, including how molecules behave) and examples of everyday substances in each of these states, changes of state, such as freezing, melting, evaporation, and condensation, and the water cycle. The 60 focal children wrote mostly on three themes: 22 books (37%) were on weather; 15 (25%) were on states of matter; and nine (15%) were on molecules. There was a grade difference with respect to the weather topic, with 1st graders composing the most books (11), and 2nd graders (7) and 3rd graders (4) choosing this theme to a lesser degree. For the other two themes, states of matter and molecules, the number of books across the three grades was about the same.

Furthermore, there were some differences regarding the content themes that focal boys and girls chose for their *Matter* books. For example, more 1st and 2nd grade boys than girls wrote weather books (7:4 and 5:2, respectively). However, in 3rd grade more girls than boys (3:1) focused on weather. In terms of books with the theme of states of matter, more 1st-grade girls than boys (3:1) composed such books, but the opposite was the case in 2nd- and 3rd-grade classes where more boys than girls (5:1 and 4:1, respectively) composed such books. Regarding molecule books, in 2nd grade only girls and no boys composed such books, whereas in the other grades, the numbers were about equal. Thus, overall, whereas more boys than girls composed books about states of matter and weather, girls mostly dominated in creating books on the topic of molecules.

In the *Forest* unit, children studied a temperate forest community; animals that live under and above the ground, seeds, plants, and food chains and webs; and interactions among living and non-living entities. There were only 59 books for this unit as one child moved out of the school. Because children had a choice of a range of animals, their books were on many more themes than the *Matter* unit. Snakes and chipmunks were most frequently chosen themes (nine books [15%] each), followed by turtles (seven books [12%]), earthworms and owls (five books [8%] each) and ants/termites, animals, and plants/seeds (four books [7%]) each). Regarding grade differences for the top three themes, only 1st and 3rd graders composed books on snakes, only 2nd and 3rd graders composed books on chipmunks, and whereas all grades composed books on turtles, most of them were done by 2nd graders. There were no gender differences among these more popular themes.

Content Accuracy

Besides *what* focal children wrote and illustrated in their books, we also considered *how successful or accurate* they were in expressing scientific ideas. We developed a content scoring form that covered the main ideas in the *Matter* unit, which included various macro- and micro-features of solids, liquids, and gases (e.g., hardness, shape, molecular speed); changes in states of matter (e.g., melting, freezing); weather phenomena (e.g., windy, cloudy); types of storms (e.g., tornados, blizzards); forms of precipitation (e.g., rain, snow); and aspects of the water cycle. A similar form was developed for the *Forest* unit, which covered parts and functions, needs, and behaviors of animals and plants, as well as interactions of animals and plants in a temperate forest community. We used all three modes of communication, namely, the text children wrote, the pictures they drew, and they conversations they had with us, to determine their scores. These scores, which reflected the ideas/concepts that children presented in their books, were determined as follows: a "0" when an idea was totally incorrect; a "1" for emergent understanding that may not be scientifically correct but had "seeds" of correctness; and a "2" for scientifically canonical and correct understanding (Varelas, Pappas, Kokkino, & Ortiz, 2008). Because children chose what to write on and what to include, they were not penalized for not presenting ideas; only those ideas they brought up were scored. In cases where children presented a particular idea multiple times, if the idea was not presented correctly all the times, they received a "1" and not a "2." Finally, each book received a final score, which was the average of the scores received on all ideas presented in the book.

The two analyses on the illustrated science books that the focal children composed indicated that they presented highly accurate science content and ideas for both units. All mean scores were similar (a GLM analysis showed that they were no significant main effects or interactions, $Fs < 1.6$, $ps > 0.05$). Thus, boys and girls, at all three grades, and across the two units, composed science books that contained accurate scientific ideas.

Text-Picture Relationships in Children's Multimodal Books

Another way we examined children's multimodal books was to analyze text–picture relationships. That is, using ideas by Kress and van Leeuwen's (2006) schemes for analyzing visual designs and Halliday's (Halliday & Martin, 1993; Halliday & Matthiessen, 2004) ideas regarding the "Clause as Representation" for examining linguistic text, we explored the ways in which children expressed scientific content in each mode. Students' books were coded by page to determine if each scientific idea was expressed just in the text (labeled as T), just in the picture (labeled as P), or in the text *and* the picture (labeled as TP). Ideas were tallied for each page per category, and, as a total for the whole book, which led to each book being classified into one of four ways: *Text-Picture Redundant (TPR)*, where most scientific ideas were expressed by both modes; *Text-Elaborative (TE)*, where most ideas were expressed in the text; *Picture-Elaborative (PE)*, where most ideas were expressed in pictures; and, *Text-Picture Complementary (TPC)*, where different ideas were expressed in each of the two modes.

Grade level had the biggest effect regarding the text–picture relationships that were employed by the focal children in their multimodal science books in both units. In the *Matter* unit ($(6)^2 = 13.12$, $p < 0.05$), 1st-graders' books were either picture elaborative (PE, 35%) or text elaborative (TE, 30%); 2nd-graders' books were either text elaborative (TE, 30%) or text-picture complementary (TPC, 30%); and, 3rd-graders' books were mostly text elaborative (TE, 65%). Furthermore, the number of PE books decreased as the grade level increased (35%

for 1st grade, to 15% for 2nd grade, to 0% for 3rd grade). This suggests that although young children use both pictures and words to express scientific ideas, they, as they moved up in grade, created *Matter* books that were more text dominant. Moreover, the low overall (across grades) percentage of text-picture redundant books seemed to indicate that children used the two modes (words and pictures) in different ways, employing each one to express specific ideas.

In the *Forest* unit, children's books also showed a grade difference regarding text-picture relationships $((6)^2=28.02, p < 0.05)$. However, the patterns were different from those seen in the *Matter* books. More specifically, 1st graders mostly composed books that were picture elaborative (PE, 70%), so did 2nd graders, but to a lesser extent (PE, 42%). However, 3rd graders' books were mostly text elaborative (TE, 65%), with the rest text-picture complementary (TPC, 33%). Furthermore, just as in the *Matter* books, the percentage of *Forest* PE books decreased as the grade increased (70% for 1st grade, to 42% for 2nd grade, to 0% for 3rd grade), indicating that children's books became more text dominant as they moved up in grade. However, we also have evidence that the forest community as a topic invited much higher presentation of ideas via pictures than the topic of matter did. Nevertheless, the *Forest* books were similar to the *Matter* books in that the two modes of words and pictures seemed to be used by the children to express different scientific ideas.

Our analyses also indicated that there were no significant differences between the two units, *Matter* and *Forest*, regarding the content about which focal children wrote or drew. That is, the content itself did not seem to influence their decisions in expressing scientific ideas in the two modes. In addition, there were no gender differences in either unit regarding the text-picture relationships in their multimodal books.

Linguistic Features of Children's Multimodal Books

Here, we examine the extent to which the focal children's multimodal books reflected their appropriation of the scientific linguistic register in the two units. In our analysis, we documented typical features of the genre (Pappas, 2006). For example, two types of processes or verbs are realized most commonly: *relational verbs* of attribution and identification (*is, are, has, have, resembles*) to explicate characteristics of a class, or to classify members, or define parts or aspects of them; and *material verbs* of doing to express, usually the concrete, "real" actions related to the topic being covered—for example, the typical features of the states of matter; the typical attributes of animals; the usual processes involved in weather phenomena; the typical behaviors of animals; and so forth (Eggins, 1994; Halliday & Martin, 1993; Halliday & Matthiessen, 2004). Other processes were also coded as "Other." For example, three other types of verbs—mental process verbs (verbs of cognition [verbs of thinking, knowing, understanding], affection [verbs of liking, fearing, hating]), and perception [verbs of seeing, hearing]) (Eggins, 1994; Halliday & Matthiessen, 2004)—are less common in science texts because participants' "inner" feelings, intentions, and motivations are not a topic of concern. However, because including particular features in particular texts in particular genres is never an all-or-nothing phenomenon but a matter of degree, sometimes children included these less common verb types. In these cases, if children incorporated them appropriately, they were coded as "Typical" instances; if they seemed not so, they were coded as "Atypical."

A similar approach was used for coding nouns, pronouns, and the tense of verbs. That is, the predominant type of nouns found in such texts is a generic one (not a particular one, except when an exploration or experiment is described [Pappas, 2006]). Two types of pronouns were coded: general pronouns ("you") and children's atypical use of pronouns ("I"). In addition, the common tense of verbs of the scientific register is present tense, which we coded in a very broad way (e.g., simple present tense, as well as those that included modal operators ["can be"]. We also included other verb forms or verbal groups, in which the Finite operator is present tense [Halliday & Matthiessen, 2004]). Children's use of logical connections was also noted, as they are also common in this genre. In addition, although not aspects of linguistic register, the number of words (length) and words per units (complexity) for each book were computed.

To capture the main trends of children's use of linguistic features in their books, we collapsed several categories of the register analysis for both units: all counts for different processes using *typical* language were included under "Typical Processes"; a similar approach was used for "Typical Verb Tense" and "Typical Nouns." For each of these variables, each book received a score that represented the ratio of the number of times a particular *typical* entity (i.e., process, verb tense, or noun) was found in the book over the total number of times that a particular *atypical* entity was found. "General Pronouns" and "Atypical Pronouns" were analyzed as indicated above, and were scored as counts of occurrences in a book. Children's use of logical connections was not frequent and therefore did not reflect any useful assessment of their appropriation of the genre so it was not analyzed.

Children's Use of Scientific Linguistic Registers

Children in all three grades were very successful in their use of the scientific register in both *Matter* and *Forest* books. Over all grades, they almost always used typical processes, typical verb tense, and typical nouns. Although their scores on these features were very close to the "ceiling" (maximum score of 1) for each of these three features, there were some differences. Regarding the use of typical processes, there were differences by grade level and by gender: 1st-graders' typical process use was significantly less than 2nd graders ($F(2, 51) = 4.054$, MSE = 0.002, p = 0.023, partial eta squared = 0.14); and girls had higher use than boys ($F(2, 51) = 5.98$, MSE = 0.002, p = 0.018, partial eta squared = 0.11). For the other two features, there were only effects for unit, namely, children used more typical verb tense ($F(1, 51) = 2.97$, MSE = 0.003, p = 0.091, partial eta squared = 0.06) and typical noun features ($F(1, 51) = 7.76$, MSE = 0.013, p = 0.007, partial eta squared = 0.13) in the *Forest* unit than in the *Matter* unit.

Overall, children's use of general pronouns ("you," "we") was also very high, and use of atypical pronouns ("I," "me," "we") was quite low in their books. For typical pronoun use, there was a significant interaction of unit by grade ($F(1, 51)$ = 9.4, MSE = 11.8, p < 0.001, partial eta squared = 0.27): 3rd-graders employed more of this feature than 1st and 2nd graders (3rd-graders averaged nine typical pronouns, whereas 1st and 2nd graders averaged two and one pronouns, respectively) in the *Matter* books. For atypical pronoun use, there was main effect for gender ($F(1, 51) = 3.64$, MSE = 2.75, p = 0.062, partial eta squared = 0.07), with boys using more atypical pronouns than girls, as well as an interaction of unit by grade ($F(1, 51) = 4.47$, MSE = 2.79, p = 0.016, partial eta squared = 0.15), with 3rd graders showing more use of atypical pronouns than 2nd-graders in the *Forest* books.

In summary, overall, the findings of the linguistic register analysis showed that most of the focal children reached the ceiling in all linguistic measures of scientific genre. The small differences found between units, grade levels, and gender groups, showed that girls appropriated the scientific genre more than boys as they did better in using typical processes and avoiding using atypical pronouns. Furthermore, there were changes across grade level: 2nd graders did better than 1st graders in typical process use, and 3rd graders did better than 2nd and 1st graders in typical pronoun use. In addition, we found that the *Forest* books included more typical noun use than the *Matter* books. Finally, these findings support the claim that all focal children, independent of content, gender, or grade, had mastered the use of the typical verb tense.

Length and Complexity of Children's Multimodal Books

As indicated above, besides examining children's appropriation of scientific linguistic registers, we also determined the length (words per page) and complexity (words per unit) for each book. Although there was some difference between the *Matter* and *Forest* books, 2nd graders had on the average (taking both *Matter* and *Forest* books together) about 17 words per page, whereas 1st graders had about 11 words per page, and 3rd graders had 27 words per page. It is important also to note that the difference between *Matter* and *Forest* books in terms of the number of words per page was only significant in 1st grade (9 and 14, respectively). This makes sense given the fact that *Matter* books were composed early in the year when 1st graders were learning to write, whereas *Forest* books were composed at the end of 1st grade. Thus, our data show that children in higher grades composed similar length books as children in lower grades (in terms of number of pages), but their books were denser in terms of the linguistic text.

Furthermore, children in higher grades also composed more complex written text manifested by the number of words per unit, but for this factor both the curricular unit and the gender of children made a difference. More specifically, 2nd and 3rd graders' *Matter* books had higher complexity than 1st-graders' books; and the 3rd-graders' *Forest* books were more complex than those of the 1st and 2nd graders'. Regarding gender by grade, girls' text complexity did not differ across grades, but boys' text complexity differed across grades, with 3rd-graders' complexity higher than 1st and 2nd graders.

Snapshots of Children's Multimodal Science Books

In this section, we offer examples of children's science books that illustrate some of the findings presented above. Although all the analyses were based on the whole books children composed at the end of each of the two units, we focus here on one or two pages from a child's book to discuss various dimensions of these analyses. Below, we use the following conventions: The child's actual words during the conversation with a project member where the child presented his or her book are indicated by quotation marks; quotes from a child's book are in italics and in quotation marks.

Example 1

First-grader John was the only child to write about weather forecasters in the *Matter* unit. He chose the topic because he wanted "to be one when I grow up . . . and it's so interesting." The major ideas in John's book consisted of reporting what weather forecasters did, that they saved people from terrible storms such as hurricanes and tornados, as well as animals and plants, and that they work at various places, for example, at TV stations, outside, and in helicopters. Figure 5.1 shows the first two pages of his book.

John's linguistic message reflects several features of typical scientific register: his use of present tense verbs ("*tell*," "*could call*"), generic nouns ("*weather forecasters*," "*meteorologists*"), material and relational processes ("*save*," "*can be*," respectively), and two instances of general pronouns ("*we*" and "*our*"). He also used verbal processes ("*tell*" and "*could call*"), which would be appropriate and typical in his book. His clause, "*we could call weather forecasters meteorologists*," is an interesting emergent version of the more common structure, "weather forecasters are called meteorologists."

On the left-hand page, John's picture and text express some similar ideas, but his picture also refers to additional ideas, as articulated below, which are not shared in his text. The right-hand page, which has no illustrations, provides more information about weather forecasters. John's picture has a weather chart showing a sun, cloud, sun rays, and a TV weather forecaster, all of which he has labeled. On top of the chart is a TV channel—NBC 9—and temperatures—101 °F and 72 °C (which he called "citrium"). John offered a very long explanation for this picture: "The clouds are being sucked up into the sun. And um there's only one

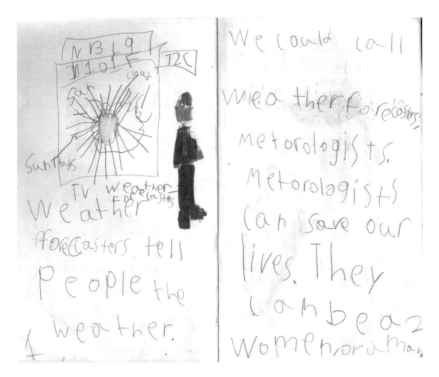

FIGURE 5.1 First two pages of 1ˢᵗ-grader John's book that he composed at the end of the *Matter* unit.

cloud left and that one it's half way sucked in. So it's going to be pretty clear outside. And it's going to be clear and no clouds are being left until next day water evaporates. So people // he tells the people to take cups or big jugs of water out on the street so they can make clouds again . . . it would evaporate like rain into the sky." John's idea that "clouds being sucked up into the sun" is not a scientifically canonical one. However, although it is unlikely that any weather forecaster would suggest to people to take jugs of water out on the street, John's idea that the evaporation of water creates clouds is, of course, accurate.

Example 2

Third-grader Dante expressed many scientific ideas in the text and pictures in his *Matter* book entitled "Solids, Liquids, and Gases." On page 3, he had a total of eight scientific ideas (Figure 5.2). Two of his text scientific ideas, *"You can make a cloud with your breath when it is cold"* and *"Gases are all around us,"* were also depicted in his illustration. What Dante did differently than some of the younger children (1ˢᵗ and 2ⁿᵈ graders) was to elaborate to a greater extent in his text only. He expressed five additional ideas in his text that were not represented in his pictures:

"*Gases are easy to push down*"; "*Gases have more room for molecules*"; "*You can't grab gases*"; "*Gases turn into liquids which is called condensation*"; and, "*Sometimes you can smell gases.*"

All the ideas that Dante brought up in this page of his book were scientifically correct and related to a variety of concepts found on the content scoring form we used, such as compressibility of gases, molecular distance, condensation and the effect of heat, composition of matter, etc. He also used typical linguistic registers to express these ideas. For example, he used several instances of general pronouns ("*you*," "*your*"), material and relational processes ("*make*," "*grab*," and "*are*," "*is called*," respectively). Moreover, all of his nouns are generic ones (e.g., "*gases*," "*liquids*," "*molecules*"); and all of his verbs are in the present tense.

FIGURE 5.2
Page 3 of
3rd-grader Dante's
book that he
composed at the
end of the *Matter*
unit.

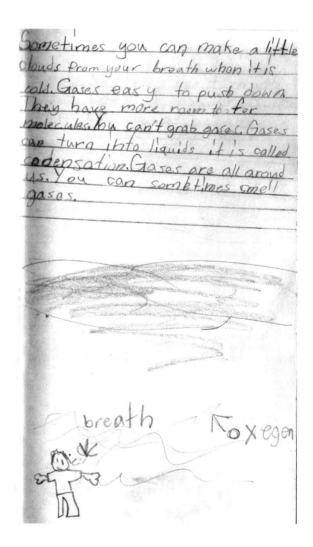

Example 3

In his *Forest* book entitled "Tortugas [Turtles]," 2nd-grader Cesar communicated many of his ideas about turtles in both his text and pictures, while introducing and then reinforcing certain ideas only in pictures throughout his entire book. For example, on one page (Figure 5.3a), Cesar wrote correctly about turtles walking slowly, and in his picture, he depicted a turtle participating in a footrace versus a person who clearly won.

Cesar also depicted the turtle's body parts including its flippers, shell (upper carapace), head (including eyes and the mouth), as well as the tail. This is, in fact, one of the reasons that children composed more picture elaborative *Forest* books than *Matter* books: their images of animals, plants, and the environment of a forest community often presented more ideas than those presented in their text.

On a later page (Figure 5.3b), Cesar provided more of his understanding of turtles' shell as protecting them and providing camouflage as the shell he has colored green blends into the green-colored background. Thus, on these pages, Cesar presented his scientifically canonical understanding of parts of a turtle's body, along with his knowledge of the shell's functions and the concept of camouflage.

Cesar used typical scientific language to express his ideas. Although his "*the turtle*" in the Figure 5.3a translation and "*the shell*" in the Figure 5.3b translation might initially be seen as non-generic nouns, the rest of his sentence in Figure

FIGURE 5.3a First page of 2nd-grader Cesar's book that he composed at the end of the *Forest* unit. English translation of Spanish text: The turtle(s) walk slowly.

5.3b, "*so that they can cover themselves*" indicate he was treating the singular forms as classes (of turtles and shells of turtles, respectively). Thus, these were instances of generic nouns. He used typical material processes ("*walk*," "*cover*"), and all verb tenses were in the present tense.

Example 4

Third-grader Yesenia in her *Forest* book entitled "My Chipmunk Book" had a page (Figure 5.4) with a brown chipmunk nursing pink babies in an underground home. The sun (in yellow) is shining above the chipmunk's home. The text reads: "*Chipmunks are mammals. That's why their babies are born alive and naked like us. Usually, the female and male make the babies. The first time they move is by jumping.*" Yesenia said of baby chipmunks, "They are pink when they are babies."

On this page, Yesenia presented all scientifically canonical ideas about chipmunks: some ideas were only presented in her written text (i.e., chipmunks are mammals; their babies are born alive; both a male and a female is needed for babies to be born; they first move by jumping), an idea was presented both in her text and picture (babies are naked and thus pink), and an idea was only presented in her picture (chipmunks have a tunnel as a home). She also employed typical scientific registers: she used generic nouns ("*chipmunks*," "*mammals*"), material and relational processes ("*make*," "*move*," a couple of instances of "*are*"), present-tense verbs, and one general pronoun, "*us*."

FIGURE 5.3b Page from 2nd-grader Cesar's book that he composed at the end of the *Forest* unit. English translation of Spanish text: The shell is so that they can cover themselves.

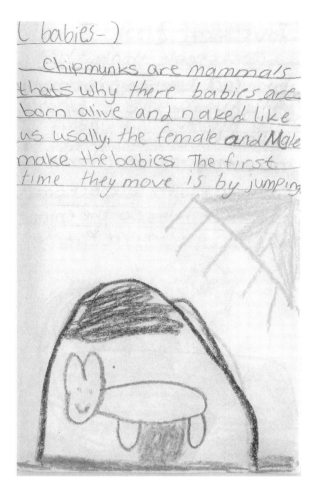

(babies-)

Chipmunks are mammals thats why there babies are born alive and naked like us usally, the female and Male make the babies The first time they move is by jumping

FIGURE 5.4
Page from
3rd-grader
Yesenia's book
that she composed
at the end of the
Forest unit.

Example 5

Ingrid, a 2nd grader, composed a *Matter* book called "Changes of State." In one of the pages (Figure 5.5) she wrote, "*Evaporation* [as a heading] *Evaporation is when a liquid turns into a gas. There is only one solid that can evaporate that is ice.*"

In her written text, Ingrid correctly defined evaporation, specifying initial and final states of matter associated with this process. She also named correctly ice as a solid, but she claimed that only ice can evaporate. In the *Matter* unit, most of the examples of change into the gaseous state referred to water, so understandably Ingrid had developed this idea. What is interesting, though, is that in her text, Ingrid implied that there is another change before evaporation, namely melting, that is making the ice turn into a liquid. Although Ingrid did not write anything about that, she showed in her picture water—liquid water—which turned into "*water vapor*" and moved upwards. Thus, her picture and her words complement each other

FIGURE 5.5
Page from 2nd-grader Ingrid's book that she composed at the end of the *Matter* unit.

evaperation

Evaperation is when a liquid turns into a gas. There is only one solid that can evaperate that solid is ice.

water vaper

communicating almost accurate scientific ideas. And, all of her ideas are expressed via scientific registers—she uses generic nouns ("*evaporation*," "*liquid*," "*solid*"), material ("*evaporate*") and relational ("*is*") processes, as well as present verb tense.

Example 6

In her *Forest* book entitled "Frogs," 1st-grader Stephanie represented canonical ideas about the animal she had chosen as the focus of her book. She composed a book about frogs because she "wanted to know about them." On one of the pages (Figure 5.6a) she presented her ideas about frog reproduction. She expressed in typical scientific registers certain ideas in words (mother frog lays eggs; it takes a long time; it can lay up to more than 4,000 eggs), and others in her picture, having drawn small circles with black dots in them for which she explained, this "is the egg and the white circle around it is jelly . . . to protect it."

On another page (Figure 5.6b), Stephanie addressed food chain ideas—what frogs eat, and what they are eaten by. Both in words (which were in bold) and in her picture, she listed frogs' food (flies, butterflies, and snails) and enemies (snakes and otters), but it was only in words that she expressed a class of animals "*insects*."

A mother frog lays her eggs. It takes a long time because a female frog can lay up to 4,000 eggs.

FIGURE 5.6a
Earlier page of 1ˢᵗ-grader Stephanie's book that she composed at the end of the *Forest* unit.

Since different insects have different forms, she could not draw insects like she drew all the other specific animals. In fact, it was through her pictures that she revealed canonical understandings of form and features of the five animals she listed in her written text. She also explained that a frog catches things by "its tongue because it's really sticky and long . . . the tongue is fast," associating form and function—the characteristics of an animal's feature (length and stickiness of its tongue) with its function. Furthermore, although the labels in her picture correspond to her written words, they also reveal another idea, namely, that enemies of an animal are the animals that eat that animal. Similar to her other pages, Stephanie uses scientific language—material ("*eats*") and relational ("*have*") processes, generic nouns ("*flies*," "*butterflies*," "*frogs*"), as well as present-tense verbs.

Example 7

Second-grader Leonara composed a *Matter* book entitled "Todo Sobre Moléculas [Everything about Molecules]." On her final page (Figure 5.7), Leonara wrote,

FIGURE 5.6b
Figure 5.6b
Later page of
1ˢᵗ-grader
Stephanie's book
that she
composed at the
end of the *Forest*
unit.

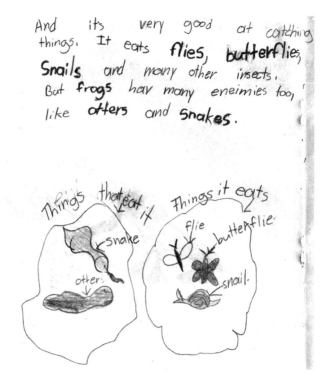

And its very good at catching things. It eats flies, butterflies, Snails and many other insects. But frogs hav many eneimies too, like otters and Snakes.

Things that eat it   Things it eats
snake   flie butterflie
otter   snail

"*In the clouds, when it rains and the molecules fall, the droplets sometimes return again to the droplets.*" In the picture, Leonara represented droplets as small blue dots in the clouds, as well as floating freely in the air, claiming, "When it's raining . . . the cloud fills up and when the sun comes . . . the same little drops that go up to the clouds." Leonara's text, picture, and conversation on that page showed us her understanding of the idea of the water cycle (even though she did not use this term)—one that involves two directions with the same substance (water) being in the clouds and falling as rain and evaporating from the ground. However, this is an emergent scientific idea, as it does not include any changes of states associated with the water cycle—liquid to gas (vapor) and vice versa. Nevertheless, Leonara did use scientific registers to express all of her ideas—material processes ("*rains,*" "*fall*"), generic nouns ("*molecules,*" "*droplets*"), and present-tense verbs.

Example 8

First-grader Vittoria chose to "write about the storms I've been in," and she entitled her *Matter* book "What's the Weather Today?" On one of the pages of her book (Figure 5.8) she focused on snow. As she discussed that picture in her book conversation, she explained why she had drawn a sun saying, "because I said '*sun*' [in the written text] and it melts." The blue entity with the bubble labeled

En las nures (uando
llueven y los Maleculas
Cainen las gotitas
a reses regresan
otravez en las gotitas

FIGURE 5.7
Final page of 2nd-grader Leonara's book that she composed at the end of the *Matter* unit. English translation of Spanish text: In the clouds, when it rains and the molecules fall, the droplets sometimes return again to the droplets.

snow to the bottom left corner is "snow that's about to melt"; the pink box-looking object is a container to collect snow, "then you save it, then put it in the little container . . . it melts and it evaporates . . . half of the snow"; and the two vertical arrows represent "water vapor going to the clouds."

This page shows Vittoria's canonical understanding of characteristics of solids (e.g., ice), and of the process of melting. Solids (like snow and ice) have their own shape, but liquids (when ice melted in the container on the right of the page) do not. Liquids spread on the bottom of the container they are in—an idea that is shown in the picture Vittoria drew and not in her written text. The idea that melting requires heat is communicated in both modes, although the change of state of matter involved in melting is presented by a combination of words ("*ice*," "*snow*," "*melting*") and image (becoming liquid water). Yet another idea, that water evaporates from the open container ("*keep the lid off*" as Vittoria wrote) and forms clouds, is shown in her

FIGURE 5.8
Page from
1st-grader
Vittoria's book
that she com-
posed at the end
of the *Matter*
unit.

picture with the blue vertical arrows pointing upwards to a black cloud. With a
dynamic interplay between words and images, Vittoria offered canonical scientific
ideas, all expressed in scientific linguistic registers. More specifically, she used a series
of material processes (all imperative, present-tense verbs, e.g., "*save*," "*put*," "*keep*,"
"*wait*," etc.) to relate the various steps of the exploration she communicated.
Moreover, to express these procedures, she correctly used particular nouns (e.g.,
"*container*," "*lid*") as well as typical generic nouns ("*snow*" and "*ice*").

Example 9

Third-grader Andres had chosen snakes for the focus of his *Forest* book. On the
page titled "A Body of a Snake" (Figure 5.9), Andres wrote, "*Near the tail of a snake*

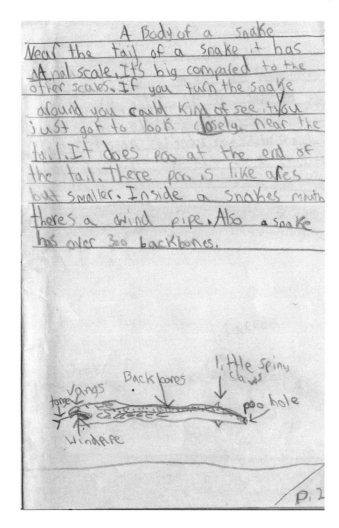

FIGURE 5.9
Page from
3rd-grader Andres'
book that he
composed at the
end of the *Forest*
unit.

it has anal scale. It's big compared to the other scales. If you turn the snake around you could kind of see it. You just got to look closely near the tail. It does poo at the end of the tail. Their poo is like ours but smaller. Inside a snake's mouth there's a wind pipe. Also a snake has over 300 backbones." His picture is a pencil drawing of a snake with body parts labeled (from left to right): *"tongue," "fangs," "wind pipe," "back-bones," "little spiny claws,"* and *"poo hole."* The picture was not colored because as Andres reasoned, readers would not be able to see the parts clearly if they were covered with crayon. For Andres, the picture played an important role, "people can know how // how to // where things are and so they won't get confused. Like somebody says that the spiny claws are in front, they could just look at this book and say 'No they are not, they are at the back.' They could show it to the kid that said that they were in the front."

Andres's written text on this page communicates several canonical ideas, some of which are also shown in his picture (poo hole, windpipe, and backbones). However, his picture also includes three other body parts (tongue, fangs, and little tiny claws) that are not mentioned in the written text. Furthermore, his picture allowed him to capture the relative location of all the parts of a snake's body. Thus, although like other 3rd-graders' books Andres' book was text elaborative, pictures, as a mode of communication, had a particular role to play that words did not. His text reflects the use of scientific linguistic register: he used generic nouns ("*snake*," "*scale*," "*tail*"), material ("*turn*," "*does* [*poo*]") and relational processes ("*has*," "*'s*"). Besides using present-verb tense (the past-tense "*compared*" is appropriate in this context), he also employed several instances of the general pronoun "*you*."

Children's Sense of Audience of Their Multimodal Books

So far we have discussed aspects of the focal children's multimodal books from both units. We now turn to a discussion about the sense of audience demonstrated by 3rd graders from both classrooms (a total of 46 students) in their *Forest* books. In our conversations with children over their books, we asked them questions focused on deciphering their meanings and not on evaluating their content knowledge or the form of their books. Thus, as indicated above, typical interview questions for each page included: asking how they decided on the topic of their book or the content on particular pages; asking about their pictures (their use of color, line, or other visual elements); asking how they decided what ideas to say in their writing and what ideas to show in their pictures; and so forth. Finally, at the end of each interview, children were asked to identify the part of the book that they thought other children at their grade level would like the best and to explain why they might like it. Relying on these retrospective interviews, children's conception of audience, the connection between their sense of audience and their semiotic choices during the composing process, and their notion of audience response (i.e., response from other 3rd graders) to their finished books were investigated (Dong, 2010).

Audience is considered an essential aspect of composing processes (Berkenkotter, 1981; Hayes, 2000); moreover, it is seen to affect the quality of writing (Berkenkotter, 1981; Ede, 1984; Roen & Willey, 1988). Most studies on audience awareness have been done at the college and secondary level (rather than elementary level), have focused mostly on persuasive writing (rather than informational writing), and have examined mono-modal written communication (rather than multimodal texts). Thus, exploring 3rd-graders' sense of audience of their science multimodal books, offers new insights in this aspect of composition.

According to Dong (2010), a new multidimensional perspective is needed for this audience-awareness investigation informed by four major interrelated sociocultural theories of language use: dialogism (Bakhtin 1981, 1986), reader response (Rosenblatt, 1978; Sipe, 2008), discourse community (Johns, 1990; Porter, 1986; Swales, 1990), and multimodality (Kress & van Leeuwen, 2006). For Bakhtin, in writing, authors are in a dialogic relationship by responding to what has been said before them by other authors, namely, relying on prior voices for meaning and the particular rhetorical semiotic resources involved. Authors also anticipate a response to their eventual audience (Nystrand, 1986). Thus, Bakhtin offers a connection between the notion of responsivity and speech genres that incorporates both a backward and a forward response, which draws on authors' knowledge of genre conventions of a particular communication situation. In addition, such a view entails authors' reliance on their understanding of the discourse community to which they belong to (Berkenkotter, 1990; Johns, 1990; Kirsch & Roen, 1990; Porter, 1986; Swales, 1990). Finally, because multimodal texts are involved, children's composing had to do with their learning to orchestrate various semiotic resources and modes available—learning the sign-making process in the science discipline (Kress et al., 2001) that uses multiple means of representation (Lemke, 1998, 2004). Thus, because children created both verbal text and visual images in their books, the concept of sense of audience needs to be broadened so that the author is seen as author/illustrator and the reader is conceived of as reader/viewer (Pappas, Kiefer, & Levstik, 2006).

A Sense of "Other": A General, Potential "They" as Audience

Children demonstrated a sense of audience in various ways, which affected their semiotic choices in composing their books. Using a qualitative analysis, Dong (2010) identified seven major areas of this audience awareness. One such finding was that in their book conversations, children frequently mentioned "they" (or, occasionally, "people" or "somebody") as they talked about their rationales for having made certain choices as authors. For example, in Example 10, Jacinta and the interviewer talked about a page with the heading "*Move and Eat and How They Look*" from his book "Owls." Note that in the following examples emphasis (bold) is added to highlight references to audience.

Example 10

Interviewer:	How come you decided to put titles on your pages?
Jacinta:	If **somebody** read it, **they** will know what I wrote.

The text on Jacinta's page tells about what owls eat ("*rats, snakes, insects, beetles, little birds, mice, and spiders*"), how owls move ("*they fly and walk*"), and what they look like ("*they look furry,*" "*they have big eyes*"). In the picture there is a brown owl and a green snake on a brown log. Thus, the heading does indicate the main topic of this page.

A page from Katia's book "Chipmunks" states that chipmunks are rodents and mammals. Katia used a similar way to talk about her audience—see Example 11.

Example 11

Interviewer:	How did you decide to include this [pointing to the text] in your writing?
Katia:	'Cause I wanted to tell **them** what they were. **They** might not know what they were.

And, as indicated above, sometimes the young authors employed "people" instead of plural pronouns such as "they," as in Example 12 below. The interviewer asks Jonah about the beginning sentence (which is also the topic sentence) of the verbal text on a page of his book "Termites." This page is about termites' enemies.

Example 12

Interviewer:	You put [pointing to the text] "*Some more things I know about termites are their enemies.*" Can you tell me why you wrote that sentence?
Jonah:	I put that so when **people** read the book **they** will know what I'll talk about on this page.

Jonah explains here that his audience, "people," will appreciate the foregrounding of the topic.

As a pronoun, "they" did not have a grammatical antecedent in the conversational contexts; moreover, it was also clear from this discourse that "they" referred to those who might read the child authors' books. This inference was confirmed by several students when the interviewers explicitly asked whom "they" referred to. For instance, in Example 13 below, Yesenia told the interviewer about the cover of her chipmunk book on which bushes, a tree, a chipmunk in its tunnel, and the sun are depicted. In addition, the word "*chipmunks*" is written on four corners of the cover.

Example 13

Interviewer:	Why did you do that [pointing to the word "*chipmunks*" in each of the four corners]?
Yesenia:	So that they can know that it's [the book's] mostly about chipmunks.
Interviewer:	Who are "they"?
Yesenia:	The people that read my book.

From these examples, it appears that the young authors, when composing their multimodal science books, engaged in some internal dialogue with others regarding what to put in words and what to put in pictures on each page. "They" seemed to refer to a general, potential collective of people with certain anticipated characteristics that the authors seemed to be able to envision. In the book conversations, terms that children used most frequently to refer to general audience were: "they," "them," and "people"; less frequently used were "you," "somebody," and "readers." Altogether 36 of the 46 students (or 78%) mentioned a general audience at least once using one or more of the above terms (only 10 students [22%] did not).

Thus, the young authors demonstrated a sense of what Bakhtin calls the "other" in the dialogic encounter. Moreover, this "other" was, in most cases, the unspecified or "unconcretized other" (Bakhtin, 1986). This notion of the unconcretized other was most explicitly expressed by Yvonne, who wrote "Earthworms." The text on page 1 of her book reads: "*If you studies about Earthworms, you would know they have five hearts.*" Below is an excerpt (Example 14) from her book conversation:

Example 14

Interviewer:	When you say "*if you study about earthworms,*" who are you talking to?
Yvonne:	The people who are going to read the book.
Interviewer:	Who are going to read your book?
Yvonne:	I don't know.

Kimberly also expressed this notion of the indefinite audience. On p. 6 of her book "Food Chains," she had written: "*Did you know you can make your own food chain? You make a food chain every time you eat or drink ...*" Below is what she told the interviewer about her use of "you."

Example 15

Interviewer:	Who are "you"? [pointing to the first sentence]
Kimberly:	Well, whoever reads this. It's *you* now [pointing to the interviewer].

To Yvonne and Kimberly, "they" (or "you") is not predetermined or identifiable; it is simply "whoever" reads their books. Moreover, this general, somewhat abstract, notion of collective audience can be concretized and actualized when someone is actually reading their books, as Kimberly said to the interviewer, "It's you now." Only when a specific individual is engaged in the actual act of reading or viewing do these young authors pinpoint a specific audience. In other words, the audience for these young children is a general, potential collective "other."

Young English Language Learners' Multimodal Academic Communication of Scientific Ideas

English language learners (ELLs) are individuals with a first language other than English who are still in the process of learning English. They constitute an ever-increasing population in the nation (Kindler, 2002). In this part of the chapter, we again examine *Forest* multimodal books and conversations, focusing on the ways in which nine ELLs (four 1st graders and five 3rd graders) communicated scientific ideas in this context (Ye, 2009). As indicated above, children created their books at the end of this integrated curricular unit, which was enacted in mainstreamed classrooms. Thus, they were provided with comprehensive content and language input (Krashen, 1985, 1995) as they engaged in various curricular activities. However, in exploring ELLs' information books, we analyze the *output* (Swain, 1995) or *languaging* (Swain, 2006) products that they created, which is also seen as an important critical facet to second-language acquisition because it "pushes learners to process language more deeply—with more mental effort—than does input" (Swain, 2000, p. 99).

Another key feature of ELLs' development is their learning of academic language (MacSwan & Rolstad, 2003; Wong-Fillmore & Snow, 2002), or, as Ye (2009) argues, *scientific academic communication* beyond just language. More specifically, Ye (2009) examined how ELLs communicated scientific ideas through three modes (text, picture, and conversation) and the various types of reasoning and informing (as types of communicative functions) that were realized in each of these modes. Using an interpretative analysis, Ye found that the ELLs presented both declarative knowledge informing about various behaviors, actions, and characteristics of entities found in a forest community *and* a range of scientific reasoning. Their reasoning included: identifying mechanisms and/or causes; comparing two entities/phenomena by identifying similarities/differences; providing specific examples to illustrate a more general claim; relating purposes associated with particular features of organisms and systems; identifying process, timeline, or sequence; recounting experiences of one's own or others; and associating two or more entities implicitly without indicating any of the above reasoning subtypes. Overall, their pictures were the major mode used to communicate scientific ideas, with text playing a secondary role, and conversation used to communicate the least number of new ideas. Most of the scientific ideas in their books realized an informing function. The most sophisticated type of reasoning—identifying mechanisms and/or causes (Hammer & Van Zee, 2006)—was the one prominently realized both within and across ideas. Below we illustrate some of the above findings by focusing on excerpts from the vignettes of two ELLs—see Ye (2009) for fuller details and discussion. Norberto and Fen are both 1st graders, and both wrote on owls, but each expressed scientific ideas differently.

Norberto: Informing and Reasoning Through Writing and Drawing

Norberto's information book was entitled "All the Things in the Forest," a text-picture complementary book (which covered many forest animals). His book had nine pages (in addition to the front cover), with two pages having only text. Norberto started each page with a heading that noted the topic (usually an animal, e.g., owls, earthworms, squirrels, etc.). He was one of two ELLs who communicated the highest numbers of scientific ideas in their information books (he included 69). He also stood out among the other 1st graders because he had the most writing on each page. Most of his ideas were communicated in text and the majority of the ideas realized the informing communicative function. Pictures were the major mode for him to express inter-idea reasoning, but in contrast to the other 1st graders, he used text most frequently to realize reasoning.

His first page was about owls—see Figure 5.10. In his conversation about his book, Norberto explained why he had presented owls in his information book: "Owls belongs in the forests."

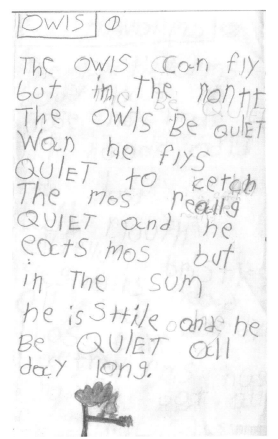

FIGURE 5.10
First page of 1st-grader Norberto's book that he composed at the end of the *Forest* unit.

All the eight ideas communicated on this page realized informing either via identifying typical actions (ITA) or characteristics/attributes (IRP) of owls. However, two types of reasoning were also realized at the inter-idea level, making comparisons (Com) and identifying mechanisms and/or causes (M/C). The text takes up most of the page, and his picture consists of only a little owl standing on a small tree at the bottom of the page. He provides the heading "Owls," with the following text: "*The owls Can fly but in the nontt [night] The owls Be QUIET Wan [when] he flys QUIET to cetch [catch] The mos [mouse] reallg [really] QUIET and he eats mos [mouse] but in The sum [sun] he is sttile [still] and he Be QUIET all day long.*" Because owls as birds can definitely fly, this is probably why Norberto had put this salient characteristic right at the very beginning of the page. Although the rest of the writing includes several emerging spellings that may challenge readers to understand his writing, he had made owls' quietness a dominant theme in his writing by correctly spelling and capitalizing all the words "quiet." He had written one idea, that owls are quiet at night, at the beginning. At the end of the page, he had written another idea: "*but in the sun, he is still quiet . . . all day long.*" This represents inter-idea reasoning—making comparisons (Com)—comparing owls' quietness at different times of the day.

In the picture, he had drawn an owl standing still on the tree and looking up, which matches the idea in the text that owls are quiet. Moreover, for Norberto, owls fly quietly to catch their prey, mice. Thus, this was another example of inter-idea reasoning (identifying mechanisms and/or causes [M/C]): due to their quietness owls could catch their prey.

Fen: Reasoning and Informing Through Drawing

Fen included 49 scientific ideas in her picture-elaborate information book entitled "Screech Owls." In her conversation on her book, she brought up slightly more new ideas than expressed in her book. Fen had the smallest percentage of informing ideas among all the nine ELLs, but exhibited the highest percent of reasoning among the 1st graders. Text, conversation, and pictures played almost equal roles in realizing intra-idea reasoning, though pictures were slightly more prominent than the other two modes. Providing attributes or characteristics of an entity (IRP) was the major type of informing that she used.

Fen's book had 11 pages (including the front cover). Eight pages (except the front cover) included pictures (which usually took half or a whole page) that contained labels and/or captions to help readers understand what the drawings stood for. She either positioned text at the top of a page with pictures at the bottom, or she created a two-page spread with pictures on the left-hand page and text on the right-hand page. On page 6, Fen provided a schematic representation of food chain, where she depicted and wrote about owls eating pack rats and rats eating cheese. On page 7 (Figure 5.11), she communicated about the same food chain but this time she situated animals in their habitats.

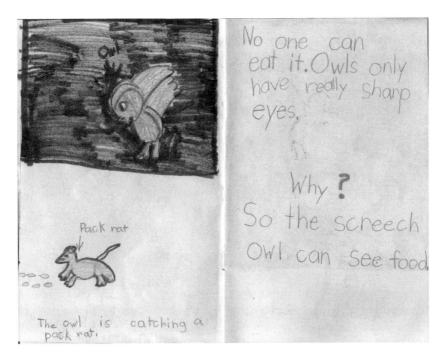

FIGURE 5.11 Page 6 of 1st-grader Fen's book that she composed at the end of the *Forest* unit.

One inter-idea reasoning instance—identifying mechanism and/or causes (M/C) —emerged during her book conversation. In a black background to indicate that it was night, Fen had depicted a side profile of a flying owl that was looking down at a running rat at the bottom of the picture, which was eating pieces of cheese. When asked why she had colored the background black, Fen not only informed the interviewer that owls prey at night, but also explained why owls need to prey at night (Example 16).

Example 16

Interviewer:	Okay, how about // I see you use the color black. Is there a reason why you chose that color?
Fen:	Because they come out at night.
Interviewer:	Interesting. How did you decide to write on that page in those words?
Fen:	Because . . . I think that's really cool because um if the owls come out in the morning, then every // all the animals can see owls. And then he // he sees it and then he runs away from it.

The last unit above is an instance of causal reasoning, as Fen explained: "Because . . . if owls come out in the morning, then . . . all the animals can see owls . . . and then he runs away." Therefore, owls need to prey at night and the black background of her picture represented this idea. Similarly to other pages, Fen had used labels ("*owl*" and "*pack rat*") with arrows pointing to the two entities. At the bottom of the page, she had written a caption to inform about the owl's action, "*The owl is catching a pack rat.*"

Thus, both Norberto and Fen included informing and reasoning communicative functions in expressing scientific ideas, but Norberto relied more on text whereas Fen used more pictures. They both created books that referred to owls, but Norberto had owls as just a sub-topic of his book whereas Fen's whole book was on owls. It is clear, however, that both children were knowledgeable on the topic and were "in charge" of their book composition.

Discussion

In this chapter, we explored young, urban children's multimodal science books that they composed at the end of each of two integrated science-literacy units, *Matter* and *Forest*. Overall, the analyses indicated that these children were quite competent in including accurate scientific content, using a variety of ways to represent and relate their ideas in both text and pictures, and appropriating the typical registers of science. With respect to the 3rd-graders' sense of audience, their book conversations showed that they were aware of the "THEYs" who could be the potential readers/viewers of their books. And, the ELL children, Norberto and Fen, were also capable in expressing a range of scientific ideas (informing and reasoning) in diverse ways, employing text and especially pictures to show their knowledge and expertise.

The illustrated information books that children composed revealed much about their understandings of the science concepts and processes that the two units centered on, and gave us a strong sense of the meaningful ways in which young children compose—and view themselves, in terms of audience awareness—their informational text and images. Each of the books was unique, but, as the examples illustrated, the books were also thematically coherent. That is, most of the books had a clear theme, and their pages related to that theme. And particular themes were more pronounced in some classrooms than others, despite the variation found within each class.

Furthermore, children presented science ideas that were mostly accurate and canonical. It did not matter whether they were girls or boys, or 1st, 2nd, or 3rd graders, or whether they wrote about ideas related to the *Matter* or the *Forest* unit; on average children received very high content scores. And their books attest to their having achieved some profound understandings—about molecular positioning and movement, about properties of different states of matter, about changes of state and factors that affect them, about various types of storms, their origins, and their impact, about animals in the forest, attributes they have and their functions, and about relationships among living and between living and non-living entities in a forest community.

In addition, looking at the pictures in the children's books, we come to appreciate the sophisticated ways in which children think about ideas. Even in 3rd grade where we found a significant increase in text-elaborative books, a fourth of the *Matter* books and a third of the *Forest* books were text-picture complementary. And picture-elaborative, along with text-picture complementary, books were more prevalent in 1st and 2nd grades. Thus, children communicated via their images important science ideas. This was especially evident in ELLs' books, as they relied the most on this mode to express scientific understandings. All of the children's conversations also revealed the thought and attention that they had often given to elements of their images, such as size, color, position, orientation, and so forth.

It is also important to underscore that almost all children, at all classrooms, showed in their books that they were able to use the linguistic registers of science, even though none of their teachers explicitly taught these linguistic features. There is a debate in early literacy research and practice regarding whether it is necessary to explicitly teach the linguistic features of informational, scientific texts for children to acquire them (e.g., Martin & Rothery, 1993; Purcell-Gates et al., 2007). Yet, the children in the present study easily realized them in their texts without such direct instruction. We think this is because the ISLE units provided many multimodal ways for children to read, write, draw, talk, and do science in meaningful, authentic contexts.

Children used generic nouns, present-tense verbs, relational and material verbs, and the scientific terms in their books, because they had been immersed in many authentic ways of "sciencing." They were read children's informational books that reflected these linguistic registers, and they had many opportunities to write in scientific ways in their journals or to engage in creating class charts or semantic maps, and so forth, all of which were integrated with their hands-on explorations. Such an interpretation is supported by Purcell-Gates and her colleagues' (Purcell-Gates et al., 2007) recent study, where authenticity was related to children's appropriation of scientific registers, but few differences were found between children in classrooms that provided explicit instruction versus those that did not. Other studies have also shown children's capabilities in employing informational genre structures (Donavan, 2001; Kamberelis, 1999; Wollman-Bonilla, 2000), but most researchers have not also analyzed any images that might have been incorporated in the children's texts.

However, as Kress (1997) has argued, children have a ravenous appetite to make meaning in a plethora of ways; they are constantly scrutinizing all aspects of their world for potential uses in representation. For example, Dyson (1999) has found that young children were able to create complicated forms of text by incorporating multiple forms of media. Certain forms and images are salient to them—"liftable" (p. 395)—for use in their own texts. In the examples we presented in this chapter, children used in their texts and pictures elements they had seen and heard about from the information books that their teachers had read aloud to them, from the hands-on explorations they had engaged in, from the multimodal texts (semantic map, mural, journal) they had produced in class as a group or individually. These curriculum genres were for children sources of ideas, wordings, registers, and images that they incorporated in their own multimodal texts.

In sum, we believe that we still have a lot to learn about the ways young children think about scientific ideas, concepts, processes, and phenomena, and express their meanings when they are offered opportunities to do so as authors of authentic illustrated information books. In such curricular contexts, young children were easily able to demonstrate an audience awareness as they expressed their ideas in diverse, multimodal ways. ELL students were also successful in this venture—they were seen as knowledgeable, "achieving," and sophisticated science learners, who showed a sense of empowerment during the conversations around their information books. As teachers and researchers continue to work together to explore children's writing and drawing, we may come to appreciate and realize more of the children's intriguing ways with words and pictures in interdisciplinary science and literacy instruction.

References

Bakhtin, M. M. (1981). *The dialogic imagination: Four essays by M. M. Bakhtin* (M. Holquist, Ed., M. Holquist & C. Emerson, Trans.). Austin: University of Texas Press.

Bakhtin, M. M. (1986). *Speech genres and other late essays* (C. Emerson & M. Holquist, Eds., V. W. McGee, Trans.). Austin: University of Texas Press.

Bazerman, C. (2004). Speech acts, genres, and activity systems: How texts organize activity and people. In C. Bazerman & P. Prior (Eds.), *What writing does and how it does it: An introduction to analyzing texts and textual practices* (pp. 309–339). Mahwah, NJ: Lawrence Erlbaum Associates.

Berkenkotter, C. (1981). Understanding a writer's awareness of audience. *College Composition and Communication, 32*(4), 388–399.

Berkenkotter, C. (1990). Evolution of a scholarly forum: Reader, 1977–1988. In G. Kirsch & D. H. Roen (Eds.), *A sense of audience in written communication* (pp. 191–215). Newbury Park, CA: Sage.

Dong, H. (2010). *A sense of audience in young children's multimodal information books.* Unpublished dissertation, University of Illinois at Chicago.

Donovan, C. A. (2001). Children's development and control of written story and informational genres: Insights from one elementary school. *Research in the Teaching of English, 35*, 394–447.

Dyson, A. H. (1999). Coach Bombay's kids learn to write: Children's appropriation of media material for school literacy. *Research in the Teaching of English, 33*, 367–402.

Eggins, S. (1994). *An introduction to systemic functional linguistics.* London: Pinter.

Ede, L. (1984). Audience: An introduction to research. *College Composition and Communication, 35*(2), 140–154.

Gee, J. P. (2004). Language in the science classroom: Academic social languages as the heart of school-based literacy. In E. W. Saul (Ed.), *Crossing borders in literacy and science instruction: Perspectives on theory and practice* (pp. 13–32). Newark, DE: International Reading Association.

Goldman, S. R., & Bisanz, G. L. (2002). Toward a functional analysis of scientific genres: Implications for understanding and learning processes. In J. Otero, J. A. Leon & A. C. Graesser (Eds.), *The psychology of science text comprehension* (pp. 19–50). Mahwah, NJ: Lawrence Erlbaum Associates.

Halliday, M. A. K. (1993). Towards a language-based theory of learning. *Linguistics and Education, 5*, 93–116.

Halliday, M. A. K. (1978). *Language as social semiotic: The social interpretation of language and meaning.* London: Edward Arnold.

Halliday, M. A. K., & Hasan, R. (1985). *Language, context, and text: Aspects of language in a social-semiotic perspective.* Victoria, Australia: Deakin University Press.

Halliday, M. A. K., & Martin, J. R. (1993). *Writing science: Literacy and discursive power.* Pittsburgh, PA: University of Pittsburgh Press.

Halliday, M. A. K., & Matthiessen, C. M. I. M. (2004). *An introduction to functional grammar.* London: Arnold.

Hammer, D., & Van Zee, E. (2006). *Seeing the science in children's thinking: Case studies of student inquiry in physical science.* Portsmouth, NH: Heinemann.

Hayes, J. R. (2000). A new framework for understanding cognition and affect in writing. In R. Indrisano & J. R. Squire (Eds.), *Perspectives on writing: Research, theory, and practice* (pp. 6–44). Newark, DE: International Reading Association.

Honig, S. (2010). What do children write in science? A study of the genre set in a primary science classroom. *Written Communication, 27*, 87–119.

Howes, E. V., Lim, M., & Campos, J. (2009). Journeys into inquiry-based elementary science: Literacy practices, questioning, and empirical study. *Science Education, 93*, 189–217.

Hull, G. A., & Nelson, M. E. (2005). Locating the semiotic power of multimodality. *Written Communication, 22*, 224–261.

Johns, A. M. (1990). L1 composition theories: Implications for developing theories of L2 composition. In B. Kroll (Ed.), *Second language writing: Research insights for the classroom* (pp. 24–36). New York: Cambridge University Press.

Kamberelis, G. (1999). Genre development and learning: Children writing stories, science reports, and poems. *Research in the Teaching of English, 33*, 403–460.

Kindler, A. L. (2002). *Survey of the states' limited English proficient students and available educational programs and services: 2000–2001 Summary Report.* Washington, DC: U.S. Department of Education, Office of English Language Acquisition, Language Enhancement and Academic Achievement for Limited English Proficient Students. Retrieved October 1, 2003, from http://www.ncela.gwu.edu/states/reports/sea reports/0001/sea0001.

Kirsch, G., & Roen, D. H. (1990). Introduction: Theories and research on audience in written communication. In G. Kirsch & D. H. Roen (Eds.), *A sense of audience in written communication* (pp. 13–21). Newbury Park, CA: Sage.

Krashen, S. D. (1985). *The input hypothesis: Issues and implications.* London: Longman.

Krashen, S. D. (1995). *Principles and practice in second language acquisition.* New York: Phoenix ELT.

Kress, G. (1997). *Before writing: Rethinking the paths to literacy.* London: Routledge.

Kress, G. (2000). Multimodality. In B. Cope & M. Kalantzis (Eds.), *Multiliteracies: Literacy learning and the design of social futures* (pp. 182–202). London: Rutledge.

Kress, G. (2003). *Literacy in the new media age.* London: Rutledge.

Kress, G., & van Leeuwen, T. (2006). *Reading images: The grammar of visual design.* London: Routledge.

Kress, G., Jewett, C., Osborn, J., & Tsatsarelis, C. (2001). *Multimodal teaching and learning: The rhetorics of the science classroom.* London: Continuum.

Lemke, J. L. (1990). *Talking science: Language, learning, and values.* Norwood, NJ: Ablex.

Lemke, J. L. (1998). Multiplying meaning: Visual and verbal semiotics in scientific text. In J. R. Martin & R. Veel (Eds.), *Reading science: Critical and functional perspectives on discourses of science* (pp. 87–113). London: Routledge.

Lemke, J. L. (2004). The literacies of science. In E. W. Saul (Eds.), *Crossing borders: Literacy and science instruction: Perspectives on theory and practice* (pp. 33–47). Newark, DE: International Reading Association.

MacSwan, J., & Rolstad, K. (2003). Linguistic diversity, schooling, and social studies: Rethinking our conception of language proficiency in language minority education. In C. P. Bratt & G. Richard (Eds.), *Sociolinguistcs: The essential readings* (pp. 329–334). Oxford, UK: Blackwell.

Martin, J. R., & Rothery, J. (1993). Grammar: Making meaning in writing. In B. Cope & M. Kalantzis (Eds.), *The powers of literacy: A genre approach to teaching writing* (pp. 137–153). Pittsburgh, PA: University of Pittsburgh Press.

Newkirk, T. (1989). *More than stories: The range of children's writing.* Portsmouth, NH: Heinemann.

Norris, S. P., & Phillips, L. M. (2003). How literacy in its fundamental sense is central to scientific literacy. *Science Education, 87,* 224–240.

Nystrand, M. (1986). *The structure of written communication: Studies in reciprocity between writers and readers.* Orlando, FL: Academic Press.

Pappas, C. C. (2006.). The information book genre: Its role in integrated science literacy research and practice. *Reading Research Quarterly, 41,* 226–250.

Pappas, C. C., Kiefer, B. Z., & Levstik, L. S. (2006). *An integrated language perspective in the elementary school: An action approach.* Boston: Pearson Education.

Pappas, C. C., & Varelas, M., with Gill, S., Ortiz, I., & Keblawe-Shamah, N. (2009). Young children's multimodal books in integrated science-literacy units in urban classrooms: Language and visual images for meaning making. *Language Arts, 86,* 201–211.

Porter, J. E. (1986). Intertextuality and the discourse community. *Rhetoric Review, 5,* 34–47.

Purcell-Gates, V., Duke, N. K., & Martineau, J. A. (2007). Learning to read and write genre-specific text: Roles of authentic experience and explicit teaching. *Reading Research Quarterly, 42,* 8–45.

Riley, H. (2004). Perceptual modes, semiotic mode, social mores: A contribution towards a social semiotics of drawing. *Visual Communication, 3,* 294–315.

Roen, D. H., & Willey, R. J. (1988). The effects of audience awareness on drafting and revising. *Research in the Teaching of English, 22,* 75–88.

Rosenblatt, L. (1978). *The reader, the text, the poem: The transactional theory of the literary work.* Carbondale: Southern Illinois University Press.

Schleppegrell, M. J. (2004). *The language of schooling: A functional linguistic perspective.* Mahwah, NJ: Lawrence Erlbaum.

Sipe, L. R. (2008). *Storytime: Young children's literary understanding in the classroom.* New York: Teachers College Press.

Sutton, C. (1992). *Words, science and learning.* Buckingham, UK: Open University Press.

Swain, M. (1995). Three functions of output in second language learning. In G. Cook & B. Seidlhofer (Eds.), *Principle and practice in applied linguistics: Studies in honour of H. G. Widdowson* (pp. 125–144). Oxford, UK: Oxford University Press.

Swain, M. (2000). The output hypothesis and beyond: Mediating acquisition through collaborative dialogue. In J. P. Lantolf (Ed.), *Sociocultural theory and second language learning* (pp. 97–114). Oxford, UK: Oxford University Press.

Swain, M. (2006). Languaging, agency, and collaboration in advanced second language learning. In H. Byrnes (Ed.), *Advancing language learning: The contribution of Halliday and Vygotsky* (pp. 95–108). London: Continuum.

Swales, J. M. (1990). *Genre analysis: English in academic and research settings.* New York: Cambridge University Press.

Unsworth, L. (2001). *Teaching multiliteracies across the curriculum: Changing contexts of text and image in classroom practice.* Buckingham, UK: Open University Press.

Varelas, M., & Pappas, C. C., & the ISLE Team. (2006). Young children's own illustrated information books: Making sense in science through words and pictures. In R. Douglas, M. P. Klentschy, & K. Worth, with W. Binder (Eds.), *Linking science and literacy in the K-8 classroom* (pp. 95–116). Arlington, VA: National Science Teachers Association.

Varelas, M., Pappas, C. C., Kokkino, S., & Ortiz, I. (2008). Students as authors. *Science & Children, 45*(7), 58–62.

Wellington, J., & Osborne, J. (2001). *Language and literacy in science education.* Buckingham, UK: Open University Press.

Wollman-Bonilla, J. E. (2000). Teaching science writing to first graders: Genre learning and recontextualization. *Research in the Teaching of English, 35*, 35–65.

Wong-Fillmore, L., & Snow, C. E. (2002). What teachers need to know about language? In C. T. Adger, C. E. Snow, & D. Christian (Eds.), *What teachers need to know about language* (pp. 7–54). Washington, DC: Center for Applied Linguistics.

Ye, L. (2009). *Exploring young English language learners' multimodal academic communication of scientific ideas.* Unpublished doctoral dissertation, University of Illinois at Chicago.

Yore, L. D., Bisanz, G. L., & Hand, B. M. (2003). Examining the literacy component of science literacy: 25 years of language arts and science research. *International Journal of Science Education, 25*, 689–725.

6

DRAMATIZING AS A TOOL
FOR THINKING AND SPEECH[*]

*Maria Varelas, Christine C. Pappas,
Eli Tucker-Raymond, Justine M. Kane, Jennifer Hankes,
Ibett Ortiz, and Neveen Keblawe-Shamah*

In this chapter we explore young children's ways of developing and communicating scientific understandings through their engagement in drama activities. We present how young children and their teachers drew upon, developed, and expressed scientific ideas as they enacted two drama activities: one in the *Matter* unit where children acted out molecules in the three states of matter (solids, liquids, and gases), and another in the *Forest* unit where children acted out animals, plants, and inanimate entities as part of a food web in a temperate forest.

Using Drama in Learning Science

Turner and Bruner (1986) claim that performing arts, like theater, help fill in gaps in meaning. People use their experiences to mediate and understand their participation in drama, and drama helps people mediate and understand their experiences in the world. In dramatizing, children's experiences with constructs and entities of the curriculum are mediated by and mediate their enactments of the drama. That is, what children learn in a drama has to do with what they already know about the subject, but at the same time, it contributes to that knowledge. Thus, classroom drama activities are a unique kind of semiotic tool where meaning is expressed and developed simultaneously in visual-spatial-kinesthetic and linguistic modes of communication. In spite of successful use in language arts, reading, and social studies, drama has not been used widely in science teaching and learning (Alrutz, 2004).

[*] The chapter is an abridged version of the following journal article: Varelas, M., Pappas, C.C., Tucker-Raymond, E., Kane, J., Hankes, J., Ortiz, I., & Keblawe-Shamah, N. (2010). Drama activities as ideational resources for primary-grade children in urban science classrooms. *Journal of Research in Science Teaching, 47*, 302–325. This article was one of just five JRST articles to be included in the 2011 reading list of the National Science Teachers Association.

The science drama activities we developed and enacted in the six classrooms constitute a particular curriculum genre that shares certain characteristics of drama as an art form (Pappas & Zecker, 2001a, 2001b). In these activities in both units, children acted out a role. They enacted representations within some general guidelines that their teacher provided or co-constructed with them. Although it might be argued that children play the roles of students in classrooms everyday according to guidelines about what it means to go to school (Schank & Abelson, 1977), what makes these activities *drama* is that children enacted *representations* of the scientific content knowledge they were supposed to be constructing. That is, they engaged with others as actors (molecules or forest entities) in a larger goal-directed scene (water changing states of matter or interacting entities of a food web) that was aimed at mediating and transforming their understanding of the scientific concepts they were representing. In other curricular activities, children enacted scientific practices, in that they observed phenomena, recorded data, developed explanations, and so forth, but they did so as themselves, as students. In the drama activities, children were asked to become "the things" they were learning about.

These drama activities were like "process drama," "a mode of learning" that allows learners to use imagined roles to "explore issues, events, and relationships" (O'Neill & Lambert, 1983, p. 11), where there is no a priori detailed script (Schneider, Crumpler, & Rogers, 2006). They were improvisational drama in which the actors became in part co-playwrights and co-directors, deciding and enacting what to do and how, and using audience suggestions to guide their performance (Weltsek-Medina, 2007). This participatory process not only generates fun, but also creativity, thinking, and imagination.

In some ways, dramatic enactments of scientific ideas enable children to do a kind of "imagining" in science (Warren, Ballenger, Ogonowski, Rosebery, & Hudicourt-Barnes, 2001) that they may not do with language alone. Warren and her colleagues define imagining as "inhabiting a created world to explore what might happen or how something might react" (p. 544). Imagining requires "playing around" with what representations would look like, what they would mean, and why. When children use their bodies to imagine how molecules move and bond to each other in different states of matter or how animals, plants, and inanimate entities relate to each other in a forest community, they spend time on concepts, constructing and representing contrasts between them and other concepts. They have to think about what makes each concept unique, which ones are related, and which are not.

Moreover, dramatizing creates hybrid spaces where students bring into the classroom their own everyday funds of knowledge and Discourses that scholars have linked with increased participation and learning for students in urban settings (Barton & Tan, 2009; Moje, Ciechanowski, Kramer, Ellis, Carrillo & Collazo, 2004). As drama activities are enacted, conversational spaces develop, defined by traces of multiple discourses (Bakhtin, 1981) that come together as everyday and scientific ways of thinking, communicating, and acting become interwoven with each other. The participatory-interactive structures that are nurtured in dramatizing may be particularly beneficial to students of color, such as African American students whose life experiences may incorporate the Black Cultural Ethos (BCE) (Boykin, 1986; Nobles, 1980). School contexts that incorporate features of BCE, such as sociality, movement, and variability, have been associated with higher achievement of African American students (Parsons, 2008).

Furthermore, as Winner (1982) wrote: "Both producing and perceiving art require the ability to process and manipulate symbols and to make extremely subtle discriminations . . . the arts are viewed as fundamental ways of knowing the world" (p. 12). Art is not only a mode to express feelings and emotions, but it is also cognitive—it fosters in students flexible, creative ways to think about and depict meaning (Efland, 2002).

The Nature of Drama and Ways of Studying It

During drama, people create imaginary worlds that allow them to link their own experiences with the unknown, or outer, social world (Henry, 2000). As these links are established, actors move back and forth between the actual and imaginary worlds. The dramatic enactments allow them to use specific perspectives to see the world, perspectives they have not used in real life. Bolton (1984) called this state of belonging to two different worlds, the world of image and the world of reality, *metaxis*.

During metaxis, learning occurs at multiple levels. The performed meaning (Geertz, 1973) that actors develop and express unfolds in the cross-section of the two worlds that the actors live in during the drama, which, in turn, constitutes a particular form of meaning. In this chapter, we show how the classroom drama activities offered children opportunities to create, and temporarily live in, and in-between, imagined and real worlds of science, namely, the world of molecules and the world of forest animals and plants.

Furthermore, each enactment occurred within the setting of the classroom and school, which means that children's participation was governed by particular norms. The classrooms differed in their physical layouts, in the ways that the teachers introduced, participated in, and gave directions for the dramas, as well as the nature of the two drama activities. Thus, children's involvement in the drama activities was not only shaped by the scientific concepts and affordances of dramatic representation, but was also influenced and shaped by the affordances of spatial arrangement and conventional practice of the settings children were in and in the ways they knew that they were allowed to operate in such settings. In this chapter we present ways in which the physical, material, and social arrangements of the schooled settings where drama took place mediated the dramatic enactments and the scientific ideas that the children in the six ISLE classrooms represented. (See Chapter 1 for details about the demographic make-up of the classrooms.)

Studying Dramatic Enactments

Drama is a form of communication and like any communicative activity can be analyzed across three dimensions (Halliday, 1978; Jewitt & Kress, 2003; Kress & van Leeuwen, 2001, 2006):

- Ideational (how ideas shared relate to each other and capture the world);
- Interpersonal (how people interact with each other as they engage with ideas);
- Textual (how the communicative activity itself is organized as a recognizable and coherent text defined in an expansive way to include artifacts that represent ideas expressed in visual, auditory, and/or kinesthetic forms).

We used these three dimensions to map out a potential place of the drama genre in elementary urban school science classrooms of young children. In doing so, we examine and discuss the possibilities and challenges that arise as children and teachers engaged in scientific knowing through such experiences.

What underlay our analysis is an assumption that emotion, feelings, and affect are integrally intertwined with reasoning, thinking, cognizing, and interacting with others (Varelas, Becker, Luster, & Wenzel, 2002). That is, as we attempted to understand the ways drama activities engage children with scientific ideas and become ideational (and interpersonal and textual, as described above) resources for them, we kept in mind that these activities might also be, at the same time, affective resources that offered children and teachers opportunities to feel and express such emotions as happiness, surprise, anger, sadness, disappointment, excitement, joy, satisfaction, anxiety, or guilt. Our goal was not to detangle affect from thinking and communicating, but rather to fold it into our interpretations of how drama activities "play out" in urban primary-grade science classrooms.

Furthermore, our goal was to explore the "togetherness" of dramatizing, and understand how children's and their teacher's ideas and contributions in a particular classroom came together and shaped the meanings created during dramatizing. We did not address individual children's understandings and participation in the drama activities, but rather how ideas, actions, behaviors, and emotions were collectively enacted, developed, and transformed.

An Overview of the Two Drama Activities

In the *Molecule* drama activity in the *Matter* unit (see Chapter 1 for a unit outline), students move their bodies through different-size spaces at different speeds in different kinds of relationships to their fellow classmates. As a solid they move slowly, minimally within the small ice cube marked out via masking tape on the floor, which is placed in a large masking-tape cup, while they are locked at the elbow, heads pressed together in a close huddle. As a liquid they still hold hands, expanding to the edges of the cup in which the ice cube is held, but they move faster and more loosely. As a gas they separate and run around the whole classroom forcing the teacher to close the classroom door so that they do not escape. We infused in the *Matter* unit elements that we did not expect the children to master, such as the idea that matter consists of molecules that "behave" differently in different states—an idea that explains the macroscopic characteristics of different states. We did so in order to help children begin to think about ways to explain what they "see" because science *is* the "dance" between data and ways of understanding data (Varelas, 1996). However, we did not discuss that water is an exception to the behavior of most substances when they change from solid to liquid, in that water contracts (i.e., its molecules come closer together) instead of expanding when it melts. Thus, in the *Molecule* drama, children acting as molecules were further away from each other when they were liquid water, which is a scientifically incorrect idea when pertaining to water, but correct for most other substances.

In the *Food-Web* drama activity in the *Forest* unit (see Chapter 1 for a unit outline), children, taking on the roles of animals, plants, and non-living entities that are indicated on nametags they wear, find a place in a "web" of various entities connected by red strings. (Although abiotic factors are excluded from scientifically canonical food chain/webs, the ISLE teachers allowed children to include such factors in order to strengthen their beginning understanding of the importance of abiotic factors in an ecosystem.) In their left hands, children hold the strings of the entities they eat/need for survival, and in their right hands, they hold the strings of the entities that eat/need them.

There were differences between the *Molecule* and *Food-Web* drama activities. The two activities drew on language, gesture, space, movement, and visual resources differently because the teachers and children were attempting to accomplish different goals. For instance, in the molecule drama, *proximity* and *speed* were important aspects of representation. In the food–web drama, the representations of *individual status* and *direction of the relationship* from each entity to another, such as the caterpillar eats the leaf and not the other way around, were important. Children also had different levels of experience with the concepts that they were enacting. In most classes, except Jennifer's 3rd grade and Begoña's 2nd grade, the *Molecule* drama was done before children had any prior discussion on how molecules behave at different states of matter. The *Food-Web* drama was done toward the end of the unit after children had discussed plant–animal interactions and plant and animal needs for survival in temperate forest ecosystems.

Dialectic Relationship Between Ideas and Enactments

Children used their bodies as more than just an object or a symbol. They used their bodies to actively construct and transform for themselves what it meant to be a molecule in a liquid or a chipmunk in a food web. Both drama activities also offered children affordances for expressing and constructing scientific ideas in conversation with their teacher and their peers about the phenomena and topics they were studying. As such, their conceptions of molecules or food webs were being constantly revised during the activity, changing how children dramatized their roles over multiple iterations. Children's ways with actions and words provided them opportunities to negotiate ambiguity and both re-enact and re-articulate understandings.

Language as a Mediator of Ideas and Actions

When Sharon Gill asked the "actors" in her 1ˢᵗ-grade class (the group that was acting as molecules at that time) to show her what happened when they were water vapor, they considered important features of molecular behavior along with other children in the class who performed the role of "audience-directors." (Conventions of transcription are given on p. 15.)

Excerpt 1 ("C" denotes Child):

1	C(actor):	Invisible?
2	Audience:	[Talking all at once]
3	Ms. Gill:	What do you think they should do guys?
4	Audience:	Get out!
5	C(audience):	Get out of the can.
6	C(audience):	Move out.
7	C(audience):	Move out all over the place.
8	C(audience):	Move out, move out, move out.
9	Audience:	And walk around the classroom.
10	Audience:	Be crazy.
11	Actors:	[Some Cs are slowly turning in or near the masking-tape cup on the floor. Most are moving slowly at the front of room, looking at each other and the floor. There are two girls standing on the edge of the container.]
12	C(audience):	Go to San Francisco!
13	Audience:	Move out!

At the beginning of Excerpt 1, an actor was puzzled with how to act out a macroscopic property of gases, namely, that some gases are invisible. However, other students in the audience-director group considered two microscopic properties—the relative distance of molecules (units 7 and 12) and their speed (unit 10). At that point, these ideas did not evolve into articulated understandings about how molecules behave in the gaseous state; they were, nevertheless, tools students used to imagine what being a molecule in water vapor might be like. Thus, children used the drama activity to begin to theorize about the movement, relative distance, and speed of molecules. This excerpt also shows the reciprocal nature of meaning making in which students in the class were engaged. That is, they employed both kinds of tools, kinesthetic and language, to engage with ideas. As one group acted out molecule behavior, the students in the audience modified the group's actions through verbal commands. Each group needed the other to enact the "ideal" behavior of molecules.

In Jennifer Hankes' 3rd-grade class, children "turned up the heat" in the *Molecule* drama by making a motion with their hands as if turning a knob and an (increasingly louder) swishing sound with their mouths, as they changed states of matter. When a group was acting out water in a liquid state, Jennifer posed a question to focus the children's thinking and acting: "Pretend to turn up the heat even more. What's going to start happening?" And children contributed:

> Excerpt 2:
> 1   Michelle: Y'all gonna get hot.
>   . . .
> 2   *Child*:   <u>*Go faster!*</u>
>   . . .
> 3   Child: Disappear.
>   . . .
> 4   Ramona: They gonna pop off and turn into water vapor.
> 5   Ms. Hankes: So if we're starting to boil, what's happening to us? We're coming out of the glass and we're becoming a what?
> 6   *Children:*   <u>*Water vapor!*</u>

Thus, in Excerpt 2, children linked the concept of heat (unit 1) with molecular behavior in the gaseous state (unit 2) and the scientific term for the water in that state (unit 6), as Ramona made a connection with the everyday experience of boiling water where bubbles (of water vapor) break off from the liquid water and "pop off" (unit 4). At another time, when another group was an ice cube and Jennifer asked, "If it gets warmer in here what's going to happen?" (which guided her students to link important ideas such as temperature and molecular behavior), students made a swishing sound. As she prompted her students for more information by asking, "We're gonna start to do what?" children offered "melt" and "get looser." In this way, children related the macroscopic process (melting) with the microscopic process (molecular bonding becoming looser) when solids turn to liquids, as they connected the scientific term of the process with the actors' actions ("get looser").

In the *Food-Web* activity, again in Jennifer's 3rd-grade class, children considered themselves as particular entities and, as they had to decide how they would be connected with each other, they debated discussing ideas they have read about or were thinking through at that moment. The drama activity also became a resource for student questioning and sense-making.

> Excerpt 3:
> 1   Ms. Hankes: Now, what eats the turtle?
> 2   Child: Fox.

3	Jamilia:	Me! [snake actor]
4	Deangelo:	How he [fox actor] going to get through my shell? . . . Nobody could eat me because I could go in my shell. That's why I ain't got no predators.
5	Ms. Hankes:	Deangelo has a good point. However, does that completely protect the turtle from all predators?
6	Lawrence:	No, the poison could get him.
7	Latessa:	Because in the book the fox had gone inside his [turtle's] shell and had grabbed it.
		. . .
8	Yvonne:	I thought all food chains started with a green plant.
9	Michelle:	I'm a green plant.
		. . .
10	Ms. Hankes:	Are there other connections? What else did we learn ate turtles?
11	Child:	Mole.
12	Ms. Hankes:	Remember mole is tiny little mammal.
13	Child:	Owl.
14	Child:	An owl eats mice.
15	Child:	They eat mice and rabbits.
16	Child:	Chipmunk.
17	Ms. Hankes:	The food chain does not always go with size . . . There's another creature that was mentioned in the book	
18	Ramona:	Raccoon!
19	Children:	Raccoon!
20	Amber:	Ms. Hankes, owls can crack shells because their beak is hard.
21	Ms. Hankes:	Yvonne is right. All food chains start with green plants. So if Latessa were not here would we have a food chain?
22	Children:	No.
23	Latessa:	Does that mean I [seed actor] will be in every time the food chain starts?

In Excerpt 3, as children were deciding on how to create their food web, many animal characteristics were considered, such as turtles' shells or owls' beaks, informed, in this case, by read-aloud books read in the unit (for information books read in the *Forest* unit, see Chapter 1). Deangelo, as he played a turtle, contended strongly that a fox could not eat him, and the teacher acknowledged his point, but also challenged it and encouraged further thinking on this. Latessa took up this opportunity by making an intertextual connection to a book the class had read (*Look Out for Turtles!* [Berger, 1992]) to argue otherwise (unit 7). And although the discussion at that moment was about animals eating a turtle, Yvonne brought up the idea that green plants are part of the food web (units 8–9 and 21–23), leading to Latessa's question about her role (playing a seed) in a food web (unit 23).

In her 3rd-grade class, Neveen Shamah also engaged her students in thinking about the scientific ideas and meanings represented in the *Food-Web* drama. One of her students, Sally, was the turtle, but Sally was not included in the dramatic enactment and was ignored by Neveen because the food chain that was constructed revolved around trees, and turtles did not "eat trees." In Excerpt 4a, Neveen continued asking her students to expand the already formed food chains and web, and Sally continued trying to include herself in the action.

Excerpt 4a:

1	Ms. Shamah:	Okay. Is there anything else? That the grass would eat // or be eaten by the grass? I'm sorry. Is there anything else that the grass would // why do I keep saying it wrong? Is there anything that eats the grass?
2	Sally:	[Off camera.] A // a termite.
3	Ms. Shamah:	[To termite Andres] You eat the grass also?
4	Sally:	Who do you eat?
5	Andres:	Wood.
6	Ms. Shamah:	Hold the // sorry. Here you go, Miss Grass. [Hands one end of string to a C and the other end to grass actor.]
7	Jacinta:	[Reaches with left hand.]
8	Ms. Shamah:	No, they eat you.
9	Jacinta:	[Takes string in right hand.]
10	Ms. Shamah:	Okay. Anything else eats the grass?
11	Sally:	A termite.
12	Alita:	[To Andres] Termites eat grass?
13	Andres:	No.
14	Ms. Shamah:	Nope. What else eats the grass but they're not here?
15	Child:	Worm.
16	Ms. Shamah:	The worm, right?
17	Sally:	Where are you, Miss Wormy or Mr. Wormy?
18	Ms. Shamah:	(★★★ ★★★). There is a worm, but whoever was the worm	
19	Sally:	I'll be the worm! And the turtle.
20	Ms. Shamah:	So come here, Sally. You can be the worm.
21	Sally:	[Rises and joins the web.] Yey!
22	Child:	She's a worm.
23	Ms. Shamah:	[Hands Sally the "worm" nametag.] Right now, put that on your neck.
24	Andres:	[Being a termite] I'm dying. The sun's killing me.

In unit 1 of Excerpt 4a, Neveen asked what ate the grass. By using "the," the definite article, to describe grass, Neveen foregrounded the *person/actor* playing the role of grass and not grass as a plant. However, the metaxic moment was retained, as the children continued to occupy real and dramatic worlds at the same time. Sally, still trying to participate offered "a termite" (unit 11) as an answer to what else might eat grass, knowing that her friend, and tablemate, Andres, was also still sitting in the audience on the periphery of the web. But Alita foregrounded the imaginary scientific world by asking Andres whether *termites* ate grass. Andres answered in the negative and did not rise to participate in the drama. He adhered to what he had learned about termites, that they ate wood. Neveen's question in unit 14 also complexly evoked both the ontological/scientific world and the world of the students' imagining. Even though the original actor playing the worm was absent that day, Sally, as the worm that day, was finally included in the food web. Andres, by unit 24, was still not a part of the food web. Enacting the imagined/ scientific world, he realized that if he were not eating wood, then he would not be eating at all and would also be exposed to the sun, something to which termites were sensitive. By occupying both worlds, the children and Neveen were able to address characteristics of various forest entities and their relationships.

As already seen in Excerpt 3 when Latessa in Jennifer's 3rd-grade class referred to the turtle read-aloud, the drama activities also provided sources of intertextuality that can be seen as similar to metaxis. Juxtaposing various texts is like being in two worlds and attempting to make sense of ideas by making connections between the two texts/worlds. The drama activities encouraged intertextuality that in turn allowed children to engage further with representing scientific concepts. As Neveen continued working with her students to construct a food web, she referred them to the information books the class had been reading.

Excerpt 4b:

25	Ms. Shamah:	What are you? Groundhog! What does the // what does a groundhog eat?
26	Kira:	(★★★ ★★★).
27	Ms. Shamah:	Okay. But we learned about other things that they eat. [To class.] What does the groundhog eat from the books we've read?
28	Sally:	Look up there, man [referring to class animal charts].
29	Ms. Shamah:	Nobody remembers? Didn't you make a list? [To Kira.] What was on your list?
30	Kira:	Vegetables and herbs and seeds.
31	Ms. Shamah:	And seeds? Okay.
32	Yesenia:	Oh, we got the seed.

In unit 27, Neveen referred to the information books of the unit that were read aloud to the children. This reminded Sally of the charts that the children had made on animals from each of the vertebrate classes. On these charts, the class had noted information on mammals, amphibians, reptiles, fish, and birds. The information included physical characteristics, what they eat, their enemies, their homes, their babies, and a "cool" idea about them. By turning to these texts, Sally acknowledged their relevance and usefulness and used them to move the drama activity forward. Furthermore, in unit 29, Neveen hinted at a journal entry that children wrote before starting the *Food-Web* drama, namely, the journal entry where children listed what the entity that they would "play" in the drama eats/needs, and what it is eaten/needed by. This hint helped Kira (unit 30) contribute to the expansion of the food web.

Serendipity of Ideas and Enactments

Back in Sharon Gill's 1st-grade class, Sharon also made sure that children linked scientific ideas to the *Food-Web* drama. At the beginning, she named the entities she wanted to have as part of the web and asked the children representing those entities to come up. However, she also asked children to say what one or another animal ate. Sharon let the children talk to figure out amongst themselves who ate what. She later intervened.

Excerpt 5:

1	Ms. Gill:	. . . Okay. So we have a caterpillar here. We have dry leaves. Anyone eat these things?
2	Child:	[Raises hand.]
3	Ms. Gill:	If you do, come on.
4	Child:	I eat |
5	Ms. Gill:	If you're supposed to be up here, you need to come. Come on.
6	Children:	(*** ***). [Several Cs approach web.]
7	Ms. Gill:	Uh oh. (*** ***). There you go. (*** ***). Okay. Everybody freeze. Can anyone help Jasmine? She's a butterfly, and she doesn't know where to go. Tell her some place. Tell her // give her some place to go.
8	Child:	Flowers!
9	Children:	Flowers! Flowers!
10	Child:	Get over there.
11	Child:	Get over there.
		. . .
12	Ms. Gill:	Okay. Um. [Unclear to whom, probably Alam, who is a tadpole.] Okay, why are you holding on to the string?
13	Child:	It could eat |
14	Ms. Gill:	Unhuh. Excuse me!

15	Children:	[Become quiet.]
16	Ms. Gill:	Why are you holding in there?
17	Child:	Me?
18	Ms. Gill:	No, (★★★). I just want // I just asked you a question. I just need an answer. Why are you there?
19	Alam:	Because um tadpoles eat underwater plants, and he's a plant.
20	Child:	Not underwater plant.
21	Alam:	But I don't know where the underwater plants are.
22	Jasmine:	Frogs. Frogs. [Points toward actor frog. Alam, the tadpole, then walks to frog.]
23	Child:	Hey frog, do you eat me?
24	Child:	No I	
25	Ms. Gill:	He doesn't // okay I guess. (★★★ ★★★). Why would you go back there to frogs?
26	Alam:	Because they're underwater and (★★★) there // [starts walking away from frog.] I need just (★★★ ★★★)	
27	Ms. Gill:	No. No. No. #Just tell me why you went there.#
28	Child:	[Bird actor] #Birds eat tadpoles.#
29	Ms. Gill:	Okay. Freeze. Everybody else is quiet. <Why does the chain go toward the frog?>
30	Alam:	[Raises hand.] I'll answer.
31	Ms. Gill:	Demario.
32	Demario:	Because uh // because uh, uh the tadpoles are younger than the frogs. And I don't know why he went there but I think (★★★ ★★★) stay close.
33	Child:	I know. I know.
34	Ms. Gill:	Okay.
35	Child:	Cause he (★★★ ★★★) the frog family. The frog life cycle.

In Excerpt 5, Sharon and her children shared authority when deciding where different students would fit in the web. She asked the class where Jasmine, the butterfly, should go (unit 7). She let them figure out the food web in a way that seemed reasonable to them, but she also asked them "why" (unit 12), and she insisted on an answer (unit 18). As Alam, who was playing a tadpole, tried to find a place along a string in the food web, he and some other children considered what tadpoles eat, that underwater plants are different from ground plants (units 19 and 21), and finally that a tadpole is part of the frog family, the frog life cycle (units 32 and 35). These are science ideas that were initiated and debated by children because they were engaged in acting out the drama in a way that made sense to them and at the same time made sense to Sharon, their teacher. However, these ideas did not necessarily emerge in other classrooms. This is one of the limitations, but the beauty, too, of the process drama that does not have an a priori script. Ideas and enactments emerge as the participants (children and teacher) think about them and act in ways that stimulate certain ideas and not others. That is why dramatizing should be used and considered as one of the various curriculum genres that need to be enacted to support teaching and learning of science.

Although the drama activities did not have a script that the children were supposed to follow, they had guidelines that enabled children to act out in their own ways. Thus, the dramas offered various unplanned and serendipitous opportunities for nurturing the children's developing knowledge about the behavior of molecules. For instance, the students in Group 3 in Neveen Shamah's 3rd-grade class were covering some distance around the room as gas molecules, but were not moving fast. Neveen asked a question to challenge children's actions.

Excerpt 6:
1   Ms. Shamah: Does gas move slowly?
2   Group 3:   [Children start to move faster. Luz bumps on a table.]
3   Ms. Shamah: Luz bumped into a table. Does that happen? Do gas
                       molecules bump into each other?
4   Children: Yeah.

Luz's unexpected bumping on the table (unit 2) offered Neveen the chance to highlight for the class an important science idea, namely, that molecules bump into other matter and into each other, thereby expanding their understandings.

Moreover, mismatches in actual and ideal behavior of the actors afforded opportunities to talk about molecular behavior. In Sharon Gill's 1st-grade class, on a day after the whole class had enacted the drama activity in front of each other, Sharon took small groups one at a time out into the hallway and told them to be either a solid, liquid, or gas. The rest of the children sat at their desks and were supposed to guess what state of matter the group was dramatizing. As groups tried to depict the state they were supposed to be, opportunities arose for the class to discuss and describe the behaviors of molecules in liquids and gasses.

Excerpt 7 ("C" denotes Child):
1   Ms. Gill: [Picks an all-boy group and goes out into the hallway
                     with it.]
2   Actors: [Three boys come in the room bouncing up and
                     down and about 1–2 feet apart.]
3   Audience: [shouting] Liquid! Liquid!
4   Ms. Gill: How many people say gas?
5   Audience: [No hands go up.]
6   Ms. Gill: How many people say liquid?
7   Audience: [All hands go up.]
8   Ms. Gill: What are you guys?

9	Actors:	Gas!
		. . .
10	Ms. Gill:	[Calls an all-girl group that disappears to the hallway.]
11	Actors:	[Four girls come in 2–3 feet apart. The second girl does the breaststroke and blows up her cheeks.]
12	Audience:	Gas! Gas! Gas!
13	Actors:	[Girls in group run around the room.]
14	Ms. Gill:	Now, group. Boys and girls in the classroom, you were right, they came in like gas, but actually they were supposed to be liquid.
15	C(audience):	That's what I thought they were.
16	Ms. Gill:	Yeah, they don't know the difference. What was wrong with that group?
17	C(audience):	They were too crazy.
18	C(audience):	Too riled up!
19	Ms. Gill:	What were they doing that gas does?
20	Actors:	[Still moving around the room.]
21	Ms. Gill:	What does gas do?
22	Audience:	Run fast.
23	Ms. Gill:	And what does liquid do?
24	C(audience):	Slower.
25	C(audience):	Kind of closer together.
26	Ms. Gill:	They're closer together, aren't they? Okay, girls, you girls need to go back to acting school.

In Excerpt 7, the interactivity of ideas and actions, of the real and imagined worlds, and of the actors and the audience all come to the fore. In Sharon's earlier drama enactments the day before, the audience had acted as the "knowers" dialoguing with the actors about what to do and how to move. In contrast, in this present enactment of charades, the audience switches roles and become guessers. However, all students are allowed, ultimately, to decide what counts as a faithful representation. In units 2–9, the boys, thinking that they are representing gas molecules, bounce up and down and are far away from each other, but are interpreted by the audience as the behavior of liquid molecules. In lines 10–14, a second group is also judged by the audience to render liquids unfaithfully. The differences between what the actors were doing and what the audience thought they should be doing offered opportunities for children to talk about the behavior of molecules in different states. As Sharon engaged the children in thinking about the actions of the group and the "actions" of gas and liquid, the children were engaging with ideas related to molecular behavior, comparing liquid and gas molecules' relative speed ("slower," unit 24) and closeness ("kind of closer together," unit 25).

Differentiating Between Imagined (Scientific) and Real (Model) Worlds

As the children in the various classes were engaged in the drama activities, they had to juggle the physical affordances of the actual 3D settings they were in with ways of being and moving that were faithful to the scientific system and phenomenon they were representing. At times they had to differentiate between imagined and real worlds and the teachers played important roles in initiating and supporting such differentiations.

In four out of the six classrooms (the two 1st grade and the two 3rd grade classrooms), when children were pretending to be molecules in the *Molecule* drama and were told to melt, at least one student got closer to the floor by bending the knees and squatting or falling all the way to the floor. In a 1st-grade classroom, when this happened, the teacher, Sharon Gill, said to the class that instead of falling down, they had to "stretch" to show that they were melting. In Jennifer Hankes' 3rd grade, when she told a group of children to melt, all four of them sank to the floor to which Jennifer responded, "We could melt like that, but instead we're gonna loosen our bonds." Melting *down* is a representation of the process in the ontological world. When a chunk of ice melts, it does not stand up any more, it flows downwards on the surface it is on. However, in the imaginary scientific world, melting means that bonds are loosened up among molecules, which, of course, explains the "flowing" property of liquids.

Continuing with Jennifer's class, let us revisit Excerpt 2 in a more elaborated form as it appears below in Excerpt 8a.

Excerpt 8a:

1   Ms. Hankes: Now we're a little bit looser. But we're still staying in the glass, aren't we? We're in the glass and we're still moving. All right. Pretend to turn up the heat even more. What's going to start happening?

2   Children: (*** ***)

3   Ms. Hankes: Whoa, whoa. You know, can I have somebody raise their hand? I couldn't hear. I heard so many good ideas. Michelle.

4   Michelle: Y'all gonna get hot.

5   Ms. Hankes: We're gonna get hotter and when molecules get hot what do they start doing?

6   Child: Go faster!

7   Ms. Hankes: They start moving faster [as she (and students) begins to move arms and legs faster] and what's gonna end up happening to them?

8   Children: (*** ***)

9   Deangelo: Disappear!

10   Ms. Hankes: What? Ramona?

11	Ramona:	They gonna pop off and turn into water vapor.
12	Ms. Hankes:	So if we're starting to boil, what's happening to us?
13	Jamilia:	[Starts to jump.]
14	Child:	[Makes a swishing sound.]
15	Ms. Hankes:	We're coming out of the glass and we're becoming a what?
16	Children:	Water vapor!
17	Ms. Hankes:	[She (and students) begins to leave the classroom. She walks with her arms outstretched.]
18	Actors:	[Walk randomly around the room, including back into the cup.]
19	Ms. Hankes:	You're a gas now. You're out of the cup! You're out of the cup.
20	Deangelo:	Get out of the cup!

As Jennifer was scaffolding the dramatization of the various states of matter, and changes from one to another, Jamilia jumped up (unit 13) to turn into gas, which Ramona had described as "pop[ping] off and turn[ing] into water vapor" (unit 11). Jumping and "popping off" movements are consistent with a vertical orientation (in the direction of gravity) that, of course, the children are used to when being in the classroom, like walking, standing, sitting, and so forth, all characteristics of the ontological/real world in which they were dramatizing science. However, the cup with the ice cube outlined on the floor where the children's dramatization was taking place, was oriented on a horizontal plane. These children's movements reveal more attention to the *macroscopic* behaviors of substances. Ice melts downward; water vapor goes up. This was yet another example of metaxis that unfolded during these drama activities. In addition, many students (and teachers) in all of the classrooms represented water vapor by spreading their arms, as if they were flying, a modification to fit the constraints that kept them tethered to the floor. Spreading their arms was accompanied by the recognition that gas molecules "fly everywhere." (In fact, one boy in Sharon's 1st-grade class also made noises like a motor as he "flew out of the cup" as water vapor.)

As Jennifer continued working with her children, yet another way of being in both the real ontological world and the imaginary scientific world, emerged as children used typical everyday movements to represent scientific concepts.

Excerpt 8b:

21	Ms. Hankes:	You're a gas now. You're flying around the room. You take the shape of the container you're in. We could be over here. We could be over there. If we were small enough we could slide under the door. All right? Turn it back, cold.
22	Lawrence:	[Slows down his movement.]

23	Chantrelle:	[Wraps her arms around herself as if she is cold.]
24	Ms. Hankes:	What's going to happen to our water vapor? We're not moving as fast anymore. [She slowly walks back to the masking-tape cup.]
25	Actors:	[Follow Ms. Hankes.]
26	Ms. Hankes:	[Reaches out to hold hands.]
27	Child:	Turn into a cloud.

Chantrelle's way of playing being cold (unit 23) comes from the ways we often behave when we are cold in real life. Eventually Jennifer modeled for Chantrelle (and other children) how to use the scientific world, instead of the real, everyday world, as a resource for their acting; Jennifer reached out to hold hands with the group members to act out being a liquid (or a "cloud" as a child said in unit 27) in the scientific way.

In a similar situation, Anne Barry needed to help her 1st graders differentiate between the "freezing" directive in the classroom as part of classroom routines (i.e., when she wanted to get students' attention, Anne asked them to freeze by stopping what they were doing and not moving) and the "freezing" of molecules that the children were acting out. Later on they changed from liquid to gas as they evaporated.

Excerpt 9:

1	Ms. Barry:	Yep. Okay. You're melting. All right. Good. What you might // might you be moving around in the glass a little bit? Move your feet a little bit. You can move out of the ice cube. Over there. Okay. Very good. Now this group. I want you to go to frozen. Be frozen. Not like we do in the classroom though. Frozen like an ice cube. That doesn't mean you stop. So how do you bond? You lock you hands. Get in that ice cube. You're frozen. Come on. Get in that ice cube. . . .
2	Ms. Barry:	You're turning from a liquid to a gas. All right. Where are you going as a gas? Come on.
3	Children:	[Begin to separate from each other and move about.]
4	Ms. Barry:	You can't go out the sides. You gotta go out the front // the top. Where are you going? You're gas. Come on you're a // evaporation. Where are you going? Not out // you gotta go out the top of the glass. Only way you can go. Come on. Evaporate. Where can you go?
5	Children:	[Leave the masking-tape cup/glass and move about the room.]
6	Ms. Barry:	Good. Where can you // oh you don't walk in the glass but you go out the top.

In units 4 and 6 of Excerpt 9, we see another instance of the tension between the two orientations, the vertical one that the children were used to as part of their everyday lives and the horizontal one in which the cup on the floor was outlined. Thus, the children first tried to escape from any place inside the cup as they perceived it as open and they could not "see" any sides (that would make it impossible for gas to pass through). However, Anne kept reminding and articulating for them that, in the imaginary scientific world they were in, evaporation only happens from the opening (top) of a cup, and thus they could only move out from that direction.

Furthermore, over time, students' dramatic enactments drew more and more on the rules of the drama genre itself, the imaginary scientific world that they were acting out, and not those that were dominant in other parts of schooling, the real world they were living in. For example, across all classrooms in the *Molecule* activity, students in the first groups were reluctant to run around the room when they were told to be gas molecules. In other activities in the classroom, students were explicitly told that they should only walk and not run in the classrooms. In the later dramatizations, participants had the benefit of watching, commenting on, and listening to remarks about previous groups, and were able to push the acceptable limits of their bodies' movements in the spaces of the classroom. As more and more groups of children became actors in the activity, they began to run faster and cover more space.

On yet a different level, in Neveen Shamah's 3rd-grade class, children's gendered lives were also obvious during the first formation of a group. Boys and girls giggled when they had to be with someone of the opposite gender holding hands or being too close when they were representing a solid. In this case, their teacher admonished them, "Do we care that he's a boy and she's a girl? No. We are molecules. Do it for science!" Thus, children's bodies had both physical/material and semiotic social dimensions (Cheville, 2006). That is, children were inscribed with the rules of the cultures and social institutions (Foucault, 1979; Luke, 1992) that they were a part of, and such rules were different from the rules of the scientific system they were enacting. The teacher had to help them differentiate between these two rule systems. This is another challenge that dramatizing presents similarly to other forms of modeling. Differentiation is needed between the two systems/worlds involved in any modeling situation if students are to develop canonical scientific knowledge and understandings.

The Humanness of Dramatic Modeling

One of the distinctive characteristics of dramatizing as a form of modeling is that the people themselves are involved in the modeling, populating the real world in which they perform and, thus, infusing the imagined, in our case scientific world, with human elements, such as feelings, attitudes, actions, and behaviors toward each other and toward the entities they pretend to be. In the *Food-Web* drama children negotiated interpersonal relationships as they pondered and discussed scientific relationships between forest entities to explore interdependence. In some ways, as the children became animals, plants, and inanimate entities, they did not forget who they were—children who wanted higher social positioning, or more power, than their peers. Their *places* in the food chains and webs they were enacting could not always be divorced from such feelings and opinions.

In Neveen Shamah's 3rd-grade class, Andres was made fun of as a "t-t-t-termite." As the web was beginning to take shape, he said: "Damn, this sucks, I'm gonna be all the way at the end." Sally also teased him about this, and his group-table members (especially Sally) had teased him the day before when he was assigned to be termite and the class was figuring out who ate whom. In Excerpt 10a, Andres is already a part of the food web, and Neveen is leading the class through imagining what it would be like to disrupt the food web by killing off an entity in the forest community.

Excerpt 10a:

1	Child:	Nothing eats me.
2	Ms. Shamah:	Nothing eats you?
3	Kira:	I didn't eat any animals.
4	Child:	The owls.
5	Sally:	Termite eats you.
6	Ms. Shamah:	Oh termites eat you. Where's the termite?
7	Sally:	Right there. Hi, t-t-t-termite.
8	Dante:	Hi, t-t-t-termite.
9	Ms. Shamah:	The only thing you eat is wood, termite. Right? So what are you holding on to?
10	Andres:	Uh the ant and the frog.
11	Ms. Shamah:	You eat them or they eat you?
12	Andres:	No they eat me.
13	Ms. Shamah:	Oh they eat you. So you have nothing to eat.
14	Sally:	You're gonna die, termite. You're gonna die.
15	Children:	(★★★ ★★★).
16	Ms. Shamah:	You don't have anything to eat. Here you go. Here, hold it. [Tries to toss end of string to termite Andres.] Here you go. Give that to him. Okay. Are you happy now? [To class.] So let's say this. The termites // we'll do this really fast. The termite only eats what?
17	Children:	Wood.
18	Ms. Shamah:	Wood. Okay. Tree's dead. [Puts arms around the tree C's shoulders.] You're dead tree.
19	Child:	Bye, bye.
20	Ms. Shamah:	You're dead. Okay. What do you think is gonna happen eventually to all the termites?

21	Children:	(★★★ ★★★).
22	Ms. Shamah:	Sally. Since you're raising your hand and everyone else is yelling. Where'd my tree go? You're supposed to be dead. I'm sorry, Sally. Go ahead.
23	Sally:	They're gonna // they're gonna end up dying because that's their only // the tree's their only food.

Sally continued to react to the forest entities, relating feelings (in a humorous way) to her sense of being better than others. As we saw earlier in Excerpt 5a, Sally was playing both a turtle and a worm. At a certain point (not included in the above excerpt), she said to another child: "Ha, ha. I eat you either way [as turtle or worm]." Later on, in Excerpt 10b, as Neveen hinted to the conversation that the class had about worms not having a particular sex but being both males and females, Sally did not like the name "Herman" (unit 33) that the teacher called her, which was the name of the worm in the website (http://www.urbanext.uiuc.edu/worms/) that the class had explored. While discussing that website, the children had associated the name "Herman" with being both female ("her") and male ("man"). Sally rejected being both male and female, as it seemed to disrupt her status as a girl.

Excerpt 10b:

24	Ms. Shamah:	Okay. What do you need?
25	Richard:	I eat worms.
26	Ms. Shamah:	You eat worms.
27	Sally:	Oh come on, Richard.
28	Ms. Shamah:	Right here. [Hands string to C.] All right, Miss Worm. Well I can't say "Miss," right? Can I say "Miss Worm"?
29	Children:	No.
30	Katia:	Female!
31	Child:	Herman.
32	Ms. Shamah:	Herman. Here you go, Herman. [Passes end of string to worm Sally.]
33	Sally:	I don't like the name "Herman."
34	Child:	Herman! Herman!
35	Ms. Shamah:	Sorry. Okay. Here you go. Here you go. Do you get the idea of how this is going?
		. . .
36	Ms. Shamah:	Okay. Miss Beaver over here. [Puts arms around beaver actor's shoulders.] She needs the wood. But // hold on. If the wood is gone // if all the trees are gone, what's gonna happen to her? [String between beaver and tree is dropped.]

37	Sally:	Miss Beaver's gonna drop dead.
38	Ms. Shamah:	Is she?
39	Children:	No.
40	Child:	She has more (*** ***).
41	Sally:	[Still connected to beaver with a string] She's gonna eat me! She's gonna eat me! [saying excitedly]

As the conversation continued in Neveen's class, this time other classmates teased *Sally* as they repeated the "Herman" name that Sally did not like (units 33–34). Moreover, as Neveen engaged the children in thinking about what would happen to forest entities when others disappear, Sally realized that when the beaver was not connected to the tree, the beaver was still connected to her so it would survive (unit 41). Although the beaver would eat her, she was excited she could save the beaver.

In Excerpt 10c, Dante (playing a prairie dog) found himself with a new, higher status in the food chain when the hawk was gone. An appreciation of the intricate relationships that determine survival in the forest community is expressed as he empathizes with the prairie dog's survival.

Excerpt 10c:

| 42 | Ms. Shamah: | If the wo // the hawk is gone, what's gonna happen to all the prairie dogs, the owls, the beavers #*** ***#. |
| 43 | Dante: | #I'm gonna survive! I'm gonna survive!# [as prairie dog actor, beaming with joy, smiling, and jumping up and down]. |

Similarly in Jennifer Hankes' 3rd-grade class, Joe and Jamilia's bantering continued when they were dramatizing the food web. While Jennifer was handing out red string, various students were discussing who would eat whom. Joe, who was playing a raccoon, kept talking in a teasing tone about eating Jamilia who was a snake, and Jamilia argued back that she ate him.

Excerpt 11a:

1	Joe:	I'm gonna eat Jamilia. I'm gonna eat Jamilia. I'm gonna eat Jamilia.
2	Jamilia:	Unhuh. I eat you [to Joe]. I eat Taliesha [who was a frog].
3	Joe:	[off camera] I eat you.

Later on, as Jennifer worked with her students to enact more branches of the food web, dramatic roles *and* scientific entities and relationships were mixed again. Jennifer called the robin up and anybody who ate it.

Excerpt 11b:

4	Jamilia:	Me?
5	Tasha:	What about an owl?
6	Children:	[The earthworm and termite came up.]
7	Child:	Amber [water].
8	Child:	What about plants?
9	Child:	Tree.
10	Ms. Hankes:	Mary [termite], what do you need to eat?
11	Mary:	Yvonne [tree].
12	Ms. Hankes:	What would happen if the robin died? Raise your hand it you would have nothing to eat as of right now.
13	Deangelo:	Owls eat different kind of stuff though.
14	Ms. Hankes:	Now imagine if Yvonne, trees, didn't exist. Who would not be able to survive?
15	Child:	Termites.
16	Child:	Humans.
17	Ms. Hankes:	Seeds.
18	Tasha:	Ms. Hankes, I [seed] made the tree.
19	Ms. Hankes:	Okay, you're right. This is a good point here. She makes the trees but doesn't // in order for Tasha to exist, doesn't there also need to be a tree to make the new seeds?
20	Amber:	And the water.
21	Ms. Hankes:	And the water. So if water didn't exist would any of us be here?
22	Children:	No.
23	Amber:	Ms. Hankes, everybody got me [water].

Children became the forest entities in some ways, but played out their real world identities in other ways. In Excerpt 11b children used each other's names to refer to what forest entities needed to survive. These hypothetical entities children pretended to be had the children's own names. The children were themselves, but at the same time they were not, they were forest entities—a state of metaxis. Some children were needed more than others in this pretend setting where they were plants, animals, water, sunlight, but at the same time, they were Jamilia, Joe, Yvonne, Deangelo, and Taliesha.

Drama in Science Education

In this chapter we explored meanings that children made in dramatic enactments of molecular behavior in different states of matter and of food webs in a forest community. These meanings were not generated in individual children's minds. They were collaboratively and interactionally constructed among the members of these classrooms—among the children themselves and between the teacher and children. Thus, we saw how children's multimodal ways of dramatizing science ideas become means of negotiating ambiguity of meaning and developing and communicating understanding.

In the drama activities we explored, children's whole bodies became central, explicit tools used to accomplish the goal of representing the imaginary scientific world. Furthermore, children's bodies operated on multiple mediated levels in these drama activities: as material objects that moved through space, as social objects that negotiated classroom relationships and rules, and as metaphorical objects that stood in for water molecules in the various states of matter or for entities in a food web. Children simultaneously negotiated meanings across all of these levels, and in doing so, acted out the drama as they thought and talked science.

Moreover, in the drama activities, scientific ideas became aesthetic objects, entities filled with thought and feeling. According to Dewey (1934), aesthetic experience involves "interpenetration of self and the world of objects and events" (p. 34). By dramatizing science, children's bodies and scientific concepts of molecules and forest entities became intertwined, showing how scientific ideas share features with works of art as aesthetic entities. Molecular behavior in various states of matter and interactions among animals, plants, and inanimate entities in a forest community turned out to have unity, intensity, harmony, rhythm, balance, and order—all elements of beauty in aesthetics (Flannery, 1991).

At times, tacit knowledge led children to act in a particular way. That is, their everyday, material, place-based, real-world experiences have helped them develop knowledge that they first used to think about, encounter, and construct the imaginary world of scientific entities that the drama activities immersed them in. One challenge associated with dramatic representations is that there is not always an "exact fit" (Duit, 1991, p. 666) between the representation and the scientific idea(s). In these cases, their teachers intervened and showed them what to do, differentiating at times and uniting at other times what the children were doing and the scientific entities and behaviors that they were representing. In this way, children were helped to differentiate the model world and the real world, and at the same time build bridges between the two—an important factor in the success of modeling as an instructional tool (Coll, France, & Taylor, 2005; Duit, 1991; Gilbert, 1993). However, we do not know whether all individual children constructed this differentiation. What we know is that as more and more groups enacted the dramas, they collectively represented the scientific world more and more accurately. For example, whereas earlier groups in various classes "melted" by falling down, later groups "melted" by loosening hand/arm bonding, spreading, and moving faster.

Givry and Roth (2006), exploring the interplay among talking, gesturing, and using contextual structures, claim that conceptual change may come in three different forms: "(a) evolution in the use of modalities . . . (b) evolution into the same modality . . . and (c) evolution of the link between different modalities" (p. 1105). In dramatizing, as different children over time engaged in both the real world and the world of science that they were acting out, children evolved in the bodily-kinesthetic modality they were using to represent scientific constructs. Furthermore, language played an important role in being in both words and in coordinating them. Teachers asked questions that fell in a range of categories that Chin (2007) specified as approaches that stimulate productive thinking; for example, asking students to provide more information (pumping), asking questions based on a statement or question by a student (reflective toss), asking questions as forms of feedback to a child's contribution (constructive challenge), asking questions that guide students to develop links among ideas (association of key words and phrases), asking questions that stimulate multimodal thinking, and asking questions that encourage students to focus more and zoom into their thinking.

Although there were guidelines for both drama activities, the enactments of these activities were different in different classrooms. There are no scripts for improvisational plays; the actors make these plays while interacting with the audience, creating characters and events that create the plays. In similar ways, the children created the drama activities, along with their teachers. They negotiated various representations as they tried to get inside the worlds they tried to understand and learn. They were the entities in the imagined worlds; in fact, they *became* the entities as time was going by and as they kept "playing science." In this way, the children populated these drama activities with their intentions and their meanings (Bakhtin, 1981). Maybe this is one of the reasons why dramatizing was enabling for the children's learning. We know from the various studies on modeling and its use in science teaching and learning that students' *own* modeling is important to their understanding—as Coll and colleagues (2005) noted: "enabling students to construct and critique their own models effectively supports conceptual development outcomes (Abell & Roth 1995)" (p. 187)—albeit insufficient as "many of students' personal analogies and explanations . . . [could be] unsuccessful at leading them to scientifically accepted ideas about the concepts" (Yerrick, Doster, Nugent, Parke, & Crawley, 2003, p. 459). The children in our study made the drama activities their own but had not originally conceived them.

Students' representations in space provided referents for the science talking and thinking. Their roles, as actors, guessers, directors, and viewers, allowed them to engage with science content from multiple perspectives. Although all the children in a class enacted the same script, each one acted out her or his role differently and made it her or his role. That is exactly the power of performing arts: each actor becomes the role in his or her own way, capturing the uniqueness of the ideas to be communicated to the audience. However, this is a challenge at the same time, as it leads to the serendipity of the scientific ideas that are explored, discussed, and developed as part of drama activities.

In these drama activities, the children had no "formal" stage. Their stage was their classroom, the place in which they lived, breathed, argued, teased, struggled, got bored, felt good, and where they were with classmates and friends every day. Because that was their classroom, they knew of certain norms and rules that governed that space and that precluded them from some of the actions they might do in the imaginary world of molecules or forest entities.

The drama activities provided opportunities for children to link scientific constructs with each other. They considered similarities and differences among solids, liquids, and gases, and they associated transfer of heat with changes in states of matter. They discussed animal characteristics vis-à-vis the place of an entity in a food web, and they considered the importance of certain entities for other entities in the forest. In some ways, the dramatizing offered an opportunity to create hybrid science learning spaces that Barton and Tan (2009) called for. In these drama activities, the physical space of the classroom where the children spent many hours of their days was transformed into a space where they enacted scientific ideas. This space was familiar to them and, thus, invited them to be a part of it in a different way so they could explore science. Albeit the challenges that the classroom space, which was governed by different rules, raised for engaging with scientific ideas in canonical ways, the acting out of science in this space also transformed the classroom into a more fun place to be.

Most students see science as rational, cold, unexciting, and lacking any emotional content. Drama, though, is totally different. Dramatic enactments contribute to infusing science with emotions, excitement, fun, interaction, and shorten the distance between object of study and subject, providing a more holistic experiential approach to learning science. Such forms of engagement with ideas, topics, and fields of study may be more empowering to children, especially the ones who are members of particular cultural and gender groups, such as African Americans and women (Nobles, 1980; Rosser, 1990), groups that have been usually underrepresented in sciences and whose science education experiences have been fraught with challenges. In the drama activities we studied, the students became "insiders" of scientific phenomena and ideas, participating with their peers, and associating science with feelings of membership in collective activity. Despite being short-lived, these "interactional rituals" (Olitsky, 2007) were characterized by the mutual focus that students had during them on particular "big" science ideas, like the micro-level characteristics of different states of matter and the ways in which animals and plants are connected in a particular environment.

Moreover, dramatizing, as a particular form of modeling, offers an opportunity to expand science education beyond dualisms—thinking and feeling, reason and emotion, mind and body, objectivity and subjectivity, masculine and feminine—dualisms that Brickhouse (2001) problematizes as she synthesizes her own and other feminist scholars' research. Although uncovering how the domination of one of the two ends of these dualisms has shaped science and science education over time is an important contribution of feminist scholarship, continuing to think along these divisions limits people's learning, which is antithetical to feminist pedagogy. To support science learning for all, we need to understand how the two ends are embedded into each other and to appreciate their interplay, along with designing curriculum and instruction that nurtures such interplay. In this chapter, we identified ways in which one example of such activity, namely, dramatic enactments of science phenomena and concepts, engaged young children with each other, with science ideas, and with their social worlds.

References

Abell, S. K., & Roth, W.-M. (1995). Reflections on a fifth-grade life science lesson: Making sense of children's understanding of scientific models. *International Journal of Science Education, 17,* 59–74.

Alrutz, M. (2004). Granting science a dramatic license: Exploring a 4th grade science classroom and the possibilities for integrating drama. *Teaching Artist Journal, 2,* 31–39.

Bakhtin, M. M. (1981). *The dialogic imagination: Four essays by M. M. Bakhtin.* (M. Holquist, Ed., M. Holquist & C. Emerson, Trans.). Austin: University of Texas Press.

Barton, A. C., & Tan, E. (2009). Funds of knowledge and Discourses and hybrid space. *Journal of Research for Science Teaching, 46,* 50–73.

Berger, M. (1992). *Look out for turtles!* New York: HarperCollins.

Bolton, G. (1984). *Drama as education.* Essex, UK: Longman.

Boykin, W. A. (1986). The triple quandary of the schooling of Afro-American children. In U. Neisser (Ed.), *The school achievement of minority children* (pp. 57–92). Hillsdale, NJ: Erlbaum.

Brickhouse, N. W. (2001). Embodying science: A feminist perspective on learning. *Journal of Research in Science Teaching, 38,* 282–295.

Cheville, J. (2006). The bias of materiality in sociocultural research: Reconceiving embodiment. *Mind, Culture, and Activity, 13,* 25–37.

Chin, C. (2007). Teacher questioning in science classrooms: Approaches that stimulate productive thinking. *Journal of Research for Science Teaching, 44,* 815–843.

Coll, R. K., France, B., & Taylor, I. (2005). The role of models/and analogies in science education: implications from research. *International Journal of Science Education, 27,* 183–198.

Dewey, J. (1934). *Art as experience.* New York: Penguin.

Duit, R. (1991). On the role of analogies and metaphors in learning science. *Science Education, 75,* 649–672.

Efland, A. D. (2002). *Art and cognition: Integrating the visual arts in the curriculum.* New York: Teachers College Press.

Flannery, M. C. (1991). Science and aesthetics: A partnership for science education. *Science Education, 75,* 577–593.

Foucault, M. (1979). *The history of sexuality.* London: Tavistock.

Geertz, C. (1973). *The interpretation of cultures.* New York: Basic Books.

Gilbert, J. K. (Ed.) (1993). *Models and modelling in science education.* Hatfield, UK: Association for Science Education.

Givry, D., & Roth, W.-M. (2006). Toward a new conception of conceptions: Interplay of talk, gestures, and structures in the setting. *Journal of Research for Science Teaching, 43,* 1086–1109.

Halliday, M. A. K. (1978). *Language as social semiotic: The social interpretation of language and meaning.* Baltimore: University Park Press.

Henry, M. (2000). Drama's ways of learning. *Research in Drama Education, 5,* 45–62.

Jewitt, C., & Kress, G. (2003). *Multimodal literacy.* New York: Peter Lang.

Kress, G., & van Leeuwen, T. J. (2001). *Multimodal discourse: The modes and media of contemporary communication.* London: Arnold.

Kress, G., & van Leeuwen, T. J. (2006). *Reading images: The grammar of visual design.* London: Routledge.

Luke, A. (1992). The body literate: Discourse and inscription in early literacy instruction. *Linguistics and Education, 4,* 107–129.

Moje, E. B., Ciechanowski, K. M., Kramer, K., Ellis, L., Carrillo, R., & Collazo, T. (2004). Working toward third space in content area literacy: An examination of everyday funds of knowledge and Discourse. *Reading Research Quarterly, 39,* 38–70.

Nobles, W. W. (1980). Extended self: Rethinking the so-called Negro self-concept. In R. L. Jones (Ed.), *Black psychology* (2nd ed.) (pp. 295–304). New York: Harper & Row.

Olitsky, S. (2007). Promoting student engagement in science: Interaction rituals and the pursuit of a community of practice. *Journal of Research in Science Teaching, 44,* 33–56.

O'Neill, C., & Lambert, A. (1983). *Drama structures: A practical handbook for teachers.* Portsmouth, NH: Heinemann.

Pappas, C. C., & Zecker, L. B. (2001a). Urban teacher researchers' struggles in sharing power with their students: Exploring changes in literacy curriculum genres. In C. C. Pappas & L. B. Zecker (Eds.), *Transforming literacy curriculum genres: Working with teacher researchers in urban classrooms* (pp. 1–31). Mahwah, NJ: Lawrence Erlbaum.

Pappas, C. C., & Zecker, L. B. (2001b). Transforming curriculum genres in urban schools: The political significance of collaborative classroom discourse. In C. C. Pappas & L. B. Zecker (Eds.), *Transforming literacy curriculum genres: Working with teacher researchers in urban classrooms* (pp. 325–333). Mahwah, NJ: Lawrence Erlbaum.

Parsons, E. C. (2008). Learning contexts, Black cultural ethos, and the science achievement of African American students in an urban middle school. *Journal of Research in Science Teaching, 45,* 665–683.

Rosser, S. V. (1990). *Female friendly science: Applying women's studies methods and theories to attract students.* New York: Pergamon Press.

Schank, R. C., & Abelson, R. P. (1977). *Scripts, plans, goals, and understanding: An inquiry into human knowledge structures.* Hillsdale, NJ: Lawrence Erlbaum.

Schneider, J. J., Crumpler, T. P., & Rogers, T. (Eds.). (2006). *Process drama and multiple literacies: Addressing social, cultural, and ethical issues.* Portsmouth, NH: Heinemann.

Turner, V. W., & Bruner, E. M. (Eds.) (1986). *The anthropology of experience.* Urbana, IL: University of Illinois Press.

Varelas, M. (1996). Between theory and data in a 7th grade science class. *Journal of Research in Science Teaching, 33,* 229–263.

Varelas, M., Becker, J., Luster, B., & Wenzel, S. (2002). When genres meet: Inquiry into a sixth-grade urban science class. *Journal of Research in Science Teaching, 39,* 579–605.

Warren, B., Ballenger, C., Ogonowski, M., Rosebery, A., & Hudicourt-Barnes, J. (2001). Rethinking diversity in learning science: The logic of everyday language. *Journal of Research in Science Teaching, 38,* 529–552.

Weltsek-Medina, G. J. (2007). Process drama in education. In A. Blatner (Ed.), *Interactive and improvisational drama: Varieties of applied theater and performance* (pp. 90–98). Lincoln, NE: Universe.

Winner, E. (1982). *Invented worlds: The psychology of the arts.* Cambridge, MA: Harvard University Press.

Yerrick, R. K., Doster, E., Nugent, J. S., Parke, H. M., & Crawley, F. E. (2003). Social interaction and the use of analogy: An analysis of preservice teachers' talk during physics inquiry lessons. *Journal of Research in Science Teaching, 40,* 443–463.

7

SCIENTIFIC PRACTICES IN HOME PROJECTS

Exploring at Home, Sharing at School

Amy Arsenault, Maria Varelas,
Christine C. Pappas, and Tamara Ciesla

Research has indicated that involving families in ways that are flexible and respectful fosters children's academic learning and performance (Epstein, 1991; Epstein & Dauber, 1991; Hoover-Dempsy & Sandler, 1997; Hoover-Dempsey et al., 2005; Quint, 1994; Rosenholtz, 1989; Wollman-Bonilla, 2001). Moreover, no matter the income or ethnicity of families, they are interested in their children's educational achievement and success (Barone, 1999; Delgado-Gaitan, 1990; Quint, 1994; Taylor & Dorsey-Gaines, 1990). Despite these findings, it is rare for teachers to explicitly create the conditions or non-homework activities where parents can be involved in their children's learning at home and where teachers can learn from families' contributions (Rosenholtz, 1989).

The ISLE project provided an integrated science-literacy home project in each unit (*Matter* and *Forest*), which included, a children's literature book (which had been read aloud to students in the classroom), materials to conduct an inquiry, and a blank booklet for children and their family members to document their inquiries. Children brought home a copy of the book *Down Comes the Rain* (Branley, 1997), and carried out an evaporation exploration, studying the drying of wet paper towels for the *Matter* unit home project. Children were encouraged to consider different locations to place their wet paper towels, along with different ways to fold the towels (e.g., flat, balled-up, folded-in-half). The packet went home during Lesson 14, and at that point children had experienced in the classroom six read-alouds of information books and nine hands-on explorations. For the *Forest* unit home project, children brought home a copy of the book *From Seed to Plant* (Gibbons, 1991), and they conducted a plant growth exploration, growing lentils in a plastic cup over a period of about 10 days while recording observations and height measurements. The *Forest* unit packet went home during Lesson 9, and at that point children had participated in six read-alouds of information books and four hands-on explorations in the classroom. (See Chapter 1 for details about the chronology of the lessons in each unit.) As families completed the home projects, students shared their findings in class. Although there are studies that have examined the effectiveness of home projects in the area of science (e.g., sending home science kits; Gennaro & Lawrenz, 1992; Solomon, 2003) *or* literacy (e.g., providing lending-library books; Yaden & Brassell, 2002; Yaden, Madrigal, & Tam, 2003), it is very rare to include both science and literacy materials in home packets. In addition, it is quite uncommon to have the family inquiries be part of the ongoing classroom curriculum.

Thus, this chapter focuses on the ISLE home projects in several ways. We first discuss how these projects were introduced in the classrooms (see Chapter 1 for details on the demographic make-up of the six ISLE classrooms). Second, we identify themes that emerged from the analysis of the booklets that the 60 focal children and their family members created at home as part of these projects. Third, we discuss how children shared their family inquiries in their classrooms. Finally, we provide the results of surveys sent to parents, which were completed after the end of each of the two home projects and captured their reactions to such projects.

Introducing the Home Project in the Classroom

Teachers walked their children through the contents of the packet and tried to motivate them so they would do the project. Third-grade teacher Jennifer told her students, "You are really lucky because you'll have a special project to do at home." Her students responded with excitement and put their hands up to ask questions. Second-grade teacher Begoña not only emphasized that the project was a special one, but she also highlighted its literacy component—"You get a book to read a whole bunch of times!" Another 3rd-grade teacher, Neveen, took another approach consistent with the emphasis she had in all of the other ISLE activities— positioning students as scientists and highlighting for them scientific practices. She told her children, "You are scientists. Scientists make predictions about what they think will happen. Think of creative places to put your experiment."

Some teachers gave more specific guidance than others. Jennifer offered her children guidelines about what to include in their booklet. They needed to put their names and title on the front page, and they could do their book any way they wanted, but she stressed that they should use their book to tell, in words and drawings, how they set up their exploration. For the *Forest* unit home project, 1st-grade teacher Anne demonstrated how to plant the seeds, as did the other teachers. Neveen modeled on the board how to measure the growth of the plants. She drew a ruler on the board and stressed how it was very important to put the date and a line for each time students measured the height of their plant. A 3rd-grade student, Andres, asked, "What if the plant gets higher than the ruler?" Neveen addressed his concern by saying that she did not think that that would happen, but that if it did, he would have to make a longer ruler (the enclosed ruler was constructed out of manila folder paper and was 8 1/2 inches long). For the *Matter* unit home project, Begoña reminded students, "You also have your own private science journal [about which students expressed excitement]. You can draw on the cover. If the towels dry fast, maybe try it again and see where it takes the longest to dry." Jennifer passed out the home project packets and used one of them to show the students what it contained. She pulled out the contents one by one to describe what to do with each item. She reminded students of the experiment (in the *Matter* unit) they had done with the three paper towels in class. Chantrelle asked, "Can we do what you did [referring to the paper towel experiment done in class]?" and Jennifer responded, "Yes, but try to be creative and think of something different." Jamilia followed Chantrelle by asking, "Can brothers and sisters help?" Jennifer responded, "Yes, they can help with ideas, but remember it is your work and your writing." Latessa asked, "Should we draw and write?" Jennifer responded, "Yes because it helps me know what you did." Thus, although teachers provided some kind of introduction to children's two home project inquiries, they did it in different ways.

Children's Home-Made Booklets

After completing their home projects, children brought to school about the same number of booklets for both units (118 in the *Matter* unit; 110 in the *Forest* unit). Analyzing both the words and drawings in these booklets, several themes emerged which we present below. The first theme had to do with the type of pronouns that were used to present the work that had been done. Many included "we" and others specified the people who worked on their home project. Second-grader Rodrigo wrote in the *Matter* unit, "*I did a experiment in my Grandmom's house with my cousin . . . my mom and I checked my project.*" Another 2nd grader, Courtney, shared, "*Me and my mom did experiment from the book with the teaspoon . . . the book was right! . . . Me and my mom talked about which one would dry first and I picked the bathroom and I was right!*" Third-grader Lawrence wrote, "*I asked my mom for help . . . she said I have a green thumb.*" Such examples provide evidence of our finding that the majority of the books portrayed a level of collaboration that had taken place between children and family members around the home project. Collaboration varied from reading the book with a parent or sibling to working together on the hands-on exploration, to having the parent/family member check the accuracy of the project.

The second theme was related to the content of the booklets—both in terms of the science content presented and the linguistic registers used to present the science ideas. Some children wrote and drew about their hands-on exploration, outlining the procedures they followed and their results. First-grader Latoya had written about the paper towel experiment, "*First table, second fridge, third TV.*" She had ended her book by presenting her results, "*The flat towel dried first it was open, the towel folded in half was next, the towel on the tv was last it was folded in a square.*"

Second-grader Guillermo presented detailed observations he had made during the plant growth exploration: "*the seeds bursted and the roots have begun to grow, the roots continue to grow, there was also a green dot on top, the stem is growing taller and the roots, the roots have reached the bottom of the cup, the stem is now 3 to 4 inches, the plant was growing bigger and bigger, the little leaf on top was also getting bigger, I put water every other [day] so it can grow and we put it where it can have sun.*" Another 2nd-grader, Courtney, began her book with a table of contents, a feature commonly found in informational texts, with headings "*How to start growing; Have you seen roots yet?; Roots are here!; The sun is a magnet.*" However, her book also included a page with a heading that did not appear in the table of contents, "*How fast can the plant grow?*" where Courtney shared observations and measurements she had made about her lentils. She wrote, "*Yesterday the plant was leaning to the right, but today it is leaning to the left. It has grown a inch taller.*" Her drawings depicted two plants, one growing leaning to the right and one growing leaning to the left, and a ruler. Courtney also incorporated in her booklet observations that other children had not made. Under the heading "*The sun is a magnet,*" Courtney described the lentils' phototropic behavior, "*My plant finally has leaves . . . wherever the sun goes the leaves follow it.*"

Third-grader Sally had begun her book by specifying the location of her experiment, "*I put my plant by a window.*" She had followed this by portraying an authoritative stance, dispensing advice to the readers of her book. "*If you want to plant a seed too, you should put it by the sun. I put my seed by sunlight because it needs the sunlight to help it make its food.*" In this way, Sally not only described an experimental procedure, but she also justified it, which made her recommendation to others much more trustworthy. Although explanations did not appear in all of the booklets, many children included them for both home projects. First-grader John offered explanations along with his predictions regarding which paper towel would dry faster. He wrote, "*The first one which is hanging will dry first . . . because the droplets can fall off . . . the ball will dry last because water is trapped.*" Third-grader Kenny had ended his book by explaining his results, "*I think the towel was still wet because I kept it in my book bag too long and the wetness came off and jumped back on the towel . . . the towel in the refrigerator was wet because the water and ice . . . getting more water from the ice melting.*" Although Kenny's explanations are not fully scientifically canonical, they represent emergent understandings about "wetness" that evaporated ("came off") but condensed back again ("jumped back on the towel"), which implies a cycle.

Another example of an explanation comes from 2nd-grader Ingrid and her paper towel exploration, in which, as she stated, "*We were trying to figure out which shape evaporate the fastest.*" Writing about her findings, Ingrid returned to the question investigated, and offered an explanation of her answer. "*According to my data sheet I don't know which dried, 2 or 3 [shape] because I checked every half hour and they dried before I checked them again.*" Ingrid reasoned about her data, offering a meaningful justification of her inability to tell which paper towel dried up second and which one dried up third, and thus, to fully answer the question of the experiment. This is a different type of reasoning from the one that John and Kenny exhibited, who offered possible explanations of why their paper towels dried up in a particular order. However, both types of reasoning are important elements of scientific practice.

A third theme was related to children's reference to, or influence by, the information book sent home. Although the majority of the children did not make in their booklets *explicit* references to the book, a few did. In his *Matter* booklet, 1st-grader Alam had written, "*We read about gas turning to water with changing temperature. I wanted to test it.*" He had continued, "*Hypothesis—cold air dries slower.*" Although Alam's writing shows that he was mixing up changes of state of matter (evaporation, which was the focus of the exploration with the drying paper towels and a change from liquid to gas, with condensation, which involves gas turning to liquid), it also reveals that Alam had focused on temperature and its role in these changes of state of matter, a significant idea. Later his "*Conclusion—Hot temperature dries fast. Water evaporates fast. Cold temperature dries slower. My hypothesis is correct.*" did not specify what dried up, but did capture the essence of the concept that higher temperatures make the water evaporate faster, an idea presented in the children's book that was sent home. Furthermore, his conclusion was supported by his results that he had shared on the previous page (see Figure 7.1).

Moreover, many children who did not explicitly refer to the book that was included in the home project packet used vocabulary and scientific language found in the book. This can be especially seen in booklets created in the *Forest* unit. First-grader John wrote, "*I came home from school . . . and I saw this little sprout coming up . . . the arch [shoot] unarched to a mini shoot . . . it sprouted up a little more.*" Second-grader Ingrid shared, "*The seeds have grown one root [picture labeled water, water drops, seeds] . . . the seeds have sprouted and the sprouts are pushing the dirt up . . . the plants are bending toward the sunlight . . . the roots look like spaghetti*" (see Figure 7.2). Third-grader Rhonda offered, "*My plant is growing. I can see the roots on bottom of the dirt. Me and my mom said we can see the green stem . . . the one I measured on page 4 it grow more bigger . . . some of the flowers are blooming and some are not blooming.*" Third-grader Jonah provided, "*After a few days of sun and some water . . . saw roots break through the seed and begin growing. This is called germination.*"

The final theme captured the ways in which children showed in their booklets emotions and feelings related to their experiences during the home project. For example, 3rd-grader Kira began her book with a heading, "*What I did when I came home,*" and then continued with, "*One day, I got the cup and put half the soil and put seeds in . . . put it in my window and waited.*" The picture she drew showed her waiting by the window. Later she included the heading, "*What I did when I saw it,*" and the body of the section read "*I saw it finally grow. I screamed and hugged my mommy. She said, 'I was a good grower' . . . I ran around the house and said, 'yeah'. It was amazing!*" She had ended her last page with the heading, "*The last day of the project,*" followed by "*I will miss the flower. It was a fun project to do.*" Although expressing such affect to the degree that Kira had done is not typical in reporting

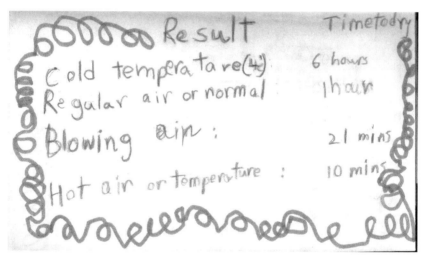

FIGURE 7.1 Two pages of 1ˢᵗ-grader Alam's home-project booklet made in the *Matter* unit.

scientific work, it illustrates this child's excitement and the positive outlook toward science, which engagement in the home project evoked for her.

Affect was also seen in the children's booklets as they reflected on how the hands-on exploration was a positive experience for them. For example, 3ʳᵈ-grader Rhonda wrote, *"I like this exploration because we have to work with our mom and dad."* Third-grader Andres shared, *"The height of the plant is amazing! We love this experiment"* in the last page of his booklet (Figure 7.3a) after a detailed record of, and reasoning for, his plant's growth (Figure 7.3b). Finally, 1ˢᵗ-grader Alam proclaimed, *"It was exciting to see the seed crack open. It was very exciting to pour the dirt into the cups."*

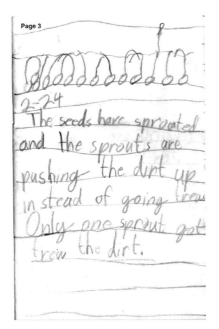

Page 3

2-24
The seeds have sprouted and the sprouts are pushing the dirt up instead of going threu. Only one sprout got threw the dirt.

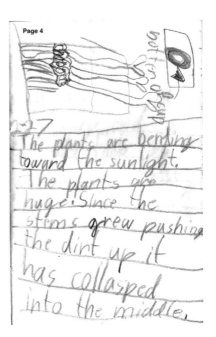

Page 4

2-27
The plants are bending toward the sunlight. The plants are huge! Since the stems grew pushing the dirt up it has collasped into the middle.

Page 5

the roots look like spagetie at the bottem of the cup and the plants look like trees in a forst growing out of the cup

FIGURE 7.2 Pages from 2nd-grader Ingrid's home-project booklet made in the *Forest* unit.

FIGURE 7.3a Last page of 3rd-grader Andres' home-project booklet made in the *Forest* unit.

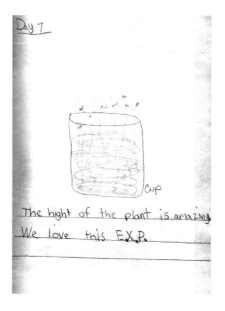

Day 7

cup

The hight of the plant is amazing We love this E.X.P.

Day 1

cup

I filled the cup with soil. Then added the seeds (lentils). Added more soil on top. I placed the cup in the Kitchen.

Day 2

cup

Observed cup with lentils (seeds) for any progress. At this time no change. The Kitchen has little light.

FIGURE 7.3b First six pages of 3rd-grader Andres' home-project booklet made in the *Forest* unit.

Day 3

Observed cup agian with lentels
Still no change. We hope some thing
will happen.

Day 4

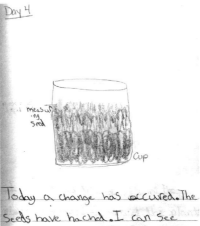

Today a change has occured. The
Seeds have hached. I can see
the roots growing. finally some thing
grawned Yah! Yah! I watered the
plant.

Day 5

I measured the grawth of the
plants (Lantils) I watered the plant
today.

Day 6

The plants grawnth has doubled
I did not water Lentils today.

Thus, various themes emerged from examining the booklets that the children created for the home projects. Children wrote about how they worked with others in conducting the explorations. They wrote and depicted the procedures they had followed and the observations they had made; they also incorporated various format features found in information books (e.g., table of contents, headings). Their booklets also revealed children's explanations and reasoning regarding predictions and results of their inquiries. Moreover, there was reference to, and /or influence by, the information book that was sent home to inform their hands-on explorations. Finally, their booklets showed emotions and feelings that the children experienced in doing the home projects.

Classroom Sharing of Home Projects

The sharing of the home projects in the six classrooms differed in length, but had some important similarities. During the time dedicated to this sharing, teachers focused on the explorations that their children had done with their family members, and took on the role of questioners who prompted students to further think about their findings.

First-grade teachers Sharon and Anne and 3rd-grade teacher Jennifer, for the *Matter* unit only, asked their students to come up to the front of the classroom and read from their booklets or share in their own words about their exploration. Several students focused on what they had done with their three paper towels, how they had shaped them, and where they had put them, but they did not engage with explaining their findings. Sharon, Anne, and Jennifer asked "why" questions to offer students opportunities to present explanations of the findings being shared. For instance, in Sharon's classroom Latoya described that she had put her paper towels on the TV (folded in a square), on the refrigerator (folded in half), and on the table (flat open), and that the one on the table had dried up first. She began to sit down and Sharon asked, "Why do you think the towel on the table dried up first?" Before Latoya answered, her classmate Kelly offered her thinking, "It was open." Sharon then asked a follow-up question, "Why do you think the flat one dried first?" Lauren responded, "The air was above the table and could touch that one." Although this is not a scientifically canonical explanation for why objects with bigger surface area dry up faster (i.e., it is not the air "touching" the surface of a paper towel that contributes to its faster evaporation, but rather the bigger exposed area which is, of course, exposed to air), it is nevertheless an emergent understanding toward explaining such data.

Later on, 1st-grader Fen took a turn to share what she had done: "I wet one paper towel. Then I squeezed out the water. I put the towel on the refrigerator door. I folded the second towel four times and then put it on the table." Sharon interrupted her, commenting, "This is interesting, let's see what happens." Fen continued, "I rolled up the [third] towel and put it on the table. The first towel [hanging from refrigerator door] was dry. The second towel [folded one on the table] was kind of dry. The third towel [rolled up one on the table] was still wet. The first towel dried up because it was completely flat open." Fen started to walk toward her desk, but Sharon wanted to hear more so she asked, "Why do you think that happened?" Fen responded, "I hanged it and it dried first." Since Fen did not actually explain *why* the flat towel dried up first, but rather just described its condition, Sharon pushed further by asking, "What helped it dry?" Fen remained in the description mode, "I put it on the flat stuff." Sharon reminded the students that they had been talking about reasons, "What have we been talking about that might have helped it?" Latoya answered, "air." Sharon continued, "Where is the air?" to which Fen responded, "Everywhere, the second paper towel was kind of dry, the third towel was still wet because the air could not get in the holes." Similarly to her classmate Lauren, Fen's explanation involved an emergent understanding, fusing the existence of air with the size of the surface area. Thus, we see in the above examples of classroom discourse that took place during the sharing of home projects, how children's presentations of their work at home became thinking devices for other children and for themselves through their teacher's persistence on explaining their results. The ideas they brought up during this sharing were revisited during the rest of the unit.

Second-grade teachers, Ibett and Begoña (for both units), and third-grade teachers, Neveen and Jennifer (for the *Forest* unit only), had their students sitting in groups of four to share their home projects. After the small group sharing, a whole-class discussion took place. In small groups, students took on the role of asking "why" questions to each other. For example, in Neveen's 3rd-grade class during the *Matter* unit, a group was talking about why some towels had dried up and others had not dried up as much. Katia asked a question to Luz, "Why do you think it dried so much?" Kira (also in the small group with Katia and Luz) entered into the conversation asking the opposite question, "Why did the other towel not dry?" In another small group discussion during the *Forest* home project sharing in Jennifer's 3rd-grade class, Corey asked Latessa, "Could plants in some way breathe?" Before Latessa answered, Joe chimed in and answered, "They [plants] don't breathe." Kenny offered, "I think they breathe because if they didn't breathe how would they live?" Joe then revised his thinking, "It could breathe through its roots." Although several emergent understandings were not further developed during this exchange, such examples provide evidence of the opportunities for reasoning that classroom sharing of the home project in small groups offered children. Such sharing contributes to the continuing development and articulation of science ideas.

Later on, whole-class discussions, that followed the small-group sharing, offered children opportunities to elaborate their thinking, with the teacher playing an important role. For instance, Vincente in Neveen's 3rd-grade class showed his drawing of a towel hanging in the backyard as he told the rest of the class how it was the first to dry because the wind blew the water vapor. Then he went on to explain how he put the second one in a jar and that was the third to dry. Neveen asked, "Did you close the jar?" to which Vincente replied affirmatively. She then asked the students if anyone had a question for Vincente. When no one responded, she continued, "Why do you think the jar was the last to dry?" Kira first answered, "No air," but since this did not make sense to Sally, she suggested a different explanation: "Maybe the water vapor evaporated and hit the top of the lid and went back down." Similarly to Kenny in Jennifer's class, Sally offered an explanation that implied that water goes through a cycle between evaporation and condensation.

Begoña's 2ⁿᵈ-grade class discussed, during the *Forest* home project sharing, how a student, Rachel, had drawn a plant that had stopped growing by depicting that its height remained the same after a few days had gone by. Rachel reasoned that the plant stopped growing because it got cold. Daniel challenged Rachel, though: "Are you sure it did not die because you did not water it?" Rachel responded, "I watered it." In order to support her children's thinking and discussing further their home-project findings, Begoña prompted the class to think about what they had been learning about the forest community by asking a general question: "What happens in the forest?" Courtney entered into the conversation stating, "some seeds don't grow" without offering a reason why. However, that was an idea expressed in the book that was included in the home-project packet, namely that seeds in packets sitting around for years will not grow if planted. Thus, possibly, Courtney may have offered yet a different factor to explain Rachel's result—the age of the seeds planted. Although this factor would probably explain why plants do not grow at all as opposed to growing to a certain height and then stopping, Courtney may have thought that the age of the seeds may also influence the resulting plants' growth over time. Another girl, Cassandra, having heard both Rachel's reasoning about the cold stopping her plant's growth and Courtney's claim that some seeds do not grow, attempted to reconcile the two ideas—"some seeds just can't take the cold."

Thus, the sharing of their home projects offered students more opportunities to think about what the results of their explorations meant, make connections, and reason. Their peers and the teacher played important roles in this process. Students learned that describing what happened was not enough. Instead, it is also necessary to construct and share explanations for the findings of hands-on explorations.

Parent Responses to Home Projects

A parent survey was sent home with children after each of the two (*Matter* and *Forest*) home projects was concluded. The survey was double-sided, with one side written in English and the other in Spanish. The parents or family members were instructed: "Please talk with your child (and whoever did the project with him or her) before completing the survey. Your feedback on these home projects will help us make them better." The survey had several parts. The first part included 10 items on a Likert scale of 1–5 (lowest to highest agreement). Three of the items (1, 3, and 5) addressed the helpfulness of the instructions, of the materials in order to do the science exploration, and of the whole project in order to have good conversations about science. Four items (2, 4, 6, and 10) had to do with the extent to which parents or family members enjoyed parts of the project—the reading of the book, the doing of the activities, the child's writing and drawing in the booklet, and the home project in general. Finally, three items (7, 8, and 9) asked parents or family members about the impact of the home project in terms of helping them connect with their child's school science, helping their child learn and have an interest in school science, and encouraging their child in engaging more with science at home. The second part of the survey consisted of two multiple-choice items to capture parents' favorite/least favorite component of the home project (i.e., the science activity or exploration, reading the book, writing and drawing in the booklet). The last part of the survey was an open-ended invitation for parents to share any thoughts they had on the home project.

Many parents returned parent surveys—104 parents (70%) returned them for the *Matter* unit and 88 parents (60%) for the *Forest* unit across all six classes—although these return rates were lower than those of the student booklet (78% and 75% for the two units respectively). The average ratings across all six classrooms on the first part of the survey (the 10 Likert-scale items) indicated that parents/guardians were very positive toward the home projects (Figure 7.4).

The item that received the lowest score in both units was Item 7: "My child shared with me the school conversation around this project." Items 3 and 8 ("The materials sent home helped us do the science explorations" and "Such home projects help my child learn and have an interest in science at school," respectively) had the highest averages in the *Matter* unit. Items 2 and 3 ("We enjoyed reading the book sent home" and "The materials sent home helped us do the science explorations,"

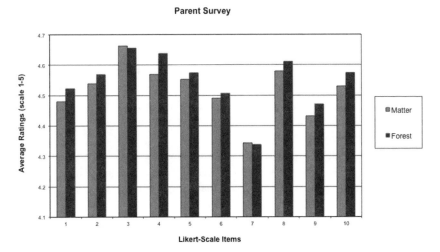

FIGURE 7.4 Average ratings across all six classrooms on the Likert-scale items of the parent survey.

respectively) were highest in the *Forest* unit. Averages by teacher ranged from 4.3 to 4.6, by grade from 4.4 to 4.6, and the averages for both the *Matter* and *Forest* units were 4.5. There were no interactions among teacher, grade, and unit.

Regarding the second part of the survey—that is, what they viewed as the favorite activities of the home project—90 parents/guardians, who answered this question, marked "*all of the above*" (the science activity/exploration, reading the book, and writing and drawing in the booklet). This accounted for approximately 38.5% of all the responses to that item for both units. The second most selected favorite part of the home project was the "*science activity or exploration,*" which accounted for 23% of the answers in the *Matter* unit and even higher in the *Forest* unit (33%). Moreover, in both units, most parents (*Matter*: 69%; *Forest*: 73%) did not find any of the activities involved in the home projects as their least favorite activity, which was the second question in the second part of the survey.

The responses that parents/guardians gave to the open-ended questions (the last part of the survey) shed more light on their reactions to the home project. Only 54 parents/guardians gave a response to that question for the *Matter* home project and 34 for the *Forest* (a total of 88 responses). Twenty-two of the surveys were answered in Spanish, primarily from Ibett's bilingual 2nd-grade classroom. Examples follow with those written in Spanish accompanied by an English translation in brackets.

> Mom: Cassandra was so excited about doing a science project at home. Doing this project helped us in what we have tried to explain to her.
>
> Dad: My son had a lot of fun doing this project. He constantly wanted to check the pieces of paper towel to see if they were dry yet.
>
> Mom: We loved doing this together! I enjoyed discussing the book and Madelyn loved writing and drawing in the booklet. We observed over 3 days and wrote down our observations. She really learned!
>
> Mom: Lawrence had already knew so much about the project and from what you told him at school. He basically knew where we were going. Me and his dad just guided him and we watched the project when he went to sleep and we had a good time together. Thanks.
>
> Dad: Student should be able to bring more science project home. Science activities a great source to student development.
>
> Mom: We learned a lot of new things about the rain and clouds and how these tiny droplets in the air always it was all very interesting.
>
> Mom: We found out my child really likes to do science experiments.
>
> Mom: It was very exciting to hear my son tell me about things I did not know.

Dad: We loved doing the project and discussing the water cycle. Keep up the good work! We would like some more such projects.

Mom: It help me and my child enjoy some time together interacting and laughing with each other. Learning new things.

Mom: Al mismo tiempo que se divierten estan aprendiendo mucho [While having fun they were also learning a lot].

Mom: Es bueno saber lo de la, lluvia, sol, y todas los cicios. Y como las plantas crecen [It is good to know about rain, the sun, and all of the cycles. And how plants grow].

Mom: Fue bueno para hija porque descubrio algo nuevo [It went well for my daughter because she discovered something new].

All of the 88 responses to the open-ended question, which consisted of 152 sentences or "chunks," were analyzed. We focused on two major aspects of each chunk: (1) subject of the comment, which we coded as: adult(s) and child together, only child, only adult(s), and undetermined; and (2) impact of the home project, which we coded as: cognitive (related to understanding of, and engagement in, ideas), affective (related to feelings and emotions), and social (related to interactions among people). This analysis showed that 61 (40%) chunks had only the child (e.g., "my daughter") as the subject. The other categories (i.e., adult(s) and children together, adult(s) only, and undetermined) were evenly distributed, with approximately 20% each.

Cognitive impact was identified in 82 (44%) chunks with 77% of them being positive. A 1st-grade parent wrote, "The home project was very insightful and encouraged my son to learn much more about weather." And a 2nd-grade parent wrote, "We really enjoyed this project and learned a lot from it. I believe the integration of activity, reading, and drawing/discussion is a great way to learn. There should definitely be more of this kind of instruction. Thanks for the project!" Affective impact was identified in 91 (49%) chunks with 82% of them being positive. Comments included: "We enjoyed waiting for the seed to grow"; "I thought it was fun doing the project," and "Para nosotros todo estaba interesante. No hubo nada que no nos gustaba todo lo que hicimos lo disfrutamos [Everything was interesting for us. There was nothing that we didn't like, everything that we did we enjoyed]."

Finally, social impact was identified in 12 (6%) chunks with 92% of them being positive. Parents or family members wrote: "Gave my daughter and myself spend more time together"; "Once again, as with the evaporation experiment, we really enjoyed doing this experiment together." Overall, 78% of all the coded chunks referred to positive or neutral impact. Thus, the parent responses underscored the value of the home projects that were appreciated for their integrated nature. Moreover, parents or family members indicated that the home projects had mostly cognitive and affective impact.

Concluding Thoughts

Many of the out-of-school science experiences that children have occur at museums, zoos, and other community institutions (Aubusson, Griffin, & Kearney, 2012). Yet, "going to a . . . museum has none of the warmth of carrying out activities with the family" (Solomon, 2003, p. 231). Indeed, increasing parental involvement in learning of school-related material has been a vital feature of local, state, and national education initiatives because such involvement has been shown to positively impact children's academic achievement (e.g., National Education Goals Panel, 1999). Thus, it is important for teachers to find ways for families to be involved in their children's school learning at home, which was the goal of the home projects.

At home, children had time to reread and discuss with their families a book, which had been read aloud and discussed in class, and design and execute an inquiry that could expand on an exploration they had done at school. They also had the opportunity to write and draw about their at-home inquiry, their procedure and their findings. Because children brought these booklets to school and shared their at-home inquiries with their peers and teacher, they had opportunities to engage in conversations with both their teacher and peers re-exploring important scientific ideas and constructing and sharing explanations for the findings.

Most home projects that have been employed have been in either literacy *or* science, and have not been connected to the ongoing curriculum in which children engage at school. The two home projects described and analyzed in this chapter are an exception. Children had opportunities to do integrated science-literacy inquiries at home, which were extensions of the literacy activities and hands-on explorations that they had experienced at school. Students were eager to engage in these projects with their families, and the families indicated that they enjoyed the integrated aspects of the projects. These home projects had two features that have been seen as critical for fostering parent involvement and may have led to parents' positive evaluation of them: (1) the teachers *invited* the parents to be involved in these science-literacy experiences (Hoover-Dempsy et al., 2005); and (2) the materials and directions to conduct these projects assisted parents in *how to* participate in them with their children (Englund, Luckner, Whaley, & Egeland 2004; Pena, 2000). Moreover, in their surveys, parents or family members noted the cognitive impact of the home projects, but also marked their positive affective influence. Such projects, that facilitate enjoyment and learning of science at home, may also contribute to strengthening parents' and family members' views of science and its place in their child's life in and out of school (Solomon, 2003).

References

Aubusson, P., Griffin, J., & Kearney, M. (2012). Learning beyond the classroom: Implications for school science. In B. J. Fraser, K. G. Tobin & C. J. McRobbie (Eds.), *Second international handbook of science education* (Vol. 2, pp. 1123–1134). New York: Springer.

Barone, D. (1999). *Resilient children: Stories of poverty, drug exposure, and literacy development.* Newark, DE: International Reading Association.

Branley, F. M. (1997). *Down comes the rain.* New York: HarperCollins.

Delgado-Gaitan, C. (1990). *Literacy for empowerment: The role of parents in children's education.* New York: Falmer Press.

Englund, M. M., Luckner, A. E., Whaley, G. J. L., & Egeland, B. (2004). Children's achievement in early elementary school: Longitudinal effects of parent involvement, expectations, and quality of assistance. *Journal of Educational Psychology, 96,* 723–736.

Epstein, J. L. (1991). Effects on student achievement of teacher practices of parent involvement. In J. B. Silvern (Ed.), *Advances in reading/language research: Vol. 5. Literacy through family, community, and school interaction* (pp. 261–276). Greenwich, CT: JAI Press.

Epstein, J. L., & Dauber, S. L. (1991). School programs and teacher practices of parent involvement in inner-city elementary and middle schools. *Elementary School Journal, 91,* 291–305.

Gennaro, E., & Lawrenz, F. (1992). The effectiveness of take-home science kits at the elementary level. *Journal of Research in Science Teaching, 29,* 985–994.

Gibbons, B. (1991). *From seed to plant.* New York: Holiday House.

Hoover-Dempsy, K. V., & Sandler, H. M. (1997). Why do parents become involved in their children's education? *Review of Educational Research, 33,* 3–42.

Hoover-Dempsy, K. V., Walker, J. M. T., Sandler, H. M., Whetsel, D., Green, C. L., Wilkens, A. S., et al. (2005). Why do parents become involved? Research findings and implications. *The Elementary School Journal, 29,* 425–451.

National Education Goals Panel. (1999). *The national education goals report: Building a nation of learners, 1999.* Washington, DC: US Government Printing Office.

Pena, D. C. (2000). Parent involvement: Influencing factors and implications. *The Journal of Educational Research, 94,* 42–54.

Quint, S. (1994). *Schooling homeless children: A working model for American's public school.* New York: Teachers College Press.

Rosenholtz, S. (1989). *Teachers' workplace: The social organization of schools.* New York: Longman.

Solomon, J. (2003). Home-school learning of science: The culture of homes, and pupils' difficult border crossing. *Journal of Research in Science Teaching, 40,* 219–233.

Taylor, D., & Dorsey-Gaines, C. (1990). *Growing up literate: Learning from inner-city families.* Portsmouth, NH: Heinemann.

Wollman-Bonilla, J. E. (2001). Can first-grade writers demonstrate audience awareness? *Reading Research Quarterly, 36,* 184–201.

Yaden, D. B., & Brassell, D. (2002). Enhancing emergent literacy with Spanish-speaking preschoolers in the inner city: Overcoming the odds. In C. Roller (Ed.), *Comprehensive reading instruction across the grade levels* (pp. 20–39). Newark, DE: International Reading Association.

Yaden, D. B., Madrigal, P., & Tam, A. (2003). Access to books and beyond: Creating and learning from a book lending program for Latino families in the inner city. In G. G. Garcia (Ed.), *English learners: Reaching the highest level of English literacy* (pp. 357–386). Newark, DE: International Reading Association.

SECTION III

Evolution of Learning in ISLE Classrooms

8

LEARNING TOGETHER OVER TIME

Young Children Making Meaning

*Justine M. Kane, Maria Varelas,
Christine C. Pappas, Lynne Pieper, Jennifer Hankes,
and Begoña Marnotes Cowan*

We consider each classroom as a learning community in which children and teachers work together to engage with materials, ideas, curriculum genres, and each other to achieve learning goals. Learning communities both shape and are shaped by their members as individual children's conceptions interact with their peers' and teacher's ideas, blend, disappear, transform, get pushed away, and are negotiated. We believe that children come to appropriate accepted scientific understandings when they are given opportunities to think about their spontaneous, everyday-lifeworld ideas (Gee, 2004; Vygotsky, 1987/1934) as they engage in classroom hands-on experiences, along with ideas presented in children's literature information books, a variety of writing experiences, and dialogue with classmates and their teacher. Moreover, we believe that children express these ideas in their own unique "repertoires of practice" (Gutiérrez & Rogoff, 2003) that enrich dialogic processes.

Learning in classrooms is a communal activity—knowledge is individually owned by children, but is also collectively constructed by them and the teacher in a classroom. Studying a class's collective development of ideas offers multiple opportunities: to figure out the "otherness" in children's thinking; to realize strengths and limitations of various resources to support it; to appreciate the diversity of resources that may be needed for productive instruction; and to reveal ways in which young children use each other's ideas and their own experiences to make sense of the world.

In this chapter, we focus on children's collective and individual science learning in ISLE classrooms. We explore both how children's learning unfolded over time within classroom communities and how children individually owned ideas at the end of the units. Because there were a plethora of ideas in both the *Matter* and *Forest* units, we chose to focus on certain concepts in each of the units to examine the collective concept development in classrooms. In the *Matter* unit, we examined the concept of evaporation because it is a challenging concept and because it is critical in understanding the water cycle and how rain is made. Moreover, it is relevant to children who experience rain, evaporation, and clouds in their everyday lives. In the *Forest* unit, we looked at the relationships among plants, animals, and non-living entities in forest communities because they are critical in understanding an ecosystem. Moreover, they are relevant to children who also experience plants and animals in their everyday lives. Using two classrooms as examples (Jennifer's 3rd grade and Begoña's 2nd grade), we trace here how these concepts were constructed and realized linguistically throughout whole-class discussions in various types of classroom activity or curriculum genres (Pappas & Zecker, 2001)—see Chapter 1 for details on all of the curriculum genres enacted in the two units.

In investigating the individual meaning making, we used pre- and postconversations for each of the two units, which we had with the 10 focal children in each of the six classrooms. (See Chapter 1 for details in the demographic make-up of the classrooms.) The conversation in the *Matter* unit started with an activity, offering children objects to sort into solids, liquids, and gases, and asking them for their reason(s) for each object. After that introductory activity, we asked children a variety of questions about states of matter, changes of state, and the rain/water cycle. In the *Forest* unit, after asking children general questions about the forest and its entities, we specified two animals (earthworm and frog) and asked the children to talk about each of them since one of the goals of the unit was children's engagement and learning of particular animal characteristics. We chose these animals because they belong to different classes, and because children engaged in thinking about these animals during the *Forest* unit. Several classroom lessons were devoted to exploring earthworms, and, although frogs were not explored as long as other vertebrates were, children in all classes had shown enthusiasm for frogs. Several children wrote their own information books about frogs and had become quite knowledgeable about them.

Exploring the collective and individual meaning making of young children in urban schools is important for a couple of reasons. Their ethnicity, race, language, and socio-economic status are often associated with low achievement, especially in science and mathematics. Moreover, they, as adults, have low participation in these fields. Thus, the present inquiry may inform science teaching and learning in various ways. It expands existing research in terms of how ideas associated with matter and forest are developed in classrooms, how young learners engage with these ideas, and how students with particular underrepresented backgrounds construct these ideas in complex ways when offered opportunities to do so.

Learning Science Together in the Classroom

Collective Meaning Making of Evaporation: The Case of Jennifer's 3rd-Grade Classroom

In Jennifer's class, we focused on the development of the concept of evaporation in the context of an evaporation experiment because Jennifer happened to ask similar versions of the same question, "*What is happening to the water in the graduated cylinders?*" multiple times throughout the experiment. (See Chapter 1 for details about this hands-on exploration.) Repeating the same question allowed us to see how children's understanding of evaporation changed over time.

In Jennifer's class, the 20 lessons of the *Matter* unit spanned 29 days of science instruction. On **Day 5**, Jennifer introduced the evaporation experiment (to be conducted by children over many days) in which she placed five graduated cylinders with 100 milliliters of water at various locations in the classroom: in a closet, by a window, on a high shelf, on the floor under a table, and in a cabinet. Jennifer asked her students a question that they would be hearing repeatedly: "*What do you think will happen to the water [in the cylinders]?*" Students offered a variety of predictions. Michelle predicted that, "*it [water] will go up and make water vapor.*" In Michelle's mind, something new was formed (water vapor), but the way in which she expressed her thinking indicates that she thought the water is turning into water vapor while it is going up. Amber started a different line of thinking— the water would change temperature. Kenny followed up on Amber's comments by adding, "*The water by the window will turn warm. All the others [cylinders] will turn cold except the one on the top [shelf]; that one will be hot.*" Kimberly also continued this line of thinking: "*the sun would make it [the water] hot.*" Tamara, Lawrence, and Joe, on the other hand, thought the water would change colors "*all by itself,*" although they could not explain why. Tamara started with this idea and Lawrence and Joe followed, apparently feeding off Tamara's idea, which is something that occurs in classrooms at various times and for various reasons.

On **Day 7** (and six days into the evaporation experiment), students checked their cylinders and Jennifer again asked her students, "*What do you think happened to the water?*" Latessa thought that "*the water [level in the cylinders] is getting lower.*" Amber agreed with Latessa and said, "*I think it [the water level] went down because the hot heat dried it up, like Itsy Bitsy Spider . . . You know when it says, it 'dried up all the rain'?*" "Itsy Bitsy Spider" seemed to be a resource for Amber to make sense of heat's influence on evaporation. Michelle followed up on Amber's comment to add that "*the water was getting hotter and hotter and started going down.*" Leigh continued this line of thinking to say, "*Water rises overnight. It rises a little bit and that's why it went down.*" When Jennifer asked her for clarification, "*How does it rise if it goes down?*" Leigh answered, "*The water rises up into the room and that's why it [the water level in the cylinder] goes down.*" Jennifer focused on the idea in Leigh's comment that the water rises into the air, asking: "*The water rises up? I don't see it* *anywhere. Does anyone see water in the air?"* To that Amber responded, *"It's water vapor!"* Leigh, Amber, and the rest of the class had heard (and the class had discussed) in two read-aloud sessions of two books (*It Could Still Be Water* [Fowler, 1992] and *What Do You See in a Cloud?* [Fowler, 1996]) that water rises into the air in the form of water vapor and that water vapor is invisible.

Other students then offered more ideas. Lawrence reintroduced the idea that heat caused the water to *"dry up."* However, Deangelo countered by introducing a new idea—that evaporation was caused by wind saying, *"I think the windows and the fan blow the water and it comes out and rises up and goes to the clouds."* The "transportation" model of thinking about the water cycle—namely that rain (liquid water) is simply being lifted up (transported) to form clouds—was evident in Deangelo's thinking. Returning to heat, Michelle drew from her life experience to say, *"I left my water at home and it got lower when it got hotter."* At that moment in the discussion, Jennifer moved her students on to measuring the water in their cylinders for that day and did not pursue a consensus about what happened to the water. In this lesson, we note that several students offered ideas about the cause of evaporation. Moreover, students offered ideas, took up some ideas offered by others, came back to particular ideas offered on previous days, revised them, used different words for them, and, in doing so, continued to create varied understandings.

On **Day 10** (and 13 days into the evaporation experiment), Jennifer asked her students, *"Where's it [the water in the cylinder] going?"* Although Jennifer asked *"where,"* she meant "how" because later in the conversation, it was apparent that Jennifer sought the underlying reasons for the process rather than the destination of the water. Gianna suggested, *"air,"* but Tasha stated, *"Wind takes it. A breeze comes in the door,"* returning to an idea that Deangelo had stated in a previous lesson (Day 7). The next day (**Day 11** and 14 days into the evaporation experiment), Jennifer explicitly addressed the meaning of evaporation: *"Why do I keep calling this the evaporation experiment? What does evaporation mean?"* Jamilia suggested that evaporation meant *"it [water] goes down."* Jennifer challenged this by asking, *"So, if I pour the water out, is that evaporation?"* The students all responded, *"No!"* Kimberly next offered, *"It goes away."* When Jennifer asked, *"Where is it going?"* Lawrence answered, *"It goes down and does not come back up . . . It dries up,"* and Latessa added, *"It's soaking up."* Jennifer concluded, *"We definitely know that it's going,"* implying that it was a taken-as-shared idea (Edwards & Mercer, 1987) that the water was leaving from the cylinders even if the class could not yet understand how. Deangelo proclaimed, *"We think you're pouring it out."* Students laughed at Deangelo's suggestion since they did not really believe their teacher was playing a trick on them, and Jennifer assured them that she was not.

On **Day 12** (and 19 days into the evaporation experiment), Jennifer again asked her students to think about what was happening to the water in the cylinders. Many possibilities were offered. Amber said, *"I think that it's something to do with water vapor."* Kimberly suggested, *"Our water turned to air."* When Jennifer asked how this could happen, Kimberly was not able to explain, but Michelle thought it may have been related to air bubbles in the water: "*Air bubbles are in the water and the bubbles cause the water to turn into water vapor.*" Lawrence incorporated the role of heat in the process, "*I think heat takes water away because it dries up and water goes down . . . It dries up because of heat.*" When Jennifer asked him where the water went he said, "*It doesn't go anywhere. It just dries up,*" which suggested that he might have thought the water disappeared and did not turn into anything. In this lesson, Amber restated the same "water vapor" idea she had mentioned on previous days. Kimberly suggested that the water in the cylinders "turns to air." As noted above, Kimberly had heard in two read-alouds, *It Could Still Be Water* and *What Do You See in a Cloud?*, that water rises into the air in the form of water vapor. We do not know if Kimberly thought of air as a prototype for all gases and thought that water turned into a gaseous state, or if she had not differentiated between water vapor and air. Then Michelle offered an explanation referring to the bubbles that sometimes appear in a resting glass of water. Michelle may have been referring to her personal experience of having seen bubbles in water or she may have been referring to an idea that was also in the read-aloud of another book, *Air Is All Around You* (Branley, 1986). In a hands-on exploration called "Existence of Air" (see Chapter 1 for details) that was part of that read-aloud, students learned about the "tiny bubbles of air [that] come out of the water" (Branley, 1986, p. 26).

On **Day 13** (and 21 days into the evaporation experiment), Jennifer helped her students make connections between the evaporation experiment, a read-aloud, and the mural they had constructed to think more about evaporation. Jennifer and her students had constructed a mural that showed rivers, lakes, ponds, land with grass and trees, gray and white clouds, and a sun. She referred to questions students previously asked about water vapor such as, "*How is water vapor made?*" Then she reminded students of the read-aloud, *What Do You See in a Cloud?*, in which they read that water vapor was all around them in the air, and was invisible. Jennifer referred back to the mural and asked, "*What causes water to turn into water vapor?*" Jamilia thought it might be the water that is already in the air. Lawrence thought it might be the wind. Eventually, Jennifer pointed to the sun students had put on their mural and made the connection between the sun and students' previous ideas about heat. Although it is not scientifically accurate that heat is needed for evaporation to take place, Jennifer wanted to help her students see evaporation as similar to melting but with different states of matter involved in order to gain a basic sense of it.

On **Day 22**, Jennifer and her students discussed the evaporation experiment as part of a school Science Fair project they created based on the experiment, and this discussion enables us to see how students integrated the ideas they had been developing related to evaporation. In discussing the project with her students, Jennifer asked, "*What happened? What did you learn about evaporation?*" Chantrelle offered: "*The liquid water evaporated into water vapor.*" Jennifer then asked, "*Why does this happen?*" Terrance explained: "*It evaporates because a gas can turn into a liquid and a liquid can turn into a solid.*" "*So they [substances] can make different changes.*"

Jennifer encouraged his thinking by agreeing that water can change from one state to another, but did not challenge the apparent reversal of states in Terrance's answer.

Lawrence connected evaporation to molecules by saying, "*It's the molecules!*" Jennifer supported his contribution and asked the students again to explain, "*So why did the water evaporate?*" Yvonne suggested that heat contributed to evaporation, referring to a hands-on exploration, "*When we put heat under the water thing [pot] a lot was coming out [referring to the teacher demonstration called 'Steam and Cold Cookie Sheet'—see Chapters 1 and 6], but the cylinders only got a little, so only a little came out.*" Tasha jumped in, "*Don't you know, when we did that molecule thing [referring to the drama activity—see Chapter 1], when we got warmer they [actors in the drama] fall down [melt] when they got hotter they popped off.*" Jennifer said, "*Okay, remember that molecules are always moving. So even if the cylinders are not being heated like we heated the water in the pot, what's going to happen?*" Tasha repeated, "*They pop off.*" Lawrence added, "*They change into air.*" Jennifer asked, "*Do they change into air?*" Everyone responded, "*No!*" Jennifer asked, "*What's it called when liquid water turns into a gas?*" aiming at helping students realize that it is not "air" but water vapor (the substance remains the same). However the class's choral answer, "*Evaporation!*" signaled to Jennifer to ask yet another question, "*And what does water evaporate into?*" Everyone responded, "*Water vapor!*"

In this final conversation about evaporation, we should note Chantrelle's succinct statement that "the liquid water evaporated into water vapor" that differentiated between liquid water and water vapor. We also saw that when asked to explain why water evaporated, students drew upon a teacher demonstration where Jennifer "made rain" by holding a cold cookie sheet on top of boiling water and their experience of the drama activity on Day 18 (see Chapter 6 for more details) where students had the opportunity to act out the behavior of molecules in solid, liquid, and gaseous states. It was this latter activity that offered the class an opportunity to explore an even more sophisticated scientific idea that evaporation does not need a source of heat in order to take place.

Thus, Jennifer's class collectively moved from a "transportation" model of evaporation to a "transformation" model, a finding consistent with earlier research (Varelas & Pappas, 2006; Varelas, Pappas, Barry, & O'Neill, 2001; Varelas, Pappas, & Rife, 2006). Such a shift implies that verbs, such as "rises," "goes up," "disappears" and "goes away" to describe what happens to water are replaced by verbs such as "turns into" and "becomes" to accurately describe the water evaporation process—the change of liquid water to water vapor.

Collective Meaning Making of Interactions in a Forest Ecosystem: The Case of Begoña's 2nd-Grade Classroom

Interaction between forest entities was an important concept in the *Forest* unit. The students spoke about interactions or one-way relationships among animals, plants, and abiotic factors. They also spoke about interdependent or two-way relationships. One-way relationships are those that denote one entity interacting with or depending upon another, such as a bird eating a worm. Two-way relationships are those in which each entity gains or loses from the encounter, such as a bird eating a berry and dropping the seeds that can later grow into new plants. Children used the language of interdependence more consistently at the end of the unit and mostly to refer to mutually beneficial interactions. Teresa summed it up with "*[The community members] help each other.*" Note that our discussion below refers to various lessons that are described and depicted in more detail in Chapter 1.

From the **beginning of the unit** when Begoña read aloud *A Forest Community* (Massie, 2000) and *In the Forest* (First Discovery Book, 2002), she hoped that her students would connect the ways in which animals, plants, and non-living entities within the forest community interact with and/or depend upon one another. Begoña directed the conversation toward the forest as a community by asking, "*So what does a community do for each other?*" Her goal was to help students focus on the interactions among forest entities, and think about the ways in which animals and plants in a forest work together as a community. Many of the initial responses from students focused on the ways one entity acted on another. For example, Teresa suggested that "*leaves are food for worms,*" and Courtney added, "*If you are a worm laying on the frozen ground, some bird is going to eat you.*" Alicia, referring to the picture in the read-aloud book, *In the Forest*, noted, "*I also see that owl coming toward that rat and it might eat the rat.*" Although Alicia had misidentified a field mouse (as Begoña pointed out) as a rat, probably because of her experience living in an urban area, Alicia's and Teresa's responses identify one-way interactions between animals in a predator–prey relationship. Students also noted how animals interact with their environment. Courtney offered, "*Most of the animals like to hibernate in the winter. They go underground.*" Caitlyn suggested that crickets might hide in the grass because "*I think they would like the tall grass, anywhere they have tall grass, because they do not want to be found [by a predator].*"

While Begoña encouraged these responses, she also encouraged her students to think about even more complex relationships in the forest. In **Lesson 2,** she read aloud *A Forest Community* and challenged her students to think about two-way relationships between entities in the forest by asking, "*How do the plants, animals, and insects [in particular] help each other?*" Her students brought up the relationship between plants growing and earthworms making soil healthy. Madelyn shared an experience she had at home in her family's garden that captured the two-way nature of the relationship between earthworms and the earth. "*It is in our backyard and we get vegetable peelings and stuff like that and we make a big pile of it and worms come out in it. The worms turn it into dirt.*" Cassandra then suggested, "*Like when you said the worms go to the bathroom. They also make dirt and fertilizer. It helps the plants.*" Building on Madelyn's idea, Cassandra referred to what she had learned from Begoña earlier in this lesson (that worms go to the bathroom) and connected that idea to what Madelyn described happening in her family's backyard compost pile.

As the earthworms consumed the family's vegetable peelings that passed through their bodies, they were making dirt and fertilizer that supported plant growth in the soil. Courtney also explained, "*The worms make room for the roots.*"

The interaction between animals and seeds was another example of inter-dependence in the forest ecosystem, which was discussed as the students were read *Seeds* (Saunders-Smith, 1998) in **Lesson 8**. When considering how birds help the forest community, Carolina suggested, "*The bird [could] travel with them [seeds].*" William agreed and added, "*They [birds] could poop them out.*" Cassandra noted that in addition to birds, squirrels also contributed to this process by suggesting that the reason an oak tree grew at a particular place in the forest may have been because, "*the squirrel left it [the acorn] there and forgot about it.*" Children cited this type of example of the interaction between animals and seeds several times to refer to the habits of squirrels, chipmunks, birds, and other animals to "drop" or "bury" and "forget about" seeds, allowing them to grow into plants. What was not explicitly stated in these examples, but was taken-as-shared knowledge in the class was that these animals used the seeds for food and, thus, benefitted from them. Other students seemed convinced of the mutual benefits in these occurrences. Courtney noted that sometimes birds drop seeds and "*they [birds] help the forest community as well. The seeds that fall from their mouths may grow.*" Although Courtney did not explicitly note the seeds' impact on birds, her phrase "*as well*" implies her assumption that seeds are helpful to birds, since they constitute birds' food. Courtney's classmate, Teresa, was more explicit and noted that this was a cyclical process when she stated that "*flowers grow and make seeds for the birds and the birds drop them and make more flower and it keep going back and forth.*"

In **Lesson 12**, the read-aloud of *A Log's Life* (Pfeffer, 1997) offered oppor-tunities to engage with interdependence as it described the importance of a dead tree to the forest community. David pointed out the helpfulness of this phenom-enon when he noted, "*The tree falling over helps the forest community by giving animals a home.*" Rather than seeing the death of a tree as a negative event, David recog-nized that the dead tree provided a home for forest dwellers. David connected this idea back to the conversation the class had had about seeds in **Lesson 8** when he offered, "*I just noticed something. That is another way to spread seeds. When it (the tree) falls [from the wind] the seeds spread to the ground.*" David also suggested that termites helped to consume the fallen tree "*because they [termites] like to eat wood.*"

Eventually, the young children in Begoña's class spoke about interactions among entities benefiting the forest as an eco*system*. In **Lesson 22**, the food chain/web activity offered children opportunities to discuss this particular case of interdependence. While the interactions in the food chain depicted one-way relationships among animals and plants, the taken-as-shared understanding among students and teacher was that these one-way relationships benefitted the ecosystem as a whole. Begoña asked, "*What if a big condo company came and right where this wren lives they want to knock everything down and put in condominiums with a swimming pool* *and a park, and all of these guys [animals] get killed because there's nothing there? What would the wren have to do?"* Sean offered that the wren would die because it had nothing to eat, and David suggested that it might move to another forest. Although neither Begoña nor students explicitly stated that the health of the ecosystem as a whole was at stake, the class's shared understanding was that disruptions to the food chain would upset the balance of the ecosystem, possibly causing harm to individual animals, but ultimately harming the ecosystem itself, that one forest.

The Ebb and Flow of Collective Meaning Making

As we analyzed how ideas unfolded in the ISLE classrooms, we concluded that children's scientific concepts develop over time in a non-linear fashion within complex classroom interactions. When ideas are allowed to emerge and unfold in a dialogic fashion, they lead children to question, wonder, challenge, and make connections with their everyday lives. The resulting arguments, explanations, and concepts ebb and flow over time. By ebb and flow, we mean that children seem, at times, to "get it" only to "lose it" later, and then "get it" again. Thus, learning is not a smooth, straight trajectory from lack of understanding to understanding. Nor is there a straight line between activities and developing concepts.

Moreover, children's ideas have different articulations in different activities, and particular ideas and evidence surface or emerge during classroom conversations, such as when the children and teacher are discussing non-fiction science texts that are read aloud. Different curriculum genres offer children different opportunities for making meaning. Individual children offer and defend contributions for the whole class to hear. Other children and the teacher build on those ideas, copy them, ignore them, or challenge them. Children's ideas become increasingly complex over time, as children and teachers revisit ideas, relating them to other ideas discussed previously and/or to personal experiences and making room for classroom members to share their understandings, wonderments, confusions, and epiphanies. Thus, children individually and collectively develop, transform, and appropriate scientific ideas with their peers.

Moreover, the teacher's artful orchestration of these classroom interactions is essential to the unfolding of children's understandings. As children encounter multiple ideas, materials, and activities, they negotiate, challenge, encourage, support, and persuade one another. In these interactions, children are not only constructing scientific understandings, but they are also developing ways of seeing themselves as doers of science who shape, and are shaped by, the classroom learning community. The learning communities that students and teachers created within the classrooms we studied supported students as their scientific ideas emerged and unfolded in fragile and complex ways.

Individual Learning and Meaning Making

Children's Improvement over the Matter Unit

Children's pre- and post-answers in the *Matter* conversations (involving all 60 focal students across grades) demonstrated that the *Matter* unit helped them make leaps and bounds regarding important and challenging topics related to states of matter and their changes. Although in the pretest children showed close to no canonical understanding of several important ideas, in the posttest they showed significant improvement in various ways. They demonstrated understanding of macroscopic properties of the three states of matter. Examples of how children associated macroscopic properties with states of matter include the following: solid—"*if you leave it alone, it will always keep its shape*"; liquid—"*you can pour it*"; gas—"*it's invisible.*" Children also identified an object's state of matter by comparing it to a prototypical substance in that group. For example, they frequently used air as a prototype for gas and water as a prototype for liquids. They also associated matter with the three states (solids, liquids, and gases), and started developing a microscopic understanding, or an understanding of what molecules are and how they behave in each of the three states. Examples of how children described microscopic properties include: solid—"*When it's a solid it's squished together // the molecules*"; gas—"*if it's gas the molecules are just all over the place.*" And they strengthened their thinking about changes of state of matter, especially, freezing, melting, and evaporation, relating them with experiences they had in their everyday lives. The examples that follow illustrate the children's progress.

Categorizing Solids, Liquids, and Gases

- In the pretest, 1st-grader Vittoria offered as a reason for grouping some items as liquids that they had "*water.*" In some ways, water was a prototypical item for this state of matter for the children. However, in the posttest Vittoria reasoned about the liquid group, "*they can drip over something, they can roll over stuff, like paint. Liquids run through stuff.*" Vittoria used a macroscopic property of liquids, namely, that they flow, to justify her grouping of items as liquids.
- Similarly, Fen, another 1st grader, moved from just naming the objects she had categorized as liquids, "*bubbles, paint,*" in the pretest, to providing two macroscopic properties of liquids in the posttest. She said, "*it feels liquidy and gooey.*" "*Liquidy*" meant for Fen that something moves, it does not stay in one place, which is the same property as the one that Vittoria referred to. But Fen also offered "*gooey,*" an adjective that we usually use for viscous liquids. Fen seemed to appreciate that some liquids flow more easily than others and, thus, she used two different adjectives to describe them.
- Offering his ways of justifying placing objects in the liquids group, 2nd-grader Daniel offered macroscopic properties of liquids even in the pretest. He said, "*It's not a thing that puts together. It's not hard.*" Although not giving a clear

answer, Daniel communicated that liquids cannot be held together. He also said that they are not "*hard*," probably implying that they are not "hard to break," as he had just spoken about the reasons for his solid group and he had said, "*they [solids] are hard to break.*" Although not all solids are hard to break, Daniel was trying to communicate that liquids could be more easily separated than solids. However, in the posttest, Daniel offered other, more elaborate reasons for classifying objects as liquids. He said "*Can pour it and spreads out if you leave it alone it does change, if it's not in something it stays the same shape the container it's in.*" Properties such as it can be poured, it spreads out, it takes the shape of the container were part of Daniel's thinking after the *Matter* unit.

- Similarly to Vittoria and Fen, 1st-grader Miranda, in a different class than the other two girls, used prototypical reasoning or just named the objects in a group for justifying their placement in each of the three groups (solids, liquids, and gasses) in the pretest. She said for solids: "*This one is an eraser, this one falls out tree [referring to a leaf]*"; she said for liquids: "*Water is a liquid*"; and she said for gases: "*Have air in them.*" However, in the posttest, she progressed in her thinking using macroscopic properties for two of the three states, solids and liquids, similar to those that Daniel and the girls have used. For solids, she said: "*When put it somewhere it stays there, it does not move.*" For liquids, she offered: "*Water, you can pour it.*" She stayed, though, with the prototypical thinking for gases, saying, "*Have air in it.*"

- For children, gases are indeed a more difficult state to grasp than solids and liquids. But, children like 2nd-grader Cassandra who did not know why she put some of her objects in gases in the pretest had scientific, macroscopic reasons for justifying such a placement in the posttest. Cassandra said referring to gases, "*Does not fill up to the bottom or end, it fills the whole thing up, like the balloon.*" Although Cassandra did not make an explicit comparison with liquids, the first part of her statement implied such a comparison as liquids start filling up a container from the bottom up and depending, of course, on the volume of the liquid relative to the capacity of the container, it may not fill it up. So, Cassandra understood that gases have the same volume as the volume of their container (e.g., a balloon).

- Third-grader Kenny also revealed a similar understanding. When asked to tell about the differences between the solids and the gas groups, in the posttest, he went beyond the two macroscopic reasons that he had given in the pretest, both sense-related attributes. In the pretest, he had said, "*Gases, you can't see or feel. Solids you can see, you can feel.*" In the posttest, he offered, "*A gas, they have no shape, but a solid does . . . Gas cannot be seen, gases could fill stuff up, they could fill things up no matter how big it comes.*" In addition to the invisibility of gases that Kenny had brought up in the pretest, he added the properties of taking the shape and volume of the container, although he did not name the latter as such.

- Yet, another example of how students progressed from the pretests to the posttest is 3rd-grader Kimberly who did not give any answers regarding the reasons for placing objects in each of the three groups (solids, liquids, and gases) in the pretest, but who offered macroscopic reasons in the posttest. In the posttest, Kimberly said for solids, "*They can't pour, take the shape of the container.*" For liquids, she said, "*They pour if you tip them over.*" For gases, she said, "*Doesn't pour, cannot see the gas inside.*" Shape, fluidity, and visibility were the macroscopic properties that Kimberly used to justify her sorting of objects as solids, liquids, and gases.

- Although most of the children used macroscopic reasoning in their posttest answers, 3rd-grader Joe used microscopic reasoning. In his pretest, when Joe was asked about the differences between solids and gases, he had said, "*That stuff [referring to gases] dangerous and this stuff [referring to solids] not.*" Joe's answer represents an everyday understanding that children may develop, namely, that gasses are dangerous partly because they can explode. They may have heard, for example, that they should leave their homes if a leak of (natural) gas is suspected, because there might be an explosion. And they may have seen on the news homes that have burned down because of a natural gas leak. In the posttest, though, Joe employed what he had learned in the unit about the molecular arrangement and behavior in the three states of matter. He said, "*Solids have strong attraction, gases don't have a strong attraction.*"

Matter and Molecules

- Other children also offered their developed understanding about molecules when asked explicitly about them. Second-grader Natasha, when asked what she thought molecules are, said "*tiny little things,*" in the pretest. And, although she was on the right track to start with, she gave a much more elaborate answer in the posttest revealing her understanding of molecular behavior in different states. Natasha said in the posttest, "*Molecules are little, teeny, little things that you can't see. In a balloon they bounce around, in water they stay together, but they have a little spaces. And in the solids, they // it's kind like stuck together and they barely move. They vibrate instead. All things have molecules.*"
- Although Natasha went beyond just defining what molecules are in her posttest answer, other children did not elaborate that much, but tried to emphasize that molecules are small entities that cannot be seen with the naked eye. In the pretest, 3rd-grader Michelle did not know what molecules were, but in the posttest, she said, "*Can only see them with a big stethoscope, they are small, all objects have molecules.*" Although she referred to the wrong tool for "seeing" molecules, she realized that they are very small.
- Similarly, her classmate, 3rd-grader Kenny, used the incorrect tool in the posttest, but articulated his understanding of molecules. In the pretest, Kenny did not seem to have any understanding of what molecules are. He had said, "*They're something in your nose that helps you sniff.*" In the posttest, Kenny offered, "*this is my hand, you could see // a telescope you // of my // of my hand // of my*

bone, you could see the molecules moving // yes // even though solid molecules // even though it doesn't look like it // solid, it // even though it doesn't look like uh molecules // the molecules are moving // moving in slow pace, and everything has it in them." Despite the many linguistic repairs, Kenny emphasized the idea that molecules are always moving and brought in the example of solids where the molecules are moving with "slow pace" in order to make his point.

- Similarly to Kenny, 2nd-grader Leonara, who in her pretest interview had not provided any answers except one (that liquids have water in them), offered a new understanding about matter and molecules. In the posttest, when asked what matter is, she said, "*Gas, liquid, solid.*" And when asked what molecules are, she offered, "*All objects have them // everything. Solids are squashed.*" Like Kenny, Leonara only talked about solids in her answer about molecules.
- First-grader Alam also showed improved understanding of the idea of molecules. In the pretest, Alam had said, "*Yes, you use a telescope to see the blood things // you keep it on molecules. All of them except air. Balloon has molecules, air in it does not. We use it to make jewelry.*" Although referring to the incorrect tool (telescope) and possibly confusing it with "minerals" based on his comment about jewelry, Alam had an emergent understanding of molecules before the *Matter* unit. He referred to a tool that makes things look bigger, implying that molecules are small to see with a naked eye. However, he also thought that solids (balloon) have molecules, but gases (air) do not. In the posttest, Alam shared that molecules are "*very small particles, smaller than germs. Everything has molecules in it.*" Alam used the comparison of molecules to germs to emphasize the "very small" size of molecules. Children often hear from adults that germs are extremely small and invisible. Thus, for Alam, something smaller than germs may have meant that it is indeed small and invisible. Furthermore, Alam came to realize that "everything has molecules" changing his initial incorrect understanding that solids, but not gases, have molecules.

Matter and Changes of State of Matter

- Third-grader Sally showed improvement of her understanding of matter by moving from an everyday sense of the word "*matter*" to its scientific meaning. Sally had said in the pretest that matter is "when you care about something." In the posttest, she said, "*Everything is made out of matter, all of them [referring to the various objects she had sorted as solids, liquids, and gases] are matter, it is in everything.*" Kenny, who was in a different 3rd-grade class, shared a similar idea to that of Sally's to start with. Kenny had said in the pretest that matter means "*if it's okay with you or not. It don't matter if you borrow my pencil.*" But, in the posttest, he associated matter with the three states of matter. He said matter is "solid, liquid, gas."
- The children also improved in their understanding of changes of state of matter. When asked whether liquids could turn to solids, 3rd-grader Amber

said in the pretest, "*You could just pour the liquid into another.*" In the posttest, though, she presented an elaborate understanding. She said, "*Water to ice // if you put water in it // in the freezer and then the next day you go check on it, it will be ice. It will be ice and ice is a solid. It happens by coldness.*" Amber not only used the correct example and the correct names of the objects and states involved in freezing, but she also indicated an important factor for the change, namely the difference in temperature (which she called "*coldness*").

• Regarding the same change of state of matter (namely freezing), 2nd-grader Natasha had confused in the pretest freezing with evaporation. She had said that an example of a change from a liquid to a solid is "*if you leave it [paint] out too long, it might get dry and turn hard.*" In the posttest, though, she correctly pointed out, "*Water in the freezer, you wait for a little while, and then you take it out, and then it feels all hard, and then it's hard for you to get out the ice. If you do it to something that has salt in it and water, it won't work because it takes // like when you put salt on the ground when it's snowing, it helps, and the ice melts.*" In the posttest, in addition to a correct understanding, Natasha referred to an everyday life experience that she had associated with freezing and melting, namely, the addition of salt to ice on streets and sidewalks. Natasha seemed to link these life experiences with the science she was studying and/or she was asked about in school. She had referred to an everyday life experience (paint drying out) in the pretest too, but that was an incorrect association.

• Children also progressed in understanding another more challenging change of states of matter, evaporation. Third-grader Antonia had not answered any questions in the pretest except that she had offered melting as an example of a change from solids to liquids. In the posttest, when asked whether liquids could change into gases, she said, "*Water evaporates, it becomes a gas when the water after one day it evaporates, it turns into a gas.*" Antonia seemed to refer to the evaporation experiment that children had done where they were measuring over time the water level of a graduated cylinder filled with water and had noticed that even after one day water had evaporated. Antonia correctly associated evaporation with the change from liquids to gases.

• Kenny was another example of progress from pretest to posttest in terms of the concept of evaporation. In the pretest Kenny had spoken about the change from liquids to gases in a way that we could not certainly tell whether or not he was on the right track. He had said, "*Gas place // we saw a gas place that was using the water to turn it into gas.*" However, in the posttest, Kenny said that liquids could change to gases and gave the following example: "*Little drops of water, water is a special kind of liquid. It could switch to these two things. It could switch to gas or evaporate and it could switch to a solid by freezing. It evaporates from the hot air. So heat is energy. It could force things to move like the molecules in this cup. The light has heat in it so it's turning // the molecules are turning faster.*" Kenny not only correctly named the process ("*evaporate*"), but he also brought up heat as a factor. Of course, evaporation is not dependent on heat, but its rate is affected by heat. In the *Matter* unit, as noted in Jennifer's case study earlier in this chapter, teachers did not differentiate between these two ideas as the children were young, but aimed at helping them develop the idea that heat increases the rate of evaporation, an idea that Kenny reflected in his posttest. Kenny not only associated heat with evaporation, but he also correctly thought of *"heat is energy"* and reasoned about its effect in the microscopic molecular level (*"molecules are turning faster"*).

- Lastly, 2nd-grader Nathaniel is an example of children's improved understanding of the idea of rain and how it is produced. In the pretest, Nathaniel had said, *"Rain comes from the sky and clouds,"* an obviously correct statement that does not, however, show an understanding of the processes involved in the production of rain. In his posttest, Nathaniel shared, *"Rain come from clouds // water vapor // when you cook gas comes up and goes out of door and turns to water vapor and water vapor changes to water, becomes a cloud."* Although Nathaniel did not bring up evaporation as the process of generation of water vapor, he correctly identified the process of boiling which, too, produces water vapor (steam) that could turn back to liquid water, as Kenny correctly noted, but without pointing out the needed removal of heat.

Children's Improvement over the Forest Unit

Children's pre- and post-answers in the *Forest* protocol demonstrated that the *Forest* unit helped children improve their knowledge and understanding of important topics related to life in a forest community at various levels. In particular, children showed in the posttest more knowledge of entities (living and non-living) found in the forest. They also became more articulate in describing characteristics of living entities, and functions of their features that facilitate life. Furthermore, they reasoned about many more connections among living and non-living entities revealing a richer and more nuanced understanding of a forest as an ecosystem. The examples that follow are representative of these findings.

What to Find in a Forest

- In the pretest, 3rd-grader Alita did not know what she could find under the ground in a forest. In the posttest, she offered, *"Insects, spiders, ants, worms, termites, roots."* Second-grader Cassandra offered in the pretest an unlikely list of animals she could see in a forest, possibly animals she had seen at a zoo. She offered, *"Jaguars, lions, sea animals, dolphins."* However, in the posttest, she showed her richer knowledge of forest animal life: *"turtles, fish, chipmunks, rabbits, squirrel, termites, moths, ants, mice, worms, frogs, lizard, owls."* In the pretest, 1st-grader Alam had a partially more appropriate list to start with: *"bears, fox, squirrels, chickens, bird."* In the posttest, though, he highly increased his list that included, *"deer, raccoons, beavers, bears, foxes, chameleons, beavers, cats, frogs, butterflies, fish, worms, lizards, grasshoppers, frogs, bears, tadpoles.*" Likewise, 1st-grader Enrique in another class, who really knew very little about the forest and scored very low in the pretest answering most of the time "*I don't know,*" moved away from naming just two animals as entities in the forest ("monkey, anaconda") to a long list of forest animals: "*snakes, beavers, owl, frogs, flies, worms, fox, woodchuck, deer, bug.*"

Parts of Plants

- In his pretest, 3rd-grader Kenny, thinking about trees, brought up two parts of plants, "*the trunk and the branches.*" He added that "*the trunk hold it up and the branches connect the leaves.*" In the posttest, though, Kenny listed many more parts, "*egg cells, stigma, petal, branch, leaf, pollen, stem,*" and specified the functions of some of them: "*The pollen // if bees drink it and goes to another flower the flower could grow, it is thick, it grows that plant. Leaves gives us oxygen, and the stem holds the plants up.*" Although Kenny thought of the leaf's function in human terms (presenting an anthropocentric view), he gave a biocentric answer about pollen that is also indicative of his developing understanding of connections among living entities in the forest. Christopher, a 3rd-grader in a different class, brought up a similar idea in his posttest. While in his pretest he had only discussed one part, sharing that the "*stem helps the plant stay up, like our spine,*" in the posttest, he reiterated this idea ("*the stem allows it to stand up*") and added: "*the pistil // the middle part had the nectar and bees come and take the nectar.*" Christopher used the scientific name of the part of the plant that is near the nectar. Although similarly to Kenny, Christopher may have been confusing nectar and pollen, they both brought up during the posttest a stronger emergent knowledge of plant parts and connections among forest entities.

Travel of Seeds

- Children also increased their knowledge in terms of the number of ways seeds travel. In the pretest, children either did not answer the question about how seeds travel or gave typical answers of children who had been raised in urban environments away from nature. For example, 2nd-grader Carmen said "*they have a lot of seeds in the car and they are traveling in the car,*" referring to people. In the posttest, though, Carmen said "*[a seed] drops in ground // birds grab them, while they are flying they fall down. Wind can blow them,*" offering two natural ways seeds travel that involve interactions between animate and inanimate forest entities. Her classmate, Flor, was explicit in the pretest that a seed travels "*only if you move it.*" Like Carmen, in the posttest, she offered birds and wind as two ways that contribute to seed dispersion, but she also added a third one. She said, "*There is a plant // when it's thin, it can move so the seed moves. A bird that grabs it and moves it. The wind might move it.*" For Flor, how delicate a plant is plays a role in how seeds move. Third-grader Christopher thought in a similar way as Flor in the pretest, offering that seeds travel "*if someone takes them.*" But, his posttest answer was much richer: "*Bird picks up the seeds and they fall and another animal carries it. Wind // it blows it, it gets stuck to something. Water.*" Not only more animals than birds were involved in Christopher's thinking about seed travel, but also water surfaced as another means of seed dispersion. His classmate Alita also showed improved understanding in the posttest. Whereas in the pretest she had only noted the human factor sharing that seeds travel "*if you take them with you from land to car,*" in the posttest she articulated various natural ways. She shared, "*Rain. Animals stepping on them, they will fall off. Hurricane // wind // the wind is strong, air will pick them up.*" And, 2nd-grader Guillermo, who was in a different class than Carmen and Flor, offered in the posttest yet another different way of seeds traveling along with the ones mentioned above. Whereas in the pretest Guillermo had offered one way of traveling, "*by wind,*" in the posttest he expanded his list offering, "*by wind, water, hitchhiking.*"

Origins of Plants and Seeds

- Furthermore, children showed improvement in their understanding of the origin of plants and seeds, along with the parts of a seed and their functions. In the pretest, 2nd-grader Ignacio said "*plants come from dirt*" (an answer that several other children gave). However, in the posttest, he said, "*they [plants] come from seeds.*" Another 2nd grader in a different class, Cassandra, who had brought up seeds in her pretest answer ("*plants come from seeds and roots*"), refined her answer in the posttest. She said, "*[plants] come from flowers, a squirrel eats an acorn and drops it and lands in dirt and grows.*" Cassandra's posttest answer indicated that she did not only learn that seeds come from flowers and that seeds make new plants, but she also appreciated the interaction between squirrels and oak trees, although she did not name them as such. First-grader Francisco also learned more about seeds from the *Forest* unit. Whereas he did not know where seeds came from in the pretest, he offered examples of various fruits in his answer to the same question in the posttest, saying that seeds come from "*oranges, watermelons, apples, bananas.*"
- Cassandra's classmate, Natasha, knew from the beginning that plants come from flowers, which is what she had said during the pretest. In her posttest answer, though, she revealed a more elaborate understanding. She said, "*[plants] come from the flower. When the flower's dying, then the seeds grow. Flowers are already dead, a fruit goes on top of it, and then the seeds are in that fruit, then the seeds fall out.*"

Seeds: Parts and Functions

•   Although Natasha had some knowledge to start with, she did not know what the different parts of a seed were and what their roles were. In the posttest, though, she revealed a sophisticated understanding of seeds. She shared: "*The seed coat helps it protect it from enemies. Since it's really hard, when the plant is inside of it and you wet it and grow it, instead of, like, when you plant it, it // you think that it doesn't get anything, but it does. It eats, um, the stuff that's inside its seed.*" Natasha's answer shows us that she had constructed an understanding of the two main parts of a seed, the coat and the endosperm, and their functions. Similar to Natasha, her classmate, Courtney, showed in the posttest an understanding of the seed coat and the embryo. Whereas in the pretest, Courtney had said that she did not know what the parts of a seed were, in the posttest, Courtney shared that seeds have "*seed coat, and plant inside the seed. Seed coat protects seed. Line in shell is the plant. They help it grow. Plant is growing inside the seed.*" And 1st-grader Stephanie did not know anything about seeds in the pretest, but revealed an improved understanding in the posttest, saying that a seed has "*a coat, a little plant inside, another one but I forgot what make it grow. The seed coat falls off, that is how the plant grow out of it, holds the seed together.*" Like Courtney, Stephanie pointed out the function of the seed coat, but she also talked about what happens to it as a plant grows out of a seed.

Animal Characteristics

•   Children also showed improvement in terms of their knowledge of animal characteristics for the two species (worms and frogs) we chose to ask them about both in the pretest and in the posttest. Third-grader Sally shared in the pretest that worms are like "*spaghetti but fatter. They are brown, pink, or black.*" But in the posttest, Sally revealed a richer knowledge about worms. She said, "*[worms] lay eggs and have hair. They have like lines on them. They have air pockets, and they have bristles and they don't have any teeth or eyes. And they have kind of like something that goes over // a piece of skin that goes over their mouth.*" Similarly, in the pretest she said about frogs that they are "*amphibians not mammals. Starts off as an egg. It has different colors, red, black, yellow, orange, blue,*" but in the posttest she shared more features: "*They're different colors. Mostly small and they have a kind of little tiny ear that nobody can really see that much. The girl frogs are bigger than the boy frogs. Have webbed feet and long.*"

•   Kimberly, also a 3rd grader, but in a different class, offered some similar features in the posttest, but she also showed that she had learned the correct classification of frogs. In the pretest, she had said that frogs are "*Mammals, green, have legs over them, do not stand on feet, hop, rib-bit, have a long tongue,*" but in the posttest, she shared that they are "*amphibians, live half their life in water and become land animals. Have flat legs, back legs are strong, rib-bit, green with bumps on them, sticky and long tongues.*"

- Second-grader Flor also shared more features about worms in the posttest than in the pretest. In the pretest, she had said that a worm *"looks like rope but fatter. It's pink and wiggles."* In the posttest, not only did she share more features, but she also reasoned about the function of a feature. She said that a worm is an *"animal that looks like a stick, stretches, has a line, no nose, eyes, ears, breaths through the lines he has, it has little hair that helps them move."* First-grader Enrique revealed even more improvement. Enrique did not offer an answer in the pretest about worm characteristics, but elaborated in the posttest that worms *"[have] no eyes, nose, hand, feet. Move like snakes. Have mouth. Something around it for the babies stuck together. They can feel things."* And similarly, he did not share anything about worms' enemies in the pretest, but he articulated in the posttest that worms' enemies are *"bird // when it tries to get it, it stretches so it can escape // porcupine, frogs,"* also revealing his understanding of how worms protect themselves from enemies.

- Also regarding worms, John, who was in a different 1st-grade class than Enrique, revealed more sophisticated knowledge about how worms protect themselves in the posttest than in the pretest. He said in the pretest that worms protect themselves by *"hiding in dirt."* In the posttest, though, he offered two new things he had learned about them. He said that worms *"[get to] tug of war [with birds] and have a lot of muscles. They can grow a new head in two seconds."* And 3rd-grader Amber, who thought in the pretest that worms' enemies are *"people's shoes,"* offered in the posttest an answer that showed how she had expanded her own everyday, urban experiences, by saying *"badgers and birds."*

- Regarding frogs, 1st-grader John's classmate, Fen, showed in the posttest a more sophisticated understanding of how frogs protect themselves. Although in the pretest she had correctly noted that a frog *"jumps away"* to protect itself, in the posttest she shared that *"by their ear drums behind their eyes, they can hear and jump,"* presenting a more detailed, reasoned knowledge of what helps them jump. Similarly, although in her pretest, Fen had correctly offered *"tadpoles"* to the question about what frog babies look like, in the posttest, she provided the same answer but she also elaborated: *"Tadpoles, but no legs, lay 140 eggs at time, have mouth and dot eye, get eaten by scorpion."* Furthermore, her classmate Stephanie, who did not know in the pretest how frogs protect themselves, offered in the posttest a one-word, but correct, answer: *"camouflage."* And, 3rd-grader Antonia who, when asked about what frogs' enemies were and how frogs protected themselves, had incorrectly focused on what frogs ate (*"Frogs eat all insects. They eat insects and hop away"*), offered a sophisticated answer in the posttest. She said that frogs' enemies were *"foxes anything that eats meats. [They protect themselves by] camouflage and have to hide in water for a little amount of time, go up a little so they are not recognized."*

Connections among Animals and Plants

- Finally, children also revealed in the posttest a more sophisticated understanding of connections among animals and plants than in the pretest. When asked in the pretest in what ways animals and plants might be connected, several children gave answers that revealed that they had interpreted the question to mean what were the similarities between animals and plants. For example, 3rd-grader Joe said in the pretest, *"they both live by water."* However, children did not give such answers in the posttest. Joe shared in the posttest, *"food chains begin with plants."* He had just explained what a food chain was and offered examples like fish eating plants and fish eaten by other fish. Similarly, 2nd-grader Carmen had said in the pretest that *"they both grow,"* but in the posttest, she said, *"animals eat plants."* Cassandra, another 2nd grader but in a different class, had also said in the pretest, *"both need plants."* In the posttest, she offered an elaborate understanding, saying, *"forest animals and plants both live in forest and help each other. Squirrel can drop its food in dirt, and another acorn tree grows."* Cassandra referred to a different connection from those offered by Joe and Carmen who talked about how plants help animals (as animals eat them). Cassandra talked about animals' benefits to plants. Yet, 3rd-grader Sally, who included in her pretest answer similarities and connections between animals and plants, presented in the posttest a very rich set of connections. In the pretest, Sally shared, *"Like fruit from plants and berries. Like eagles pick berries. Or like some animal that wants to eat the leaves off the plant. They both kind of living because plants grow and animals grow."* In the posttest, Sally articulated two-way relationships between animals and plants, *"Animals eat plants. The animals eat plants and leave leftovers and the leftovers from plants decompose and help out the soil so to get more mineral. And because of that the birds will have homes to live in and more plants to grow."*

- Similarly 1st-grader Alam, who did not have an answer in the pretest about ways animals and plants are connected, offered interesting relationships in the posttest by presenting examples, *"birds make seeds fall down, bees help flower by taking the nectar, plants help the animals breath better air."* And even though 2nd-grader Guillermo gave a correct response in the pretest (*"animals eat plants"*), he showed an expanded understanding in the posttest—*"spreading out the food // animal eats the seeds it has, it might fall off and grow under the water."*

- Furthermore, like Joe and Carmen, 2nd-grader Natasha (in a different class from Carmen's) showed change by moving away from similarities (pretest answer: *"Animals and plants // they drink water and they eat food"*) to connections in the posttest: *"Some animals eat // meat-eater eats a plant // animal. That means it has plants, like, plants in it, even though he eats meat. And, um, they're connected because some animals eat plants, grass and other kind of // of plants, like leaves or flowers."* First-grader Edwin, who did not give an answer in the pretest, shared in the posttest that *"plants help animals eat, help them grow and make them big and strong,"* focusing on the one-way benefit of plants to animals. Similarly, 1st–

graders Francisco and Rosa (in a different class from Edwin's) did not have any answers in the pretest, but their posttest responses focused on different connections: Francisco said, "*bees like to go on dandelions*" and Rosa said, "*woodpeckers eat bugs in trees. The tree frog lives in tree.*"

Food Chains and Webs

• Furthermore, children's responses to the question about what came to their minds when they heard food chain or food web revealed their learning during the *Forest* unit. First-grader Miranda who did not respond about this in the pretest, shared in the posttest, "*All the animals that the frog can eat.*" Second-grader Natasha who gave a limited response in the pretest ("*I think, um, a horsy's food chain is apples, grass*") showed a better understanding in the posttest ("*A worm is eating dirt. A bird eats the worm. A hawk eats the other bird*"). And 3rd-grader Alita who gave a not so meaningful answer in the pretest ("*animals and sharks*") offered an articulate answer in the posttest ("*Something that eats something. Something big eats something small. Beaver is eating a beetle. Beetle is eating the grass. Grass is drinking water*"). Although Alita portrayed limited canonical understanding (e.g., not yet appreciating that size is not the determining factor in the order of a food chain, and that abiotic factors, like water, are not needed in a food chain), her emergent ideas show her developing knowledge network on which she could build later in school. Furthermore, we note that although size of organisms had come up in the ISLE classrooms and discussed and problematized, exclusion of abiotic factors from a food chain/web was not a concept that was appropriate for these young children. Thus, the ISLE teachers have allowed children to include abiotic factors in the food chains/webs they drew, discussed, wrote about, or enacted in their classrooms.

Individual Gains of Scientific Knowledge

The gains in their science knowledge that children showed in the six classrooms where the two ISLE curricular and instructional units were enacted and studied over the course of a school year were significant. Although children did not reach, on average, the highest possible level of understanding, they demonstrated an impressive growth (both quantitatively and qualitatively) in both units, *Matter* and *Forest*. What is particularly interesting is that these children (1) had very different socio-economic, ethno-linguistic, and academic backgrounds than most children who have been studied so far in the existing literature around issues relevant to the subject matter that we focused on, and (2) were much younger than students in other research who had studied and engaged with similar scientific ideas. Both of these features challenge further what students in urban settings who are often considered underperforming, at risk, underprivileged, underprepared, unsupported,

and underserved can do when given rigorous, substantial, and meaningful opportunities to explore, discuss, present, and think about scientific concepts and processes.

In the *Matter* unit, these young 1st, 2nd, and 3rd graders engaged in many
curriculum genres (e.g., read-alouds of information books that were read to them
by their teachers and dialogically discussed in their classrooms, along with the
hands-on explorations they engaged in and the discussions around them, in
addition to the many communicating opportunities) to think about mostly
intensive macroscopic properties of the three states of matter and to differentiate
among them. This contradicts findings of other studies (Krnel, Glazar, & Watson,
2003), which, however, did not focus on children who had given any particular
attention to these ideas as part of their science instruction. Our study reveals what
understandings young children construct in classrooms with teachers and peers as
they use a variety of curricular resources. In their classrooms, these young children
developed to an important extent the repertoire of macroscopic properties of states
of matter. Furthermore, although concepts like what matter is and changes of state
of matter such as evaporation are particularly difficult for older students (Liu &
Lesniak, 2005, 2006; Nakhleh & Samarapungavan, 2005; Tytler, 2000), these
young children made sense of them and linked them with their everyday
experiences.

In the *Forest* unit, the young children we worked with reached a higher level
of understanding than in the *Matter* unit, but they also started the *Forest* unit with
more knowledge. Although limited by their experiences of living in a big city away
from natural environments, such as a forest, they developed rich understandings
of important dimensions of life in a forest and especially of the connections among
biotic and between biotic and abiotic factors. And although they did not appreciate
all the nuances of such connections, they learned about plants and their niche in
a forest community and in food chains, and they revealed a biocentric approach
to ecological knowledge sharing understandings of interconnections among living
entities beyond such relationships with humans, demonstrating a sense of
environmental moral reasoning (Kahn, 2001, 2002). Furthermore, girls' and boys'
knowledge did not appear to be different, underscoring that girls can have as much
knowledge about the environment as boys, along with caring, which contradicts
other previous findings that positioned girls as more caring and boys as more
knowledgeable regarding the natural environment (Loughland, Reid, & Petocz,
2002; Loughland, Reid, Walker, & Petocz, 2003).

References

Branley, F. M. (1986). *Air is all around you.* New York: HarperCollins.
Edwards, D., & Mercer, N. (1987). *Common knowledge: The development of understanding in the classroom.* New York: Routledge.
First Discovery Book. (2002). *In the forest.* New York: Scholastic.
Fowler, A. (1992). *It could still be water.* New York: Children's Press.
Fowler, A. (1996). *What do you see in a cloud?* New York: Children's Press.

Gee, J. P. (2004). Language in the science classroom: Academic social languages as the heart of school-based literacy. In E. W. Saul (Ed.), *Crossing borders in literacy and science instruction: Perspectives on theory and practice* (pp. 10–32). Newark, DE: International Reading Association.

Gutiérrez, K. D., & Rogoff, B. (2003). Cultural ways of learning: Individual traits or repertoires of practice. *Educational Researcher, 32,* 19–25.

Kahn, P. H., Jr. (2001). *Structural-developmental theory and children's experience of nature.* Paper presented at the Biennial Meeting of the Society for Research in Child Development, Minneapolis, MN. ERIC Document Reproduction Service, ED 453 908.

Kahn, P. H., Jr. (2002). Children's affiliations with nature: Structure, development, and the problem of environmental generational amnesia. In P. H. Kahn & S. R. Kellert (Eds.), *Children and nature: Psychological, sociocultural, and evolutionary investigations* (pp. 93–116). Boston: MIT Press.

Krnel, D., Glazar, S.A., & Watson, R. (2003). The development of the concept of "matter": A cross-age study of how children classify materials. *Science Education, 87,* 621–639.

Liu, X., & Lesniak, K. (2005). Students' progression of understanding the matter concept from elementary to high school. *Science Education, 89,* 433–450.

Liu, X., & Lesniak, K. (2006). Progression in children's understanding of the matter concept from elementary to high school. *Journal of Research in Science Teaching, 43,* 320–347.

Loughland, T., Reid, A., & Petocz, P. (2002). Young people's conception of environment: A phenomenographic analysis. *Environmental Education Research, 8,* 187–197.

Loughland, T., Reid, A., Walker, K., & Petocz, P. (2003). Factors influencing young people's conceptions of environment. *Environmental Education Research, 9,* 3–20.

Massie, E. (2000). *A forest community.* Austin, TX: Steck-Vaughn.

Nakhleh, M. B., & Samarapungavan, A. (1999). Elementary school children's beliefs about matter. *Journal of Research in Science Teaching, 36,* 777–805.

Pappas, C. C., & Zecker, L. B. (Eds.). (2001). *Transforming literacy curriculum genres: Working with teacher researchers in urban classrooms.* Mahwah, NJ: Lawrence Erlbaum.

Pfeffer, W. (1997). *A log's life.* New York: Simon & Schuster.

Saunders-Smith, G. (1998). *Seeds.* Mankato, MN: Pebble Books.

Tytler, R. (2000). A comparison of year 1 and year 6 students' conceptions of evaporation and condensation: Dimensions of conceptual progression. *International Journal of Science Education, 22,* 447–467.

Varelas, M., & Pappas, C. C. (2006). Intertextuality in read-alouds of integrated science-literacy units in urban primary classrooms: Opportunities for the development of thought and language. *Cognition and Instruction, 24,* 211–259.

Varelas, M., Pappas, C. C., Barry, A., & O'Neill, A. (2001). Examining language to capture scientific understandings: The case of the water cycle. *Science and Children, 38,* 26–29.

Varelas, M., Pappas, C. C., & Rife, A. (2006). Exploring the role of intertextuality in concept construction: Urban second-graders make sense of evaporation, boiling, and condensation. *Journal of Research in Science Teaching, 43,* 637–666.

Vygotsky, L. S. (1987). *Thinking and speech.* In R. W. Rieber & A. S. Carton (Eds.), *The collected works of L.S. Vygotsky (vol. 1): Problems of general psychology* (N. Minick, Trans.). New York: Plenum Press (original work published 1934).

9

CHILDREN'S CONCEPTIONS OF BEING SCIENTISTS

Eli Tucker-Raymond, Maria Varelas,
and Christine C. Pappas

FIGURE 9.1 Second grader Guillermo's illustrations of being a scientist.

In the top picture Guillermo, a Latino 2nd grader, has drawn an experiment he did with worms. He has written the words "dark" and "light," pointing to the two conditions for which he was testing worm preference. The bottom picture depicts him holding a magnifying glass next to a table with various labeled seeds. Asked to draw and explain himself as a scientist, Guillermo has drawn two instances from his time in his ISLE classroom in which he was testing and developing theories about the phenomena under study.

As students experience science in classrooms, they develop ideas about what science is, how it is done, and for what purposes. They also develop ideas about themselves as participating in scientific activity. For these reasons, in ISLE classrooms, children engaged in practices that simulate those of professional scientists (National Research Council, 1996, 2012). One way in which we attempted to understand children's views about what it meant for them to engage in science was to interview students, asking them to draw pictures of themselves being scientists. This is different from asking students to draw a picture of *a* scientist, a task that has been repeated with many different demographic groups and adapted to address more specific kinds of scientists (e.g., Chambers, 1983). Such tasks often lead researchers to conclude that the vast majority of students think: *white man with white hair in white lab coat*, suggesting that children of color may have difficulty seeing themselves as scientists (e.g., Finson, 2002; Sumrall, 1995). However, our interviews revealed that young children of color are able to imagine and articulate themselves as scientists in multimodal illustrations and interviews in ways that yield complex understandings of scientific and school practices, both for themselves and for scientists out in the world. (See also Walls, 2012.)

In the interview, children were told the following: "I want you to think of two times you were a scientist. I would like you to draw a picture of each time you were a scientist. We won't have time for you to do a real detailed drawing. I would just like you to give me a sketch. If you can't think of two times, maybe if you just draw one, you will be able to think of another time." After children drew their pictures, they were asked to tell the interviewer about each of their pictures and explain how they thought of themselves as scientists in each picture. They were asked to clarify if this was an occasion that had taken place in the past or something they would like to do in the future. Furthermore, they were asked the following questions: "Why do scientists do the things you showed?"; "Are there things that scientists do that you didn't put in your pictures?"; "Are there things in your pictures that scientists don't do?" The same protocol was used for all of the three interviews we had with students.

When we asked students to draw themselves as scientists, we asked them to place themselves in a world of science. In their interviews, students populated the worlds of their illustrations with goals to accomplish; actions to engage in; tools to work with; other people with whom to engage; language, both written and spoken; and feelings, emotions, and attitudes about what they were doing in the illustrations. Students created themselves as "figures" in a "grounded world" (Holland, Lachiotte, Skinner, & Cain, 1998). That is, they created themselves as actors in scientific worlds complete with practices, purposes, and values. Their, and our, attention to such elements outlines students' expressions of ideological stances toward science. Thus, the drawing and interview task allowed us to explore differently what others have called students' views on the nature of science (e.g., Lederman, Abd-El-Khalick, Bell, & Schwartz, 2002).

As students experience the world, mature, and learn, their conceptions of themselves change. They interpret themselves in new ways through new information, in new settings, and for new purposes. This means their ideas about themselves and the world are always in process. As children learn science, "they also learn a lot about who they are (and can be) and what science is (and can be)" (Barton, 1998, p. 382). That is, as children's self and world identifications develop, they are in process, only within a realm of possibility (Bruner, 1996). They cannot become people whom they view are impossible to become. But possibility emerges and is simultaneously constrained by experience. As members of young children's ecologies, teachers and researchers help construct experiences *and* possibilities for identities. As students' ideas change about who they are as scientists and who scientists out in the world are, the relationship between who they see themselves as, and who they see scientists as, changes, becoming either more similar or more different.

Finally, the student and the researcher negotiated who this student was and the scientific world in which they operated within the context of a very specific interview. The researcher was asking, "When were you this kind of person?" and the student was answering, "When I was this kind of person I engaged in activities in this way ..." Within the interview, that interaction shaped the adult and the student as kinds of people in an institutional setting (Gee, 1996). The student decided to represent his or her making sense of the interaction in a certain way, making choices about what best fit the question being asked. Of course, some of these figured worlds students drew on are not only valued, but also were supported explicitly by the ISLE project, the teacher, and the institution of schooling. Thus, children's ideas about scientist identities are subject to, and constructed within, the perspectives that regulate the settings involved.

Scientific Stances and Practices

Philosophers, sociologists, historians of science, science educators, and scientists hold various views on the nature of science (Alters, 1997). One of the contested issues centers on the interplay between theory and data, and the inductive-deductive continuum. Lederman et al. (2002) remind us that:

Scientists observe, compare, measure, test, speculate, hypothesize, create ideas and conceptual tools, and construct theories and explanations.

However, there is no single sequence of activities (prescribed or otherwise) that will unerringly lead them to functional or valid solutions or answers, let alone certain or true knowledge.

(pp. 501–502)

That is, scientists take a range of approaches to study and understand phenomena. One spectrum of approaches may lie along an inductive-deductive continuum. Inductive approaches characterize practices in which scientists learn from observations of the world and then develop theories about it. Deductive approaches characterize practices in which scientists develop theories first and then test them. This is the differentiation between two ways of knowing—knowing from thinking about something by relating ideas, concepts, constructs together, and knowing from empirical evidence (that is, of course, always theory-laden to some degree). Both inductive (data to theories) and deductive (theories to data) directions of scientific activity ought to be emphasized in science education (Varelas, 1996).

A related issue is the continuum of science as an enterprise that develops a particular type of knowledge that has particular intellectual concerns versus an instrumentalist view that considers science as solving problems, and, at times, designing products to address societal or personal needs, thus focusing more on applied concerns (Rudolph, 2005). Furthermore, Wong (2002) highlights another distinction relevant to the nature of science, namely, appreciating individual variation versus focusing on commonalities shared by scientists as a group, commonalities that represent a standard practice. He argues that it is important to teach our children in ways that highlight variation, nuance, details, uncommon features, uniqueness, and complexity so that they see science as "fundamentally human and vital" (p. 398).

Drawing Scientists

We interviewed 54 of the 60 focal children in ISLE classrooms, three times: at the beginning, middle, and end of the ISLE curriculum implementation (see Chapter 1 for a description of the classrooms and details about focal students). We analyzed transcribed interviews and pictures through a thematic content analysis. (Conventions of transcription are given on p. 15.) We attended to the following dimensions: (1) whether the activity in the drawing was in fact previously experienced, and if so whether it was experienced by the child or by somebody else, or whether the activity would be done in the future; (2) whether the activity was (would be) done at school and being related to the ISLE curriculum, at school and not related to the ISLE curriculum, outside of school, or not specified; (3) whether the activity was a hands-on one, one involving print material, one involving other media, or not specified; (4) whether or not the child portrayed and/or talked about him/herself in the drawing; (5) whether or not others were part of the activity depicted in the drawing and expressed in the talking about the drawing; (6) the artifacts involved in the activity and depicted in the drawing; and (7) the actions depicted and discussed that were part of the activity. In this chapter, we discuss these dimensions by focusing on two major areas—the stances toward science approaches and goals that children took through their pictures, and the comparisons they made between themselves as scientists and scientists out in the world.

Children's Being and Becoming Scientists

Hogan (2000) points out that students are able to be meta-cognitive about their engagement in scientific activities. They are aware of the fact that they engage in activities that are more or less scientific, and that they engage in these activities as people who act "as scientists" or not. To explain their positions to us in the interview, students must juxtapose knowledge of their own practices with those of scientists out in the world. They must be aware of the nature of their own activities as well as those of (other) scientists. In this case, their knowledge is emergent, but integrated. It is neither declarative knowledge about others, nor procedural or meta-cognitive knowledge about themselves. It is a developing integrated knowledge of their own practice in relation to other people's practices.

Stances toward Science

In this section, we discuss what the pictures and interviews revealed about students' stances toward science, or how they positioned themselves as approaching scientific activities and for what purposes in each of the three interviews. We analyzed whether in their pictures they constructed science mainly as an inductive or deductive enterprise, or whether they saw science as mainly concerned with design, solving problems, or producing knowledge for others. We used children's statements about the actions and goals of actors and events depicted in their pictures to determine what students thought about the purposes of science and their participation in it, at least in the event they represented. For each interview, we share findings from the whole group, along with examples of how two particular students responded to the interview task. In doing so, we show how students' stances toward science changed throughout the year. We categorized each illustration along one of the stances toward science that we indicated earlier. These were: Inductive Explorer, Deductive Tester, Problem Solver, Engineer, Knowledge Developer (when there was not enough information to determine whether the child was using one of the four previous specific goals), Knowledge Presenter (when the emphasis was in the sharing of knowledge with others as opposed to developing the knowledge), and Not Enough Information (when there was not enough information to determine the stance).

Children's Initial Conceptions

In the first interview (PRE) given before their participation in the two units, students created 74 pictures, and we coded 32% of them as Developing Knowledge. Recall that developing knowledge was a general code that we used when students expressed engagement in a mainly intellectual activity, but did not identify whether they may be testing theories or observing the world and developing theories from their observations. Engineering (instrumentalist view of science) accounted for 13% of pictures, which was the second most identifiable stance. Students expressed three of the stances only at 4%: Inductive-Explorer, Deductive-Tester, and Producing Knowledge. Finally, we could not identify a stance toward science in 43% of the pictures. In these cases, children did not give us enough information verbally or in pictures for us to determine a particular stance. Such responses perhaps indicate that children across grades had very emergent understandings of science. Even students for whom we did report a stance did not always talk about what we would consider canonical scientific activity. For example, one 1st grader reported learning about the American flag, many students drew and talked about pictures of themselves doing art, and others talked about going to the store or shopping. Students relied on a wide range of resources to describe themselves as being scientists.

Leonara, a Latina in Ibett's 2nd-grade bilingual class conducted in Spanish and English, did not draw a picture in the PRE. When the interviewer told her to imagine herself as a scientist and draw a picture of that, Leonara responded, in Spanish, "What do you mean by scientist?" Leonara then said that she had never had science in school before, did not know what it was, and asked the interviewer, again in Spanish, "How does science work?" Other students had similar reactions during the first interview—they did not know what a scientist was. As such, they did not have a stance toward science—at least as we had constructed it in our interviews. Later on, after participating in ISLE, Leonara was able to answer that question with clarity and confidence (shown later in this chapter).

As an example of the most common kinds of drawings in the first interview, we draw on Jamilia. Jamilia, a 3rd-grade African American girl in Jennifer's class, was an active class participant, sharing her ideas with the teacher and fellow students. Jamilia drew two pictures in the PRE, something that only eight out of 54, or 15%, students did.

Both of Jamilia's illustrations in the PRE (Figure 9.2) were hands-on explorations. As the interviewer asked Jamilia about her first (top) picture, Jamilia responded that she had drawn herself doing something she would like to do, "Making something great." She said she was doing so because she thought scientists, "Pour something and mix something . . . and things could happen." In this case, the arrow that Jamilia drew referred to the idea that the substance in her "jar . . . spilled." She also added that if one drank it, "your face will turn blue." In this way, Jamilia's top picture was like 26% of other PRE pictures, in that she referred to scientists as mixing substances to create effects. Other students' responses about "mixing" included making steam, smoke, antidotes for poison, or explosions. Although Jamilia thought that scientists participated in this kind of activity she did not know why. We coded Jamilia's illustrations as not having enough information to have a stance toward science. In the second picture (bottom), Jamilia drew herself as she "put some colored water in there and the water in the vase turned black . . . And then the flower got smaller . .

FIGURE 9.2 Third-grader Jamilia's PRE illustrations of being a scientist.

. because there was no more color water." She indicated that she had done this activity in 2nd grade and that scientists did such activities because they were "fun to do." Such drawings are similar to findings in "Draw-A-Scientist" tasks that other researchers have asked young people of all ages and backgrounds to do (Finson, 2002; Rodari, 2007) and may point to stereotypical images of science portrayed in mainstream images. However, in this case, Jamilia did not draw a generalized stereotype of a scientist, but herself.

Although Leonara specifically asked the interviewer "What's a scientist?" this was the question that all of the students had to ask themselves as part of conceptualizing themselves as scientists before they drew. Their pictures and talk reflected their answers to that question before they participated in the ISLE curriculum. The fact that there were no significant differences regarding stance in student responses across grades perhaps indicates that students in early grades do not often participate in concentrated science curricula.

Children's Conceptions Midway into the School Year

In the interview we conducted with students between the two ISLE units (MID), students drew 97 pictures—almost every single student drew two pictures. Students' illustrations showed a greater articulation of particular science experiences that portrayed either inductive or deductive approaches to study. Illustrations that depicted Inductive-Explorer stances increased to 13% and Deductive-Tester illustrations increased to 26%. Although Developing Knowledge dropped three percentage points to 29%, the number of Developing Knowledge pictures increased from 24 to 28. Producing Knowledge dropped to 1%, or one instance. Engineering also dropped five percentage points from the PRE to 8% of the total number of MID pictures. Furthermore, pictures in which we could not make a determination of stance dropped to 23%, almost half of the percentage of PRE pictures. Even though the total number of pictures drawn went up, the number of illustrations that did not have enough information went down from 32 in the PRE to 22 in the MID. The differences suggest that students were more able to communicate ideas about their own scientific practices within the interview. To create their illustrations, students had to draw on resources for what science was, indicating that they had more developed ideas of science in the MID interview than they had in the PRE.

In the MID interview, Leonara drew two pictures of herself as a scientist participating in two hands-on explorations that occurred in the ISLE *Matter* unit (Figure 9.3). She also included people other than herself in the pictures.

In the first picture, Leonara said that she drew "when we (★★★) the glass that the teacher put us to do // to observe. Like what was the change about the glass with the water and the paint." Although she used the word "paint" she was referring to an observation of food coloring in water when students observed and drew at four intervals what it looked like when a drop of food coloring spread through a glass of water. (See Chapter 1 for details on this and other ISLE curriculum genre activities.) Leonara said that she was a scientist because "we were drawing in the paper what was the change." For Leonara, in this picture, science was about observing and recording phenomena because scientists wanted to know "what's the difference . . . and that's the change, it [food coloring in water] changes little by little" over time. For Leonara, scientists did not necessarily have an idea about what would happen, but they investigated and explored phenomena to see what would happen. They were inductive-explorers.

In the second picture, like 35% of all pictures in the MID interview, Leonara drew an ongoing evaporation experiment. She brought up what her teacher had asked, "where [do] you wanna put the glass [and] the other glass? . . . and we were

FIGURE 9.3 Second-grader Leonara's MID illustrations of being a scientist.

watching careful how all the water was going down. The water was evaporating." The "glass," to which Leonara was referring, was the graduated cylinders that the water was in for the evaporation experiment. The sun in Leonara's picture was also important to her. When asked what she had drawn in the top right corner, she said:

> the sun and the window because this is the air it was going over there and the sun was <flashing> over there so it was gonna make it more down // more evaporating . . . the sun and the air make it evaporate because // we didn't saw that because it happens little by little.

In her answer to how she was a scientist, Leonara referenced details of the activity such as the window, where her group had placed their graduated cylinder, and the sun and air that contributed to water evaporating. She was able to articulate her understandings about a specific natural phenomenon, evaporation. By articulating her identification as a scientist, Leonara also indexed scientific content, thus participating in scientific discourse. Similar to her first picture, Leonara said that she was a scientist because she was "drawing here in the paper how much it was going down // evaporating // so the teacher can compare it with all the other groups that put it on the table. Um what you draw." Scientists engage in this activity to find out "how if you put it one day and then you pass one week how many it goes down, how many it evaporates, how many could evaporate just in one day, in five minutes." As in the first picture, Leonara conceptualized a stance toward science that was one of inductive exploration. Perhaps because she herself did not know what might happen, and was told to observe and record by her teacher, she adopted a stance toward science that was one of induction and exploration rather than deducting from what one already knew to predict and test an outcome. It is not that one is better than the other—both stances are prevalent in science—but that Leonara's experiences in science led to her beliefs about it.

In discussing differences between her pictures and scientists out in the world, she mentioned that she had not drawn anyone writing anything down, a practice of scientists. However, she did talk about it; thus, in this way, her recording of data and scientists' writing were similar. She also mentioned that scientists did different experiments. She said that the experiments she had done were "for the little kids. Like 2nd graders." Scientists, on the other hand, studied "other planets . . . from Pluto, from Mars [because] they're big enough." It is unclear whether it was the scientists or planets that she was referring to that were "big enough," but in any case, neither 2nd graders nor the experiments she had engaged in were the same as scientists out in the world. However, because she had done experiments, she was like a scientist. Lastly, Leonara said that scientists "don't teach." Possibly, Leonara was again referring to the distance between her classroom experiences and those of scientists out in the world. She had experienced teaching in her classroom, but that was not what scientists did. What she had done was like scientists, but scientists did other activities that occurred outside of the 2nd grade, school setting, and did not do other activities that were typical for a school setting.

In her MID interview, Jamilia also drew two pictures to represent herself as a scientist (Figure 9.4). Again Jamilia drew herself next to (on the left) the materials in both illustrations. This time, both of Jamilia's illustrations were about activities she had completed in the ISLE *Matter* unit. In the top picture, Jamilia actually represented *two* ISLE activities. In the middle of the page, on a table, is a picture of the cylinders that students used when doing the evaporation experiment. On the left is her group's tube and to the right is her teacher, "Ms. Hankes's tube." To the right is the mural her class had constructed. In her picture of the mural, she had drawn (from left to right, top to bottom) a cloud, the sun, a tree, and the ocean. Scientists participate in such activities to "find out what's true or not."

In the second picture, Jamilia drew an electronic text she had watched with the rest of her class in which they learned about solids, liquids, and gases, and molecules. Jamilia had also labeled her pictures, something that she did in her journal throughout the semester. She represented a scene from this electronic text about matter that showed how tightly packed "molecules" are in "a rock." Similarly to the first picture, scientists engaged in the activities represented in the

FIGURE 9.4 Third-grader Jamilia's MID illustrations of being a scientist.

bottom picture "to know if they are doing the right thing or not." In both cases, Jamilia depicted scientific activities as finding the right answer. There is a right answer to be found, and scientists might have some idea about what it is or they might not, but they need to make sure that they are doing the "true" or "right" thing. We coded these pictures as Developing Knowledge. Jamilia had nothing to add about differences between her and scientists during her MID interview. Such a reluctance to name differences perhaps signaled a shift to a discursive identity that was more scientist-oriented for her.

Children's End-of-Year Conceptions

In the POST interview, even though there were two fewer pictures drawn than in MID, the percentages for the following stances increased: Inductive Explorer (14%), Deductive Tester (29%), Developing Knowledge (36%), Producing Knowledge (3%), and Problem Solving (1%). Illustrations coded as Engineering dropped by more than half, to 3%, and only 14% of pictures were coded as Not Enough Information. After participating in both units, as well as sitting in the same interview for the third time in a year, students were more able to draw on intersubjective resources with which to respond to the task demands successfully. Students at all grades had clearer ideas about what science was, whether it was recording ideas, listening to others give information, or testing whether worms liked light or dark conditions. Students continued to mention observing phenomena and recording data to learn from, classifying objects, and hypothesizing about and testing phenomena under different conditions.

In the POST interview, Leonara again drew two pictures of herself as a scientist (Figure 9.5). Both of Leonara's pictures were from the *Forest* unit. They also included her classmates. Again, for Leonara, other people were important in her activity as a scientist. Other people were also more important to children across the ISLE classrooms as other people were included in 69% of all pictures. The first picture that Leonara drew was the food web drama enactment in which students were each a plant or animal in a temperate forest ecosystem.

In the top picture, Leonara said that she was a scientist because she "felt happy." For her, science activities included positive affective dimensions. She liked what she did as a scientist. She drew herself in the middle of the picture (with the dark hair) and included specific boys and girls from her class. The lines indicated the yarn strings in the food web drama, which the children held to show "if he eats he or // so she eats he so we don't get confused." She explained: "Antonia (girl on bottom right) was the bee and I was the seed, so the bee eats the seed." Scientists participated in such activities to "see what different people or animals or plants eat." Leonara then went on to explain that "if an animal or plant stops existing, like, if the water stops, the fish won't live, we won't live, and not even the plants." As in the MID interview, Leonara embedded her scientific under-standings, as well as her understandings of the explicit purposes of the activity, in

FIGURE 9.5 Second-grader Leonara's POST illustrations of being a scientist.

her answer about herself as a scientist. Being a scientist consisted of knowing things about the world, perhaps important for the survival of human beings.

In the bottom picture, Leonara explained that she thought of herself as a scientist "when we were doing the [children's own illustrated information] books and everyone wanted to copy the books [the trade books the teacher had placed on the chalk ledge] and Ms. Ortiz didn't let us." She drew herself (to the far right) and two classmates, a boy and a girl, "looking at the books for information and so we can get ideas for ourselves to make our picture." Scientists wrote books because "somebody can read that book and learn something new. Also, she can pass it to the classroom so that everybody can learn something new, read the book, or you give them information." It is unclear whether Leonara thought of herself as a scientist because she wrote the book, or because she was not allowed to copy. In either case, her conceptualizations of science included textual activities and producing knowledge for others that is communicated through words and pictures.

In response to differences between the activities she depicted and those of scientists, Leonara spoke mostly about details she did not draw, specifically in the books that she and the other students were composing. However, she also articulated differences between her activities in her classroom and scientists out in the world: "They don't have kids . . . because scientists are people they are not kids." She also explained:

> The experiments that we do are not the same as the experiments that they do . . . because they find other stuff. They don't do this. They don't do the food chain, they don't do books, they just make experiments, and see what could happen and things we don't know.

As she did in the MID interview, Leonara seemed to differentiate between "kid" activities and those of scientists out in the world. She knew that what scientists did was different from what she and her classmates had done, but that the practices were similar. She also expressed a stance toward science that was one of developing knowledge and presenting it to others. Invoking both similarities and differences between her activities and those of scientists out in the world, she revised her early statement:

> They make the books and they pass it around like the book that we read on chipmunks, on forests. But [they also make books on] other stuff like on medicine and different stuff.

Leonara indicated that she knew scientists studied and produced knowledge on a range of topics to share with others, including topics she had studied, chipmunks and forests, but also other topics her class (or possibly kids in general) did not study.

While she had not been a scientist, Leonara gave many clues that suggested she thought she simulated what scientists do. In doing so, she developed her perspective on what it meant to do science and to be a scientist. In the beginning, she did not know what science or a scientist was. She did not even attempt to draw anything at all, as others did who may have had similar lack of knowledge about the word. After she participated in the *Matter* unit, she likened science to observing and recording phenomena. She also expressed stances toward science that suggested exploration through hands-on activities in which change occurred. At the end of the year, after both units, Leonara also indicated that scientists find information through experiments, writing about, and presenting it for the benefit of others. Leonara's focus on hands-on explorations after the *Matter* unit and developing and sharing knowledge after the *Forest* unit mirrors the ratio of hands-on explorations to read-aloud activities in each unit. That is to say, Leonara's representations of what science was had to do with her developing an emergent repertoire of science practices.

In her POST interview, Jamilia again drew two pictures of her participation from ISLE units (Figure 9.6). In the POST interview, Jamilia included one event from the *Matter* unit and one from the *Forest* unit. In both cases, she drew about the project children completed at home. The top picture depicts the home project with the paper towel exploration and the bottom picture depicts the home project with the lentil growth exploration. In the top picture, Jamilia, "drew a radiator and when we had // did the paper towel experiment . . . and I drew a picture of me." She also labeled the paper towels on the radiator "A," "B," and "C." These labels reflect the names Jennifer had given to the paper towels when she did the paper-towel experiment in class. Jamilia indicated that A and B towels dried up more quickly, but in the interview, she could not say why they did, although she did say that scientists did such activities to "study" things. It seems that Jamilia's stance

FIGURE 9.6 Third-grader Jamilia's POST illustrations of being a scientist.

toward science and scientists included developing knowledge but also dimensions of exploration for which she did not anticipate any particular outcome, but studied the phenomenon inductively, and thought about which towels dried up the fastest only after doing the experiment.

In the bottom picture, Jamilia drew the plant she grew and for the first time included someone other than herself, her older sister. She reported that the plant was "growing [but] had died . . . because I didn't water it." She said scientists participated in such activities, shown in the bottom picture, "to see if it took a few days to grow." In contrast to the first picture in her POST interview, Jamilia expressed an idea about what would happen as she tried to grow the plant—it would take a few days. In this way, her stance toward science was one of deduction, or testing a prediction based on what she already knew.

As in the MID interview, Jamilia did not indicate any differences between what she did and what scientists out in the world did. Interestingly, both of Jamilia's illustrations were ISLE activities completed at home, away from school (the findings of which were shared in class). It could be that the independence and responsibility of completing the activities at home made Jamilia feel more like a scientist and perhaps less like a student-scientist or a student in science class. Such experiences may be integral to developing students' identifications with science in ways that extend beyond the classroom.

Comparisons with Scientists Out in the World

In this section, we present our findings on how students depicted themselves as similar to, and different from, scientists out in the world (although some information on this topic has been already mentioned above). We offer insights into how students perceived their own participation in science class and themselves as scientists (i.e., proximal processes and circumstances), how they perceived scientific practice in the grown-up world (distal processes and circumstances), and relationships between the two. As noted earlier, we asked children a series of questions that elicited similarities and differences between proximal and distal conceptions, including, "Why do scientists do the things you showed in your picture?"; "Are there things that you put in your picture that scientists don't do?"; "Are there things that you did not put in your picture that scientists *do* do?" These last two questions may be biased toward differences. Thus, we find it especially compelling that the ratio of similarities to differences increased after students participated in the *Matter* unit and again after participation in the *Forest* unit.

We coded the comparisons that children made between the activities they depicted and what scientists out in the world might do or not do—that is, between their proximal conceptions and their distal conceptions. We focused on actors, processes, and physical circumstances that children included in their pictures and oral descriptions. Actors included anyone else they may have depicted beyond themselves. Processes included: material (acts on or with artifacts, e.g., mixing, pouring, observing); textual (acts with print, images, or other media, e.g., reading or writing a book); cognitive (references to thinking, knowing, understanding); social (acts with other people, e.g., working with partners); affective (description of feelings, attitudes, emotions, e.g., smart, cool, excited); and verbal (verbal language, e.g., talking or answering questions). Physical circumstances included: material artifacts (tools, equipment, materials, e.g., magnifying glasses, bowls, food coloring) and physical space or place (places where activities are done, e.g., at my home kitchen).

In the PRE interview (Figure 9.7), material processes were by far the most prevalent dimension that students talked about. That is, students talked about what they and scientists did in terms of observable actions. Students in all six classes mentioned differences (42) between their actions and those of scientists slightly more than they did similarities (40). Other categories were barely mentioned. Students mentioned material artifacts 11 times total. In this category also there were slightly more differences (7) than similarities (4). As an example of similarities in material processes but differences in material artifacts, Jonah, in Neveen's 3rd-grade classroom, drew himself "mixing juices." He said that scientists engaged in similar activities to his in that they also "mix things" and "make different formulas," but that they used different artifacts, "They don't use milk and juice."

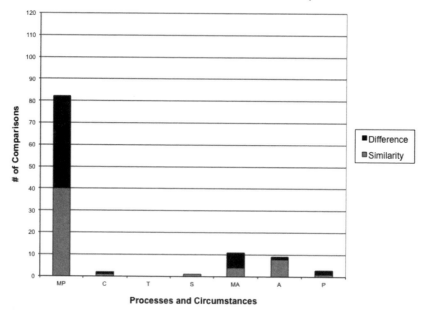

FIGURE 9.7 Comparisons of PRE proximal and distal student conceptions of being scientists. Key: MP=Material processes; C=Cognitive processes; T=Textual processes; S=Social processes; MA=Material artifacts; A=Affective processes; P=Physical space or place.

They use what they made." One category, in which students saw themselves as more similar (8) to scientists, rather than different (1), was in their affective relations to the event. For example, Antonia, in Ibett's 2nd-grade class, said that scientists "want to be creative doing something they really like to do." That is, how they and scientists out in the world felt about the activities in which they participated was similar, at least in the few instances when children called attention to it.

In the MID interview (Figure 9.8), students again mentioned material processes much more than any other category; however, all of the other categories, except place, were also more prevalent than they had been in the PRE interview. Material Processes were referenced a total of 114 times. Again, differences (58) were slightly higher than similarities (56). Cognitive processes, almost absent in the PRE interview, were referenced 36 times in the MID interview. Almost all of these reflected similarities (34) students perceived between themselves and scientists out in the world. For instance, Kenny, in Jennifer's 3rd-grade class, said that scientists engaged in experiments, like the one his class had done on evaporation, "so they could learn from it" and "teach themselves about evaporation." Similarly, in Begoña's 2nd-grade class, Natasha said that scientists "*figure out* what things can evaporate and what cannot," as well as "how water turns to steam." Textual

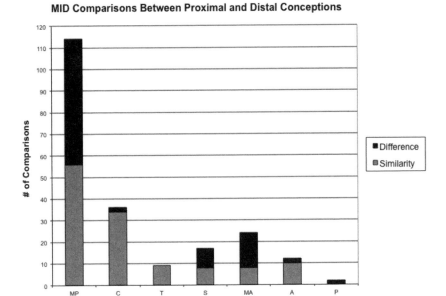

FIGURE 9.8 Comparisons of MID proximal and distal student conceptions of being scientists. Key: MP=Material processes; C=Cognitive processes; T=Textual processes; S=Social processes; MA=Material artifacts; A=Affective processes; P=Physical space or place.

processes were mentioned 9 times, and all were similarities. For instance, Jamar, in Sharon's 1st-grade class, said, "scientists have to draw every day or once a week." Sally, in Neveen's 3rd-grade class, evoked recording data when she said that scientists "fill out how many times the water evaporated." Social processes also increased to 17 total instances. Nine of these were differences and 8 were similarities. In Neveen's 3rd-grade class, Carlos noted a difference between the picture he drew of himself working alone and scientists out in the world, "Some scientists have partners to work with them so they don't do all the work." Material artifacts were referenced a total of 24 times, as differences 16 times and as similarities eight times. For instance, in Ibett's 2nd-grade class, Carmen said that scientists "do things with paper" but "don't do things with paint," as she had depicted. And according to Vittoria, in Sharon's 1st-grade class, scientists don't "have a dog . . . [like I do] to see what happens to my dog with the fleas." Affective processes increased to 12 total responses: 10 of these were similarities and 2 were differences. Place was mentioned twice, and both times students indicated that the places for their activities were different from those of scientists out in the world. For instance, Joe, in Jennifer's 3rd-grade class, said that scientists "explore the world," something he had yet to do.

In the POST interview (Figure 9.9), material processes continued to be the most prevalent dimension, even though the total number was fewer than that of the MID (88). However, the number of material processes in which students said they engaged similarly to those of scientists out in the world increased slightly from the MID interview to 59. Thus in terms of percentages, similarities of material processes increased significantly from 49% to 66%. The number of students' references to cognitive processes rose to 58. Again, the vast majority of these, 90%, were similarities. Textual processes also went up slightly to 15 total instances. Twelve of these were similarities and 3 were differences. Social Processes decreased overall to 12 total instances, but the number of similarities increased to 10. Similarities accounted for 83% of the total, a large increase from the 47% of the total in the MID interview. Students mentioned slightly more material artifacts (28) in the POST than they did in the MID interview. Again, the majority of these were differences (86%). Mentions of affective processes also increased in the POST interview to 21 overall. Nineteen of these, or 90%, were similarities students noted between themselves and scientists. Place was only mentioned once by the students in relation to differences between themselves and scientists.

Students do not just build ideas of scientists from their own particular activities and then generalize to some abstract scientist. They constantly renegotiate their identifications through the activities they engage in, the roles they take on in these activities, and the spaces others give them. Activities related to science occur in a variety of places, including, television, and other forms of mass media. Students' sources also include stories of family members dissecting frogs in their "scientist high school," and personal experiences in and out of school. These are *all* lived experiences for children. In these experiences, they are scientists some of the time,

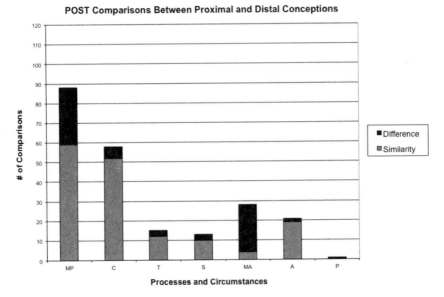

FIGURE 9.9 Comparisons of POST proximal and distal student conceptions of being scientists. Key: MP=Material processes; C=Cognitive processes; T=Textual processes; S=Social processes; MA=Material artifacts; A=Affective processes; P=Physical space or place.

and they are observers or wishers-to-be at some other times. But they always develop ideas of themselves in relation to science, scientific activity, and scientists. It is part of their meaning making.

Concluding Thoughts

To date, most of the research that has used visual images to study children's perceptions of scientists and/or science has been around for over 50 years and has focused on stereotypical indicators, specifying various characteristics students attribute to scientists, such as loners and eccentrics, and reasons that led students to these characteristics (Finson, 2002). The Draw-A-Scientist Test, DAST (Chambers, 1983), and its adaptations and supplemental interviews (Sumrall, 1995) reveal children's stereotypes about scientists in terms of appearance, race, gender, work setting, and so forth. Other scholars have questioned the methodological validity of DAST tests. For instance, Losh, Wilke, and Pop (2008) critiqued DAST methods of asking children to only draw scientists, and not other professionals, such as teachers and veterinarians. That is, DAST research does not allow conceptualizations of scientists to be compared to conceptualizations of other professionals. Another shortcoming of most DAST research is that students are not asked to explain their pictures (cf. Barman, 1999; Bulda, 2006). As such, students' drawings are interpreted by researchers removed from the interview and students' possible explanations. A singular mode can be problematic for accurate representation of young children's knowledge. Students' oral accounts of their drawings provide more information about their conceptions of themselves as scientists and about their conceptions of scientists in general. Moreover, the DAST studies offer limited understanding of children's epistemological beliefs of science and especially of children's own identities as scientists.

To adapt the Draw-A-Scientist Test to understand more fully students' views on the nature of science, Walls (2012) interviewed 23 African American 3rd graders and asked students to name their scientist, provide a story about their scientist, and provide commentary on the skin color. In addition to asking students to draw a scientist, Walls' work also used another tool: students were asked to identify a scientist from a series of photographs. Walls found that the children produced stereotypical views of science similar to previous studies, but they also expressed their own positive feelings in relation to science. The overwhelming majority of scientists that students drew were African American.

Our research assumes that students can conceptualize *themselves* as scientists in and out of school. The important quest for us is to understand why students think they are engaging in any activity they have labeled as scientific. Rather than focus on what scientists look like, we asked students to focus on what scientists *do*, *what* they did it with and for *what purposes*, and to describe the activities they, themselves, engaged in as scientists in ways that were similar to, and different from, the activities scientists out in the world perform.

Students were more able to think about and represent themselves as scientists after having participated in the ISLE curriculum. That is, students were at least more able to articulate what it meant to be a scientist after participating in just one unit of the ISLE curriculum (the *Matter* unit). Even though it was not a primary goal of the ISLE project to change students' views of themselves as scientists, this finding is consistent with other DAST studies that show treatments generally change students' perceptions of science and scientists (Finson, 2002; Mantzicopoulos, Samarapungavan, & Patrick, 2009). However, no other study has examined students' change in conceptions of themselves as scientists, except an earlier study from our group (Tucker-Raymond, Varelas, & Pappas, 2007).

As they were interviewed over time and experienced the two ISLE units, children were more likely to believe activities in which they had engaged were similar to, if not the same as, what scientists did. Moreover, the more they participated in ISLE, the more they came to associate ISLE with scientists' practices, at least in response to the questions of an ISLE researcher. Even if students did not draw themselves as engaging in ISLE, they used scientific concepts, such as evaporation or studying plants and animals in the natural world, in their MID and POST interview drawings.

Although we conducted the study with a small number of students (n=54), there were no significant differences in any of the coded categories between boys and girls, or students from different ethno-linguistic and racial backgrounds. Most of the statistically significant differences that existed were due to when the students participated in the interview—before the curriculum, after the *Matter* unit, or after both the *Matter* and *Forest* units. Additional differences were found across classrooms, but very rarely across grades. These findings suggest that any differences in students' responses were not due to ethnicity, race, language, gender, or for the most part, grade, but were instead due to their individual subjective experiences in the world and in classroom instantiations of the ISLE units. That is, how teachers and students enacted ISLE differentially in classrooms seemed to have more effect than anything else. However, even these differences existed for only a select few variables, suggesting that students' responses were highly individual. While such differences point to particular aspects of the curriculum that may or may not have been particularly salient for students, individual case studies showed students' nuanced, subjective experiences.

Students' stances toward science were more complex and recognizable the more students participated in ISLE. Not only were they able to create more canonically coherent representations of science as they participated in ISLE, they also rendered science as more about finding out answers to questions, developing knowledge, and testing hypotheses rather than building machines or finding solutions to problems. While science certainly embraces all of these stances at different moments and in different fields, students' responses reflected their experiences of ISLE curriculum emphases.

As students talked and drew about science, they primarily referred to material processes or observable actions. However, after participating in the *Matter* unit, students were much more able to mention other aspects of science, such as cognitive, textual, social, and affective processes, as well as material artifacts. What did not increase over time were students' mentions of the physical space in which they and scientists operated. Perhaps this was due to the fact that their scientist experiences happened primarily in the same place. There was also little, if any, explicit classroom discussion about where scientists do their work.

The data also indicate that students, as they participated first in the *Matter* and then in the *Forest* unit, saw themselves as more similar to scientists out in the world in terms of material, cognitive, textual, social, and affective processes. Students also recognized that scientists might use different materials than the ones they were using, but that had little effect on the way students saw the processes in which they were engaged as similar to those of scientists. That is, students may have seen the details of the specific activities as different from those of scientists, but they thought like scientists, they socialized like scientists, they read and wrote like scientists, and they were affectively engaged in the subject matter in ways that were commensurate to those of scientists out in the world. Most significant, perhaps, is the consistent increase in cognitive processes mentioned by students over the three interviews. Students' attention to cognitive processes shows that they thought of themselves as thinking like scientists out in the world.

Students rely on a number of resources to engage with the nature of science and what it means to be a scientist. However, school programs go a long way toward shaping what counts as science. Students' conceptions of science come from their experiences with science. When students are regarded as agents of their own learning and their lives are filled with rich experiences of observing, measuring, predicting, and drawing conclusions about the natural world and sharing them, they include them in their representations of science. The more young children participate in concentrated science curricula that integrate literacy rather than are separate from it, the more they develop complex views of science. Young children do see themselves as participating in science, and can also recognize differences between what they do and what scientists out in the world do. For students to develop complex views of science, they need to have practice with many different types of textual genres, practices, and content. Schools also need to take into account and address students' experiences with science content outside of the classroom.

References

Alters, B. J. (1997). Whose nature of science? *Journal of Research in Science Teaching, 34*, 39–55.

Barman, C. R. (1999). Students' views about scientists and school science: Engaging K-8 teachers in a national study. *Journal of Science Teacher Education, 10*, 43–54.

Barton, A. C. (1998). Teaching science with homeless children: Pedagogy, representation, and identity. *Journal of Research in Science Teaching, 35*, 379–394.

Bruner, J. (1996). *The culture of education*. Cambridge, MA: Harvard University Press.

Bulda, M. (2006). Young children's perceptions of scientists: A preliminary study. *Educational Research, 48*, 121–132.

Chambers, D. W. (1983). Stereotypic images of the scientist: The Draw-A-Scientist Test. *Science Education, 67*, 255–265.

Finson, K.D. (2002). Drawing a scientist: What we do and do not know after fifty years of drawings. *School Science and Mathematics, 102*, 335–345.

Gee, J. P. (1996). *Social linguistics and literacies: Ideology in discourses* (2nd ed.). Bristol, PA: Taylor & Francis.

Hogan, K. (2000). Exploring a process view of students' knowledge about the nature of science. *Science Education, 84*, 51–70.

Holland, D., Lachiotte, W. S., Skinner, D., & Cain, C. (1998). *Identity and agency in cultural worlds*. Cambridge, MA: Harvard University Press.

Lederman, N. G., Abd-El-Khalick, F., Bell, R. L., & Schwartz, R. S. (2002). Views of nature of science questionnaire: Toward valid and meaningful assessment of learners' conceptions of nature of science. *Journal of Research in Science Teaching, 39*, 497–521.

Losh, S. C., Wilke, R., & Pop, M. (2008). Some methodological issues with "Draw A Scientist Tests" among young children. *International Journal of Science Education, 30*, 773–792.

Mantzicopoulos, P., Samarapungavan, A., & Patrick, H. (2009). "We learn how to predict and be a scientist": Early science experiences and kindergarten children's social meanings about science. *Cognition and Instruction, 27*, 312–369.

National Research Council. (1996). *National science education standards*. Washington, DC: National Academy Press.

National Research Council. (2012). *A framework for K-12 science education: Practices, crosscutting concepts, and core ideas*. Washington, DC: National Academies Press.

Rodari, P. (2007). Science and scientists in the drawings of European children. *Journal of Science Communication, 6*(3), 1–12.

Rudolph, J. L. (2005). Inquiry, instrumentalism, and the public understanding of science. *Science Education, 89*, 803–821.

Sumrall, W. J. (1995). Reasons for the perceived images of scientists by race and gender of students in grades 1-7. *School Science and Mathematics, 95*, 83–90.

Tucker-Raymond, E. Varelas, M., & Pappas, C. C. (with Korzh, A., & Wentland, A.). (2007). "They probably won't be named Rachel": Young children's emergent multimodal representations of identities as scientists. *Cultural Studies of Science Education, 1*, 559–592.

Varelas, M. (1996). Between theory and data in a 7th grade science class. *Journal of Research in Science Teaching, 33*, 229–263.

Walls, L. (2012). Third grade African American students' views of the nature of science. *Journal of Research in Science Teaching, 49*, 1–37.

Wong, D. E. (2002). To appreciate variation between scientists: A perspective for seeing science's vitality. *Science Education, 86*, 386–400.

ISLE in Urban Early-Grade Classrooms

10

YOUNG CHILDREN IN URBAN CLASSROOMS

Possibilities for Sciencing

Maria Varelas and Christine C. Pappas

In this book, we shared a variety of ideas that emerged from research and practice in early urban elementary classrooms where teachers sought to integrate science and literacy in ways that both build on and extend children's knowledge, enjoyment, and identification with science. We called this project *Integrated Science Literacy Enactments* (ISLE) to capture the essence of our work: it involved designing and studying curricular and instructional *possibilities* that were *performed* in classrooms between teacher and students in ways they could only enact. As we studied enactments, we focused on a variety of curricular, instructional, and assessment dimensions. In doing so, we tried to understand how students, especially from certain ethno-linguistic, racial, and socio-economic backgrounds that are often associated with academic underperformance, function and achieve when offered various multimodal opportunities to do science at school. The previous chapters present some of the studies that we have conducted in this context and offer ways to showcase urban classrooms as vibrant communities where students, guided by their teachers, learn science and literacy. We believe that the findings provided in this book support important understandings about this process. Below we present these understandings, pointing back to the previous chapters.

Learning in the Company of Others

All chapters foreground the communal, collective ways in which meaning making and learning science ideas unfolded in the classrooms. Children built on what they knew to make sense of the new ideas that the science information texts provided, as they were dialogically shared in the children's classrooms. Intertextuality was a tool that allowed them to access meanings they had, examine them, and develop them further. As children and teacher initiated intertextual links and/or took up others' links, they both showed that they valued the knowledge and experiences that each brought to the classroom. Moreover, they also articulated scientific knowledge—offered examples, explained phenomena, reasoned, compared, and made inferences. The hands-on explorations and the related whole-class debriefings, which complemented read-alouds and various writing, illustrating, and performing activities, allowed children to work together, share understandings with each other and the teacher, challenge each other, and deal with uncertainty. Their dramatic enactments of depicting molecular behavior in different states of matter and relationships in a food web were by nature communal endeavors, where children needed to coordinate with their peers to perform the activity and develop sophisticated understandings of science ideas. This collectivity was also apparent as we tracked the development of science concepts, such as evaporation as it relates to states of matter, and interdependence in a forest ecosystem, throughout the two ISLE units.

Moreover, the books that the children wrote and illustrated individually at the end of each unit echoed ideas discussed in the classroom. Children had appropriated the linguistic features of the science genre that was dominant in the books and used in classroom discourse. The themes that they chose for their books, although they were diverse, also showed similarity within a classroom. Furthermore, "others" were prominent in their sense of audience for which they had composed their book. Similarly, in their conceptions of being scientists, others gained prominence as the school year unfolded. Children drew themselves in the company of others as they thought of themselves doing science and even when they only drew themselves, they talked about others as they narrated their pictures. The idea of working with others and learning together was, of course, the salient goal of the home projects. This experience allowed children not only to work with family members reading a text, engaging in a hands-on exploration, and documenting it in writing and pictures, but also to share these ideas in class, where their teachers and their classmates were able to further help them construct explanations about their findings.

Yet, each child participated in classroom discourse in specific ways, which became this child's niche in the classroom community. Employing particular language acts to express their thinking, individual children crafted a place for themselves that often complemented each other's. However, in the midst of communal learning, we also provided evidence of children individually owning important science ideas in each of the two units—something that current educational reforms focus on exclusively, perpetuating a culture of endless individual testing as a measure of learning.

Multimodality and Its Affordances

Children's learning was facilitated by the multitude of communicative modes used in the science lessons. Teacher and children engaged with text (written and oral), pictures, physical objects, bodily performances, semantic maps, and murals. Although, in this book, we did not have the room to discuss how semantic maps and murals were used in the classrooms and the affordances they offered, in other publications (Pappas & Varelas, 2009; Varelas et al., 2007), we have presented examples of these class experiences and products and how they supported children's own book making and articulation of science ideas.

During the read-alouds of science informational texts, both the pictures and the words became sources of intertextuality for children and teacher. As children noticed aspects of pictures or heard the teacher reading aloud about ideas related to a phenomenon, they made references to others texts, recounted their own or others' experiences, or made associations with their own explorations. Furthermore, they interacted with physical objects in a variety of ways, including: everyday items that they categorized in different states of matter; wet paper towels that they made dry up at different times; and lentils that they grew at home. In all of these experiences, they had opportunities to reason, challenge each other's actions and reasoning, and make their own the knowledge that science texts and their teacher offered them. In addition, in the drama activities, they used their real bodies to represent ideas that had similar, but not identical, meanings in the world of science versus the social world of their everyday life in and out of school. During these dramatic enactments, children voiced meanings that were not only nuanced understandings, but also reflected affective dimensions of engagement with science.

Moreover, multimodality was salient in children's conceptions of being scientists in various ways. By drawing themselves doing science, they depicted themselves, and in some cases, other actors or spectators, surrounded with texts or materials, or instruments, or tools. These drawings offered unique windows in the multimodal ways in which they were thinking of themselves as scientists vis-à-vis scientists out in the world. The oral discussion they had with the interviewer over their pictures embellished our understanding of the comparisons they were making. Similarly, in the illustrated science books that they created on a topic of their choice, children used pictures in various ways: at times their pictures depicted ideas in their text; sometimes their pictures represented new ideas not expressed in their text, thus complementing their text; and at other times, pictures were their dominant tool for communicating ideas that they chose to include in their books.

Diversity and the Many Faces of Science-Literacy Integration

As our team (see Preface) came together to design integrated science-literacy enactments, we developed units, lessons, and activities in broad strokes with enough flexibility and malleability so they can be adapted to the teachers' own practices and ways of being in the classroom. The findings of our research studies reported in this book not only confirm the variability and diversity of these enactments, but they also shed light on children's unique, communal, and multifaceted ways of making sense of science and the world.

In the drama activities, serendipity and uniqueness of children's ideas and actions in the different classrooms allowed for different science ideas to be further explored. The improvisational performances that teacher and children put together shared similarities, but were shaped by the actors and audience in each classroom. In read-alouds, different children participated in different, unique ways in classroom discourse via various language acts.

The different curriculum genres within the ISLE units also contributed differently to the ebb and flow of concept development and meaning making of a particular science idea. Moreover, within each curriculum genre, there was an important degree of variation. For example, the same hands-on exploration included variations in each classroom that offered different opportunities for students to raise ideas and debate them. Also, the dialogical nature of the read-alouds of informational texts allowed for the students' different experiences to be forgrounded and used to help them extend existing understandings and learn science. The various curriculum genres that were included in the home projects (hands-on, read-aloud, and writing and illustrating) were appreciated differently by the different families that shared their reactions to these projects. For some families one genre was more salient, whereas for others, a combination of genres allowed for a meaningful and enjoyable experience.

What is also very relevant to this theme of diversity is the unique ways in which children configured the books that they authored to communicate their science knowledge and in which they conceptualized themselves as being scientists. In their books, children used differently the two communication modes, text and pictures. They also set up their books in a variety of ways—some used a two-page spread to elaborate an idea, others organized their books in chapters, and yet others used some of features of the information book genre, such as a table of contents or a glossary. Moreover, as children portrayed themselves as scientists, they focused on different scientific practices that they have used mostly in their ISLE science lessons as the year progressed. The science-literacy enactments had different forms in each of the ISLE classrooms, and furthermore the children in a class and across classes experienced these enactments in different ways, resulting to a multitude of ways in which they associated themselves with science and science ideas.

Dialectical Relationships That Shape Children's Being and Becoming in Classroom Communities

As teacher and children engaged with science ideas using a variety of practices and tools, they not only developed scientific knowledge, but they also developed identities, seeing themselves (and being seeing by others) as particular kinds of people, positioning themselves, and being positioned, in particular ways by their classmates and their teacher. During group work on hands-on explorations or in whole-class read-alouds, children's status in the classroom shaped other children's ways of making sense of science ideas. Through their own books, some of the children saw themselves as the experts offering their audience (readers and viewers) ways to learn science content. As children participated in unique ways during the ISLE lessons, they constructed identities that evolved and strengthened over the year—identities of questioners, wonderers, knowers, and risk-takers. Moreover, both their academic identities (as students in a school) and their science identities (as doers of science in and out of the classroom) shaped, and were shaped by, the ways in which they engaged in activities (Kane, 2012; Varelas et al., 2007).

In the classrooms, teacher and children constantly negotiated power, authority, ideas, and actions. The information texts that they used were seen as authoritative bodies of knowledge only to be embellished, questioned, and made sense of through classroom participants' experiences, meanings, memories, and knowledge, and the children's hands-on explorations. Their home investigations had a place in the classroom and offered opportunities for constructing explanations. Their emergent ideas were not dismissed, or pushed aside, but were made part of the collective knowledge that was revisited and finessed over time. These were the spaces that teachers and children created together, which had both physical and symbolic dimensions, and in which knowledge was produced, or in other words, re-produced *and* transformed (Varelas, Kane, & Pappas, 2010).

Ecology of Learnerhoods

The understandings about teaching and learning of science that we outlined above can be further theorized as part of another construct that we have introduced in an earlier publication. In Varelas, Kane, and Pappas (2010), we discussed the construct of "learnerhoods" that get enacted in classrooms. A *learnerhood* is a space (much like a neighborhood) were learners come together interacting with each other during the process of learning. Like a neighborhood, a learnerhood can be defined by its physical location, the people populating it, the ways in which these people interact, and the physical and symbolic artifacts used and created in the context of these interactions.

At any given point in time in a classroom, some students are in a learnerhood, others are outside of the physical and/or symbolic boundaries that define that learnerhood, and may belong to different learnerhoods. For example, as students form alliances among ideas, as they work together to collect and analyze data, as they perform together a dramatic enactment of a phenomenon, they form learnerhoods where they support each other and are facilitated, at times, by their teacher. Learnerhoods may change composition in shorter or longer time intervals and may evolve based on the experiences of its members and on the available resources. In learnerhoods, learners engage with ideas, with each other, and with materials and artifacts. Thus, in some ways, the construct of learnerhood allows us to foreground the collectivity of thinking, acting, and engaging which constitutes an important understanding that emerged from the various studies presented in this book.

In a classroom, there is a multitude of learnerhoods that are formed and reformed all the time, using different available resources—a question by the teacher or a peer, an idea from that a family member who helped them think in the context of their home project, an insight children developed as they were moving an object during an exploration, a semantic map that the class created to capture the developing ideas on a topic. Students get in and out of various learnerhoods and hold different roles—at times, a recounting of an experience during a read-aloud, while children sit on the classroom rug, becomes the pivotal point for the whole class to discuss a science idea; at other times, children wait until they understand what other peers say in their small group before they align with a particular idea; and yet at other times, children imagine how the readers or viewers of the books they are composing might be engaged, and structure their books accordingly.

This multitude of learnerhoods in a classroom may be considered as an "ecology of learnerhoods," a system of learnerhoods forming the classroom community. Considering the classroom as the a system of *learnerhoods*, as opposed to a system of learners, enables us to pay attention not only to individual learners but also to the relationships among them and their teacher, ideas, and artifacts that evolve constantly throughout the life of that classroom and shape both teaching and learning. Considering the system of learnerhoods as an *ecology*, in a biological sense, allows us to "bundle together" important notions about classroom teaching and learning, which we identified earlier as themes that emerged in the six ISLE classrooms. In an ecological system, critical concepts include diversity, interactions and interdependence, dynamic balance, resources and energy cycles, and niche. As our practice and research in urban classrooms with young learners—the integrated science-literacy enactments—showed, such concepts are integral to promoting productive learning environments.

Diversity of curriculum genres allows multiple entry points for learners, who engage in such genres in different ways, and who construct such genres differently as a part of who they are as students and as scientists. Dialogically engaging in read-alouds of information texts, exploring with materials in the classroom and at home, acting out phenomena, and writing, illustrating, and talking about science ideas, all present to children various affordances for doing science and developing positive relationships with science. As teacher and children participate in these different practices, children interact with others and depend on others to stretch ideas, to appreciate their emergent understandings, to show a different way of thinking about an idea, to challenge their thinking, and to make them feel like experts. As these interactions take place, the goal is to reach a dynamic balance among participating children, among developing ideas, between questions and answers, between help and autonomy, and between accepting and challenging. Such balances can be reached only when the diverse repertoires of practices and experiences that children bring with them to school are validated and extended further, using resources, such as texts, people, materials, and activities. Language, in various modes (written, oral, diagrammatic, pictorial, everyday, scientific), is an essential mediating resource that allows learners to communicate with each other, form learnerhoods, and offer and receive help so that both the learners and learnerhoods can flourish and prosper. As children develop their own niches in the classroom community, they both shape this community and are shaped by it.

We hope this book inspires you to develop, practice, and understand your own enactments of integrated science-literacy approaches in your or other teachers' classrooms, and to offer your students many and various possibilities to do, talk, write, draw, act out, represent, and think science, and see themselves as scientists, or in other words, to be involved in *sciencing* in all grade levels. Sciencing in the early grades is especially important since children can, want, and do engage with all these dimensions of sciencing when offered opportunities to do so.

We also hope that this book is viewed as a contribution to the increasing scholarship that disrupts the persistent rhetoric of underperformance and under-achievement of students of color living in US urban areas that encounter economic and other hardships. As pointed out in Chapter 1, four of the ISLE classrooms included almost all Latino/as or African American students living in poverty, and two had diverse students with about half experiencing economic hardship. However, there were no statistical differences in terms of race and ethnicity in the various studies of measures of learning science and seeing themselves as scientists that we conducted. Both African American and Latino/a students thrived in classrooms where there were multimodal opportunities to engage in sciencing, as much as students whose race and ethno-linguistic affiliation do not underprivilege them. We only wish that this thriving continues to grow.

References

Kane, J. M. (2012). Young African American children constructing academic and disciplinary identities in an urban science classroom. *Science Education, 96*, 457–487.

Pappas, C. C., & Varelas, M., with Gill, S., Ortiz, I., & Keblawe-Shamah, N. (2009). Multimodal books in science-literacy units: Language and visual images for meaning making. *Language Arts, 86*, 201–211.

Varelas, M., Kane, J. M., & Pappas, C. C. (2010). Concept development in urban classroom spaces: Dialectical relationships, power, and identity. In W.-M. Roth (Ed.), *Re/Structuring science education: ReUniting psychological and sociological perspectives* (pp. 275–297). Dordrecht, The Netherlands: Springer-Kluwer.

Varelas, M., Pappas, C. C., Tucker-Raymond, E., Arsenault, A., Kane, J., Kokkino, S., & Siuda, J. E. (2007). Identity in activities: Young children and science. In W.-M. Roth & K. Tobin (Eds.), *Science, learning, and identity: Sociocultural and cultural-historical perspectives* (pp. 203–242). Rotterdam, The Netherlands: Sense Publishers.

AUTHOR INDEX

SUBJECT INDEX

Taylor & Francis

eBooks

ORDER YOUR FREE 30 DAY INSTITUTIONAL TRIAL TODAY!

FOR LIBRARIES

Over 23,000 eBook titles in the Humanities, Social Sciences, STM and Law from some of the world's leading imprints.

Choose from a range of subject packages or create your own!

Benefits for you

▶ Free MARC records
▶ COUNTER-compliant usage statistics
▶ Flexible purchase and pricing options

Benefits for your user

▶ Off-site, anytime access via Athens or referring URL
▶ Print or copy pages or chapters
▶ Full content search
▶ Bookmark, highlight and annotate text
▶ Access to thousands of pages of quality research at the click of a button

For more information, pricing enquiries or to order a free trial, contact your local online sales team.

UK and Rest of World: **online.sales@tandf.co.uk**

US, Canada and Latin America:
e-reference@taylorandfrancis.com

www.ebooksubscriptions.com

ALPSP Award for
BEST eBOOK
PUBLISHER
2009 Finalist
sponsored by

Taylor & Francis **eBooks**
Taylor & Francis Group

A flexible and dynamic resource for teaching, learning and research.